Slow Food

Our century, which began and has developed under the insignia of industrial civilization, first invented the machine and then took it as its life model.

We are enslaved by speed and have all succumbed to the same insidious virus: Fast Life, which disrupts our habits, pervades the privacy of our homes, and forces us to eat Fast Foods.

To be worthy of the name, *Homo sapiens* should rid themselves of speed before it reduces them to a species in danger of extinction.

A firm defense of quiet material pleasure is the only way to oppose the universal folly of Fast Life.

May suitable doses of guaranteed sensual pleasure and slow, long-lasting enjoyment preserve us from the contagion of the multitude who mistake frenzy for efficiency.

Our defense should begin at the table with Slow Food. Let us rediscover the flavors and savors of regional cooking and banish the degrading effects of Fast Food.

In the name of productivity, Fast Life has changed our way of being and threatens our environment and our landscapes. So Slow Food is now the only truly progressive answer.

That is what real culture is all about: developing taste rather than demeaning it. And what better way to set about this than an international exchange of experiences, knowledge, products?

Slow Food guarantees a better future. Slow Food is an idea that needs plenty of qualified supporters who can help turn this (slow) motion into an international movement, with the little snail as its symbol.

SLOW FOOD

Collected Thoughts on Taste, Tradition, and the Honest Pleasures of Food

Edited by Carlo Petrini,

with Ben Watson and Slow Food Editore

Chelsea Green Publishing Company

White River Junction, Vermont

Designed by Suzanne Church.

Printed in the United States.

First printing, October 2001

04 03 02 01   1 2 3 4 5

Printed on acid-free, recycled paper.

Library of Congress Cataloging-in-Publication Data available upon request.

Chelsea Green Publishing Company
Post Office Box 428
White River Junction, VT 05001
(800) 639-4099
www.chelseagreen.com

contents

Deborah Madison

Whenever I read the mission statement of Slow Food U.S.A., I'm always very impressed, and also somewhat amused by how much it aims to cover and how much Slow Food wants to do. Slow Food is a very big creature, large enough to accommodate more than one point of view as to what it is exactly. Like the blind men patting the elephant to determine its nature, those who are drawn to Slow Food can probably find what they're looking for based on their own interests.

To the gastronome, Slow Food might have to do with artisanal foods and wines. To the person seeking a tempo of life that is more in step with life's natural rhythms, unlike America's present fast-paced model, Slow Food offers a sympathetic response. For those whose concerns run to the historical aspects of food, traditional methods of cheese making might be of particular interest, or the examination of traditional foods and food methods found in different regions of the country. Those whose historical quests are more aligned with animals and plants will find that Slow Food, through its Ark of Taste initiative, provides a place to actively debate the merits of old breeds, from turkeys to sheep, or oysters to apples, and to become actively involved with their preservation. If your concerns are with the politics of social change, you may find yourself in harmony with Slow Food's commitment to land stewardship and food that's grown by sound and sustainable methods. And all seekers join hands at the table, for Slow Food sees the "the kitchen and the table as centers of pleasure, culture, and community." The lens through which Slow Food views the world of food is a wide one indeed.

For the past five years my focus has been on America's farmers' markets, a subject that, I've discovered, looks a lot like Slow Food. After visiting nearly one hundred markets, farms, and producers, I've come to see that what farmers' markets have to offer is no less than a way of life. The farmers' market supplies our tables with food that has great vitality, flavor, and beauty. But pick up one corner of the cloth called farmers' market, and a whole lot more comes with it. The innocent shopper who thinks she's buying salad greens, a dozen delicious pullet eggs, some pure, white locust honey, and a basket of Wolf River apples is also involved with doing a lot more as a consequence of these simple purchases.

Quite often, the foods we find at the market are grown by sound, sustainable methods. Fields are planted, orchards are maintained, and animals are raised without the use of pesticides and hormones that are damaging to the land, the farmers, and consumers. Quite often the foods we find there are traditional foods, grown from heirloom seeds, scions, and stock, chosen for optimal flavor rather than the demands of the distant marketplace: uniformity, shippability, cosmetic appearance, and long shelf life. Foods that are crafted—the fine cheeses found across the country everywhere, a rich pear butter made from antique pears in Wisconsin, or the tamales made from the farmer's own corn and chilies in New Mexico—have an integrity that surpasses the foods we commonly encounter outside the farmers' market. And a shopper at the farmers' market will hone a fine sense of the seasons and come to know profoundly that "in season" refers to where we live, not to the neverending season of the world found in the supermarket.

But in addition to the fine quality of food the market offers, a successful farmers' market also ensures a healthy rural economy instead of one that's depressed. And it fosters a positive connection between urban and rural peoples. Knowing that our food is grown nearby and not in some unknown place gives us shoppers a sense of security and connection. I've come to believe that true pleasure at the table also comes from intimately knowing the source of our food. And today it's only at a farmers' market that we have a chance to connect with someone who produces what we con-

sume. The sense of community that comes from being connected to those who produce the food we eat, and to those who, like us, take pleasure in such connections, is essential for a civilized way of life.

A great deal follows from this connection. As we come to know our local farmers and producers, we begin to place the farm in our personal landscape. Visit a farm, and it comes into focus. Suddenly the landscape of food is something to care for and protect. Issues such as zoning and water arbitration take on new meaning, and it becomes clear that the landscape can survive only as long as the health of rural, traditional farming communities is strong. Our interdependence becomes increasingly evident.

For many of the ills and anxieties that beset us in this too-fast time of disconnection, farmers' markets offer a tangible antidote. The market eases us into a more harmonious rhythm of life, starting with how we shop, for common advice tells the shopper to begin by slowing down. Shopping here is not an experience to hurry through, but one to savor. Stroll through the market and look at what's there. Linger over a cup of coffee with friends. Plan a dinner around who you've met at the market as well as what you've bought.

The farmers' market is a tremendous resource; a source of inspiration and joy. To anyone who partakes, it is about the conviviality of the table, about being part of a community and becoming involved in the big picture of sustainability through the simple act of choosing how we spend our dollars. While Slow Food is not about farmers' markets per se, the values that underlie what happens at the market are essentially the same. It's here that we have an opportunity to take part in sustaining a living food heritage and enjoying the benefits of sustainability, cultural diversity, authenticity, and integrity. Slow Food, through its mission and through the essays in this book, is about how big and important food really is. A glance at the chapter titles and you see that, like the farmers' market, it's impossible to take up the subject of food without thinking about everything else that it touches, which is, in the end, life itself.

Deborah Madison is a chef, food advocate, and the author of several cookbooks, including The Green Cookbook, The Savory Way, *and* Saturday Market, Sunday Brunch. *She also leads the Slow Food convivium in Santa Fe, New Mexico.*

The cultural goals of the international Slow Food movement are to defeat all forms of chauvinism, to re-appropriate diversity, and to indulge in a healthy dose of cultural relativism. *Slow*, "the international herald of taste and culture" and our quarterly review, first saw the light of day in April 1996 when it was published in three editions: Italian, English, and German. The eleventh review (September 1998) was also published in Spanish and French editions, and *Slow* thus began to speak five languages. Edited by Alberto Capatti—an intellectual who has played a fundamental role in the study of the history and trends of European gastronomic culture—*Slow* is now in its fifth year, and the volume you have in your hands provides an opportunity to reflect upon its importance for the development of our movement.

The table of contents of this book provides an overview of the topics *Slow* has addressed over the years, and reading the articles you will note crossovers of significant ideas. Biodiversity, defense of local cultures, the Ark project (see Chapter 1), a firm stand on bio-technologies, animal well-being—these are just some of the themes that have characterized Slow Food's activities over the past few years. From the Ark idea, for example, we have developed the Presidia, concrete initiatives to reactivate the economies connected to products on the verge of extinction. Wherever it has been applied, the Presidia project has always worked very well indeed, and we are now striving to promote it planetwide.

Over the years, *Slow* has accompanied the movement's activities, stressing how it developed from being a purely wine and food association into an organization for the defense of vegetable, animal, and cultural diversity. Not that we have ever forgotten our origins as lovers of the pleasure of food, wine, and conviviality and as revivers of a passion for slowness, such an indispensable tool for improving the quality of our lives. In its pages, *Slow* relates the Slow Food adventure and describes the prospects for the movement's future developments.

Slow Food now boasts more than 65,000 members all around the world, a vast global network of men and women capable of generating ideas and programs to defend taste and the right to a responsible, knowing form of pleasure; one that is respectful of cultural and material diversity, and one in which all can share.

Distinctive in style, *Slow* is the *fil rouge* that sews this network together, building it and representing it over the course of time. Born with the Internet but printed on paper, written by collaborators from many, many countries and produced in the small market town of Bra in Piedmont, *Slow* is not only the organ but also the cultural pulse of Slow Food.

Carlo Petrini is the president and
founder of Slow Food

Patrick Martins

Welcome to the Best of *Slow*. Since 1996, the quarterly journal *Slow* has gracefully served as the face of the international Slow Food movement, represented by members in 50 countries around the world.

Founded in 1989 by Carlo Petrini, Slow Food started in reaction to the opening of a McDonald's restaurant at the Spanish Steps in Rome. At that time, Slow Food was primarily a gastronomic organization dedicated to rediscovering and protecting the right to the pleasures of the table, and to using our tastebuds as our guides to seek out the highest achievements in taste.

A key moment in the history of Slow Food occurred in 1996 with the launch of two new projects. The Ark of Taste, inspired by Noah's Ark and its protection of animal species, turned Slow Food's focus away from pure gastronomy and towards ecology and a dedication to the land and farmers who produce the finest artisanal foods. It was now no longer enough to know good food: now we needed to know where it came from, who produced it, and how we could ensure a secure future for its existence. The "eco" part of our eco-gastronomic movement necessitated a new focus on education of the entire food continuum, from soil to table. It was then that the second project, the publication of the first issue of the quarterly journal *Slow* by the Slow Food publishing house in Italy, found its mission. *Slow* has educated members and readers around the world on uniqueness and tradition, regionalism and universality in food.

Since the inception of the journal, Slow Food has blossomed to 65,000 members, including more than 5,000 in the United States. The country that brought us Wonder Bread, Lite Beer, and individually wrapped cheese slices has come full circle. Slow Food U.S.A., a nonprofit organization, has been thrilled with the connections we've made—through the national office and our sixty-two local chapters (or "convivia")—with producers, farmers, and purveyors from around the country. From Native Americans in Minnesota who still harvest wild rice using sticks and canoes to fishermen who are working to keep Delaware Bay oysters on our tables. From Alan Foster in Oregon, who produces world-class ciders from heirloom apples with names like Foxwhelp and Brown Snout, to the Roman taffy man, who is continuing a three-generation tradition of serving New Orleans taffy to local residents out of a horse-drawn carriage.

The disturbing trend toward uniformity in food and in culture threatens to make our planet a much less interesting place to live. Yet food is only the most visible example of this trend. Tugging on that one loose thread unravels a whole host of issues related to how we choose to live our lives: from urban sprawl to family farms, organic agriculture, and farmers' markets; from the ethics of bioengineering to the re-creation of local economies and regional "foodsheds." In America, sadly, our fast-paced, technologically driven lifestyles have put culinary pleasure and conviviality on the endangered species list. Yet, as the growing membership in Slow Food attests, there is a pent-up demand in this fast-food nation for foodstuffs that embody quality, identity, variety, and taste.

I hope that you enjoy the articles that follow, selected from the first five years of *Slow* and representing some of the best journalists, food writers, and opinion leaders from around the world. While the Slow Food movement concentrates its efforts on the physical pleasures of food—holding tastings, educational workshops, and major food events—*Slow* will continue to appeal to the intellectual pleasures of readers who are curious about food culture on a global scale. Just remember that, like a spectacular meal, these articles are meant to be savored slowly, one dish at a time.

Patrick Martins is the
president of Slow Food U.S.A.

Chapter ONE

The Ark and the Deluge

BUILDING THE ARK

Carlo Petrini

Those of us who work in the wine and food industry are continually faced by the worrisome fact that small purveyors of fine food and good wine are fast diminishing, while vegetables, fruits, and products that belong to our heritage are being systematically squeezed out of production. At the root of the problem lie confused agricultural policies that fail to take natural bio-rhythms into account and narrow-minded health regulations thought up for large companies and imposed on small producers. Woe betide the noble class of gourmets if they continue to neglect this catastrophic trend. On December 2, 1996, at the Taste Fair at Turin Lingotto, Slow Food organized a conference on "An Ark of Taste to Save the Universe of Savors." This conference was organized as part of a concerted effort to oppose that state of affairs. We have invested the effort with a symbolic name: the Ark, a protective receptacle for quality products that should be saved from the deluge of standardization and worldwide distribution. It is our view that, rather than pay homage to the logic of macroeconomics, we should operate within a regional framework and promote new forms of "slow" production and supply. This is perhaps the only possible quality guarantee that pays due respect to agriculture around the world.

I am aware that there are conservative implications in the idea of an Ark. It is an over-simplification to advocate support for only homemade products and small purveyors as an absolute value, thereby overlooking existing industrial companies that operate honestly and deploy their entrepreneurial skill in an environmentally friendly way. The great risk is that we will end up in a world of our own, cut off from highly complex processes. This is an error that we should avoid. It is wrong to remain stuck in the past without looking beyond our noses. Yet that will certainly be our fate if we lose touch with basic common sense. We have much to learn from the worldwide Slow Food movement.

I am also convinced that "playing a defensive game" is not a mistaken policy at this particular moment in time. If the flood is on its way, the only solution is the Ark. The storms ahead herald death and destruction, and if we fail to realize this, our marketing, community policies, and clever intuitions will be of little use. We must build the Ark as soon as possible.

Information is the first issue. What we need to do is look after small, high-quality food purveyors from the source through to consumption. This means implementing a process of awareness that is a reward for the producer and a guarantee for the buyer. Those in the trade must be aware that they are bearers of culture. The pride and satisfaction thus derived, and the recognition of results thus achieved, are bound to contribute to a general increase in professionalism. We, the gourmets, the wine and food publicists, must do our utmost to give dignity to these makers of food culture.

As for the "sacred fire" of hygiene, if it is not handled *cum grano salis*, a tremendous gulf will be created between institutions and producers.

Safeguarding and improving agriculture and local food purveyors calls for resources. Change in the European Community (EC) contributions policy—no longer paying a system that destroys, but paying those who work conscientiously and professionally—has long been overdue and will take time and effort to implement. Frankly, at the moment I am fairly skeptical about it.

For our own part, we are working on another front, trying to involve those who choose, try, judge, and consume. This project cannot take off if we do not convince consumers to pay more for better products. It is high time we put an end to the demagogy of price. For years it has been little more than an alibi for those who produce low-quality goods in large quantities.

Suggestions

The following are some practical suggestions.

The first one derives from an idea expressed by Italian parliamentarian Carmine Nardone: the adoption of 1,500 fruit-trees that are facing extinction. Slow Food Arcigola is asking wine producers to take on this project. In our vineyards, let's try to re-create something of the environment we inherited from our forebears by planting fruit trees in between the rows of vines. This could be done in the Langhe region in Piedmont, in the Valpolicella and Chianti Classico areas, in the gardens and green areas of the wine-producing towns. We would thus be establishing the first eco-museum in Italy, a living exhibition that will give these trees a chance to survive. It's a question of saving genes in the golden age of biogenetics.

Second suggestion: a code for the Ark. We believe that the words Castelmagno, San Daniele ham, and Grana Padano stand for a heritage to be proud of. That is why we urgently require legislation that recognizes quality food products as part of a cultural heritage that should be safeguarded and appreciated. Those who work hard to pass on their knowledge and culture to future generations deserve such recognition.

Third, we believe it is essential to get a campaign of taste teaching underway. This is one of the main reasons for the existence of our organization, Slow Food Arcigola, which has always recognized and affirmed the cultural value of sensory training.

MATERIAL CULTURE · "There is a desperately serious genocide of taste and I believe that we should intervene, not least because food is closely bound to agriculture, agriculture to the countryside, and the countryside to culture. And when we speak of culture, we are obviously not referring to culture as art treasures, but material culture, which is infinitely more vast—it is humanity's overall behavior, what gives meaning to human existence. And taste is something that gives meaning."

Luciana Castellina, Chairman of the European Parliamentary Commission for Culture

QUALITY OF LIFE · "Speed and the general rat race force rush upon us, but this should not stop us from doing everything we can to defend the traditions, products, and habits of our country. This is something that not only manufacturers who refuse to standardize consumer products should try to pursue, but also local and national public institutions. . . . To say that we should protect the production of 'cultural assets' is simply not enough. For this to happen we must raise the necessary economic resources. Just claiming that certain characteristic cultivars and certain local processes should be preserved will get us nowhere. We need to make sure that those directly involved in such preservation can count on a reasonable quality of life."

Enzo Ghigo, President of the Piedmont Regional Council

Much knowledge is to be gained through the taste buds and the mucous membrane in the nose, and attaining such knowledge is an experience that is closely related to pleasure. Pleasure of this sort implies moderation and awareness and is an integral aspect of health. Moreover, all these factors together are essential to taste, which means pleasurable learning and wise enjoyment.

If we abide by such measures, we should manage to weather the forthcoming deluge. But once the Ark has fulfilled its task, it should be destroyed. We do not want to live in the Ark. Once the waters have withdrawn, we shall step out onto land and, like Noah, plant our vines. Just like him, we shall indulge in some redeeming drunken revelry. Our children will doubtless laugh at our inebriation. However, among them there will be ones who, with the strength and conviction of a member of Slow Food, will take care of us and lovingly cultivate the vine.

NEW VALUES · "I believe that a nation's wine and food traditions are part of its cultural identity. However, concrete action is necessary to raise awareness of this in daily political activity. . . . The disappearance and standardization of tastes, the lack of interest in characteristic flavors, are part of a more generalized standardization of values and the consequence of various dominating non-values. . . . So the problem is not that of building an Ark of taste for an elite, but of redefining a new scale of values."

Willer Bordon, Heritage and Environment Undersecretary for the Italian Government

An Ark product can be animal or vegetable, for example, the Red Abalone and the Gilfeather turnip. It might even be mineral, supposing a sea salt were deemed worthy of inclusion. Or it could be a food, such as Creole cream cheese, produced by artisans using time-honored methods. In some cases, an Ark product will be a dawning tradition or a new creation that captures regional flavors and heritage.

To qualify as a passenger on Slow Food U.S.A.'s Ark, a product must possess these characteristics:

- Must be a unique, high-quality product with excellent flavor.
- Must be at risk of extinction—of being lost in the world of standardized food.
- Historically, socioeconomically, or culturally, must be tied to a precise territory or locality (products are often named after their place of origin).
- Must be in limited production (although a potential for increased production is desirable).
- If a refined or crafted product (such as smoked meat or aged cheese), then must be prepared according to specific techniques that reflect tradition or an innovative interpretation of traditional methods.
- Must be symbolically important as a regional food.

No product containing genetically modified raw materials and no transgenic breed or plant will qualify for the Ark.

The Ark U.S.A. Committee will set up a data bank and collect information about cultivars, breeds, products, and producers, as well as about shops and restaurants that are selling Ark products.

Slow Food's intention is not to create a food museum but instead to develop a lively marketplace for endangered foods. Because we recognize that food culture is regional, not national, we expect Ark products to have strong regional identities. Regional foods have deep meaning in local culture and have significance far beyond nostalgia and sentimentality. In a country as large and diverse as the United States, it is likely that Ark products from Vermont will be completely unfamiliar to people who live in Tucson or the Silicon Valley.

The Ark will not become a brand name, and Slow Food will not become a "middleman." Our goal is simply to shine the spotlight on small producers of high-quality, regional foods and to identify the markets and restaurants where these products are available. Where there is the need, Slow Food U.S.A. will create Presidia to help connect producers with consumers or restaurateurs. The Presidia can also encourage small specialty growers by helping to ensure fair prices for rare foods that have not been grown or produced because they are not deemed economically viable. The well-being of these growers and producers is intensely important to the Slow Food movement.

For more information, or to nominate a food to the Ark, please contact the Slow Food national office at P.O. Box 1737, New York, NY 10021; telephone (212) 988-5146.

ONE : 2

REGION IS REASON

Hermann Scheer

In November 1996, the United Nations' Food and Agriculture Organization (FAO) promoted a world summit on food problems. The question was: How can we feed eight billion people considering the progressive degradation of land and the subsequent decrease in agricultural output?

The answer provided during the conference was totally inadequate. It was exclusively based on the intensification of agricultural development and genetic manipulation technology within the framework of further globalization, that is, increasing world trade in agricultural produce. In short, an answer based on the models of development that are responsible for the appalling present situation. What the

FAO summit was effectively doing was urging us to accelerate down what they recognize to be a dead end street.

The fast-food question is not just about McDonald's. Fast food is one of the main features of the world economy. It subscribes to the principles adopted for the Olympic Games: quicker, higher, further. In our data-obsessed society, this leads us to live in an increasingly stressful world, continuously under pressure, in constant competition with others, and in obeisance to a single rule: producing ever more quickly and cheaply. This model has no future and embodies at least two contradictions. The first relates to the problem of transportation, one of the fundamental factors of global economy and global agriculture. The transportation system is based on an absurd principle according to which apples from New Zealand are shipped to Western Europe and Perrier water to California. Food that may be produced locally is thus increasingly moved from one end of the world to the other simply because fuel prices continue to diminish.

The low cost of energy does not promote well-balanced development and is the result of a mistaken policy. Moreover, the regional character of our agricultural production is inevitably undermined by a number of factors: lifting fuel taxes on air and sea transportation, deregulation of air transportation, and increasingly high export subsidies that distort the market and promote large distributors to the detriment of small producers and distributors. The globalization of production in the agricultural market can in no way promote healthy development.

It is also time to face the fact that any attempt to make quick profits in agriculture tends to be highly destructive. The fast food to fast profit ratio inevitably squeezes the breath out of small-scale production, which is unable to compete. Moreover, the trend ends up by polluting water and soil through increased use of fertilizers and chemical products, thus endangering the future of agricultural production. As a result, the number of vegetable species decreases, our common heritage (or what we should consider as such) is privatized, and the plurality of agricultural and food species is destroyed. Ultimately this leads to patents of biogenetics, a science now included in the General Agreement on Tariffs and Trade (GATT) treaties, whose inconsistencies will be highlighted in a report by the Agriculture Commission of the Assembly of the Council of Europe that I personally chair. First of all, it should be noted that the rules pertaining to total freedom pay no attention whatsoever to social context or pre-existing international agreements, such as the commitments made at the environment summit held in Rio de Janeiro. It is unacceptable that in 1991 our governments should have signed an international agreement to safeguard biodiversity and two years later subscribe to the GATT agreements that undermine biodiversity.

The second contradiction concerns state policies that provide incentives for transportation—in the GATT agreement, for air and maritime traffic—and, at the same time, complain about the fact that high energy consumption endangers vegetable species and the environment. The Rio de Janeiro summit fostered protection policies against climate change and its consequences, while the GATT agreements encourage processes that will provoke a climatic catastrophe. By the same token, in 1992 it was declared that biodiversity should be protected, whereas the patents on biogenetics proposed at the GATT negotiations are bound to lead to the privatization of vegetable species.

We simply cannot organize the agricultural produce market according to the same criteria used for the industrial sector, and it is high time we realized this. Agricultural production cannot be increased indefinitely because the availability of land is not unlimited. Moreover, geography and soil conditions largely dictate where certain crops can be grown. Though a mere ten countries may manufacture cars for the whole world, the same simply cannot be said for food. It is absurd to apply the same criteria to agriculture and industrial production.

On the contrary, we must do our utmost to prevent this from happening. It is not true that the free circulation of agricultural produce benefits Third World countries. Indeed, if the industrialization of agriculture in the Third World follows the pattern of rich Western countries, the Third World will lose rather than gain. Should this model be adopted, experts estimate that one billion out of the three billion people who currently depend on agriculture for their living in Third World countries will lose their jobs in the next twenty years. Quite clearly, the economic, social, and political consequences would be catastrophic.

The Ark that Slow Food has built must do its utmost to stop this process from taking place. Those who intend to safeguard biodiversity in production and consumption should put up a consistent fight against the patents of biotechnology. Those engaged in giving new life to the culinary tradition of wines and food must support the new regionalization of agricultural economy. Those who are aware of quality of food production must struggle to abolish subsidies exclusively granted in relation to quantity, another aspect of prevailing agricultural policy.

What is to be done?

I would like to conclude with a few operational remarks. Let us reflect upon the meaning of the term "protection." Protecting culture, the environment, and human values is no longer enough. We need to change something in the structure of the economy, introducing new definitions and objectives.

First and foremost, we should develop direct patterns of distribution, abolish export subsidies, and use that money to support regional markets and counter patents on biogenetics. The agricultural sector must get actively involved in opposing the decrease in energy prices and the thoughtless consumption that this encourages. Individual countries should create banks in which the diversity of species can be preserved. Clean, renewable energy obtained locally from agricultural produce needs to be developed because it can considerably reduce current costs. And we must fight for the abolition of all the government directives that determine the size of apples, pumpkins and so on, since these rules only help large distributors and hinder the process of regionalization in agriculture.

A HERITAGE · "There are enormous reserves of local experience that must be preserved in view of the fact that they actually represent a cultural patrimony. When we say that we have a heritage of products, we are basically saying that we have a cultural heritage. . . . A material fact is thus a fact of civilization, with its obvious economic consequences, because a cultural heritage also has an economic value. . . . [Our local products] are the creation of a body of farmers and tradespeople who have expressed the spirit of the land, their ideologies, their way of living through their products. That's why it's a question of cultural heritage."

Corrado Barberis, President of the National Institute for Rural Sociology

GENETIC EROSION ·   " . . . 1,500 of the 7,000 varieties of fruit that we have in Italy will disappear over the next four to five years. The whole of society will pay the price of this genetic erosion, not only during the current generation but also in those to come, because it is precisely by valuing diversity that we can save the flavors and specific attributes of soil and land. . . . What we need to do is take a new, critical look at the prevailing technological model and make this a starting point for a reappraisal of biodiversity and the specific attributes of soil and land. Far from being a marginal issue, this is a new imperative, like a new social pact. . . . There are various aspects of international regulations that do exactly the opposite. In today's world a mere thirty plants meet 95% of food needs, and this is an extremely serious matter. It means that the level of genetic erosion is very high and is progressing. Every six hours another plant disappears. This is a here and now emergency. . . . On the one side we have this enormous heritage under serious threat; and on the other, article 35 of the GATT Agreement. I believe that the latter is extremely negative, particularly at an ethical level. The article was dictated by the United States and Japan, violating all the previous international conventions, and it leaves countries free to apply a type of industrial patent system to living matter. The upshot of this is that inanimate things are placed on the same level as living matter, including animals and plants of a higher order. There is no way a policy of this sort can be reconciled with the social, economic, and ethical implications of maintaining land and soil diversity. On the contrary, the tendency seems to be to transform farmers into piece-rate workers serving multinationals."

Carmine Nardone, member of the Agriculture Commission of the Italian Parliament

ONE : 3

INSIDIOUS DISTANCE

Stefanie Böge

In recent years, the world of mass food production has witnessed a constant development in farming techniques, processing methods, and transportation systems, which together have contributed to the unprecedented availability of a plentiful range of products. We can choose from a wide variety of top-quality foodstuffs of extremely widespread provenance. However, this supply system has two significant drawbacks: it involves transportation that devours huge amounts of energy and pollutes the environment; and it brings about a reduction in variety within the food supply. Rarely do these two aspects—the increase in transportation distance and the constant reduction of regional variety—feature in the debate concerning food supply. So let's take a closer look at them.

Transportation is an indispensable condition for trade exchange and the access to new sales markets. Nevertheless, low transportation costs encourage companies to turn in-house costs, such as warehousing, into external costs in the shape of product transportation. Moreover, distances tend to grow as companies look for sources of cheap raw materials and new sales outlets. The cost of transportation is negligible in relation to a company's total produc-

tion costs, so goods tend to travel ever greater distances.

Tons and kilometers

In recent decades, the food industry has experienced substantial increases in transportation distances. The total quantity of transported goods multiplied by the distance covered (expressed in tons per kilometer) has almost doubled, from 15.1 to 28.2 metric billion tons per kilometer between 1970 and 1990. (This comparison does not take into account the products' value, but gives a good idea of the increase in transport distances.) According to 1991 figures from the German Ministry of Public Transport, the transport of goods by road—the most harmful from an environmental point of view—has increased threefold, from 7.5 to 22.8 tons per kilometer, and nowadays accounts for 80 percent of the total transport of goods in the food industry, as opposed to the 50 percent of 1970. Despite these figures, food consumption has only slightly increased. Conversely, the quantity of the transported goods multiplied by the distance covered has rocketed.

So we can assume that we eat more and more food from farther and farther away. In a nutshell, the distances

THE ARK AND THE DELUGE

ONE

we consume are increasing. But the increase in transportation distances is not only due to the dynamics of the economy. It largely depends on our eating habits. Our society is undergoing structural changes (more leisure time, more singles, and more elderly people), which also involves patterns of consumption that bring about a different relationship with food. As indicated by 1990 statistics from the German Ministry of Nutrition, Agriculture and Forestry, the consumption of highly sophisticated food is on the rise, such as ready-made dishes (frozen food or dishes to warm up in a microwave oven) and industrially processed fruit and vegetables (preserves, juices), easy to prepare but very demanding in terms of production and transportation. At the same time, the needs of consumers—both male and female—are becoming increasingly personal and differentiated. We take it for granted that we can buy anything, whenever we like and wherever we are. Our relationship with the seasons and regional peculiarities has been almost entirely lost. Regional variety has been replaced by homogeneous products subjected to long-distance transportation and designed to meet consumers' requirements.

One yogurt, ten meters

What distance is currently covered by an apparently simple product such as a strawberry yogurt? Strawberry yogurt is made of milk, strawberry preparation, sugar, and yogurt cultures. It is packaged in a recyclable glass pot, closed with an aluminum film, and labeled. Yogurt is sold in cardboard trays of twenty pots each. Trays are glued and reinforced with several layers of cardboard. All these components (strawberry preparation, aluminum film, etc.) are produced by other manufacturers and are subsequently transported to the yogurt producer.

Production and distribution involve over 8,000 kilometers, and sales accounts for a further 3,493 kilometers. If we relate all these kilometers to the gross weight of a single yogurt purchased in a store, there are at least ten meters of truck transport. As we spoon down the nutritional value of the product, we are also symbolically consuming the distance covered by the transport vehicle.

Apples

The same rules apply to fresh produce, such as fruit and vegetables, which also travel enormous distances to reach our tables. A glance at the fresh produce stalls at supermarkets shows to what extent everything is available throughout the year: winter strawberries, spring pears, summer apples, and autumn gooseberries. Somewhere in the world, they are in season!

The increase in imports aims at widening the range of products offered. But since exporting countries are generally geared to selling their "best quality" products on foreign markets, the "quality requirements" of importing countries tend to increase. As a consequence, local producers have to compete with the quality (and the prices) of imported products. Local products that differ from the homogenous international model thus tend to be discarded.

The European Union and the World Trade Organization also have an impact on the standardization of food. Originally their actions aimed at reducing health risks and making sure that products complied with sanitary directives. Nowadays, in most cases, their role has changed. Take apples, for instance. Quality standards refer to three classes: Extra, I, and II. The leaf-

stalks of Extra apples must be undamaged, Class I apples can have damaged leaf-stalks, whereas Class II apples may have none at all, though their skin must be unblemished. Other rules concern the skin and the minimum diameter, which—according to the class—ranges from 50 to 65 millimeters. In Germany, only the apples included in the Federal list of admitted varieties can be put to market. In order to preserve the purity of these local varieties, an old variety cannot be sold in the European Union.

Apples are just one illustration of how an economy based on long-distance transportation is inducing a reduction in product variety. In certain European regions there are still hundreds of varieties of apples that can be used for many different purposes, yet an ordinary German supermarket will stock no more than ten varieties in the course of a year. Apples come from eight different countries (Argentina, South Africa, New Zealand, Spain, France, Italy, The Netherlands, Germany). You will often find the same varieties produced by different countries. Usually they are common varieties of eating apples that cannot be used for any other purpose.

So the whole world is represented in supermarket apples. In the first half of the year, they will mainly come from Europe and, in the second half, from overseas. Regional varieties are very seldom put to market. The distinctive feature of these apples is that nearly all of them comply with the same "quality standards": a standard size, a given color, an unblemished skin, and—this is guaranteed—the same taste.

Quality is regional

The long distances our food has to cover do not only have an impact on the environment (in terms of energy consumption, exhaust emissions, surface occupation, accidents), but also on the growing standardization of products. The "variety" you can see on entering a supermarket is only apparent, since the basic components are often the same. The only difference is in packaging and in the addition of flavoring and coloring. Fresh fruit and vegetables are of standard size and color, and the varieties on sale are very limited in number. Consumers nowa-days can no longer experience certain foods since regional products are no longer available on the market. We have based our lifestyle on long distance transportation, believing that we therefore benefit from a wider choice of products. In fact, top-quality products stand out for their regional and seasonal features. Long-distance transportation—though necessary for given specialties such as the original Parma ham—is a drawback for most food, especially staple foods. Long-distance transportation is not a sign of quality, because trade activities associated with it have far-reaching negative effects on the variety of regional products. The fact is that quality is not guaranteed by the distance covered by products, but by their regional variety.

IN THE AMERICAN ARK: WILD RICE

Barbara Bowman, Chuck Lavine, and Marcia Lavine

Wild rice, an aquatic plant that grows along lakesides and rivers, has long been a sacred and staple food for many native North Americans living in Minnesota, Wisconsin, and parts of Canada. Others who live in this area also enjoy this local specialty, which is closely associated with the region's history and geography. At one time wild rice was hand-harvested by many native peoples, including the Ojibway, the Chippewa, and the Sioux.

The true wild form of this grain is endangered for two reasons: growing conditions are fragile, and there is economic competition from lower-priced "wild rice" that is cultivated, machine-harvested, and machine-parched. Aboard the U.S. Ark is the wild rice that grows naturally, is harvested by Native Americans, and is hand-parched over a wood fire.

Wild rice isn't actually a rice. It's the highly nutritious seed of an annual aquatic grass *(Zizania aquatica)*, and the true wild variety has very specific growing requirements. It germinates and grows in cold lakes in locations where the water moves slowly. The depth of the water is critical: if it's too deep, the sun's rays will be too dim to mature the plant, and in water that is too shallow the grass develops weak stems. When the plant reaches the surface of the water, it sends out a float leaf that supports the grass as it grows. If conditions are favorable, more leaves develop above water, producing the high-protein grain, but if the water level rises or if there are high winds, the grass may be uprooted.

Autumn in Minnesota is unpredictable, and this plant is acclimated to that uncertainty. Wild rice guards its survival by producing a series of seeds that mature at different times. That way, if early seeds are destroyed by adverse weather or eaten by waterfowl, the next series has a chance to develop under more advantageous conditions. Because the seeds mature and fall in stages, hand-harvesting is sequential, with a single stand of grass being harvested three or more times. Sequentially harvested grains are large and unbroken—the marks of the highest-quality wild rice.

In Minnesota, a license is required to harvest naturally grown wild rice on state-owned land. Regulations require that rice be harvested from a canoe in the traditional manner during a regulated season. Using a pole, the driver powers the canoe through the water; meanwhile, the harvester uses beater sticks (called "knockers") to whack the mature grains into the canoe. On reservation land, the harvesting techniques are the same; however, only Native Americans may harvest the rice. In the traditional manner, after harvest the green rice is cured and then parched over a wood fire to dry the hulls and separate them from the grain.

Parching over wood dramatically affects the color and taste of the grain. Whereas commercial wild rice is nearly black, the hand-processed rice can be shades of smoky gray or beige with dark flecks. This hand-harvested, hand-parched rice cooks evenly and has an appealing toasted-nut flavor and a tealike aroma. Rinse the rice well to remove the residual chaff. It cooks a lot faster than the cultivated wild rice many of us are used to preparing.

Unfortunately for the consumer, there are several types and grades of grain sold under the name "wild rice," some not being wild at all but rather a cultivated grain grown in paddies in Minnesota, Canada, and California. The main categories, in order of decreasing mechanization, are:

1. Paddy rice, commercially cultivated—a hybrid grain always harvested by machine.
2. Lake rice, machine- or hand-harvested and machine-parched.
3. Native-harvested and hand-processed lake and river rice— hand-harvested and hand-parched. This is the product on board the U.S. Ark.

Natural rice, harvested by Native Americans and hand-parched, is now in limited production. Because it currently costs about $8 a pound retail and has minimal distribution, very few people outside the northern Midwest have ever tasted this product. It is, however, an important part of the economy for several Native American groups. Three facilities in northern Minnesota process the rice by hand-parching. There is sufficient grain and adequate processing facilities to in-crease production. Yet people simply don't know that this authentic, regional wild rice exists, a problem that hopefully the additional attention brought to wild rice by Slow Food will help remedy.

We recommend the high-quality rice that comes from Northland Native American Products: (612) 872-0390.

Chapter **TWO**

Tradition and Consumerism

SLOW FOOD VERSUS MCDONALD'S

George Ritzer

McDonald's is the leading force in the fast food industry and a model for many other sectors of society that seek to utilize its principles in an effort to duplicate its success. Among those principles are an emphasis on efficiency, on things that can be quantified rather than the quality of those things, on predictable products, settings, and experiences, and on the replacement of skilled human beings with non-human technologies. I have used the term "McDonaldization" to describe the process by which these principles have spread throughout the fast food industry, other sectors of American society, and increasingly other societies around the world. The enormous popularity of this model reflects the fact that it has much to offer, but the model also carries with it a series of problems, including an undue emphasis on speed, a focus on quantity to the detriment of quality, a loss of concern for unique goods and services, and the decline and eventual elimination of skilled human workers.

Of particular interest here are the implications of terms like "fast food" and "junk food" that are usually associated with this process. McDonaldization has led to a trade-off in which we are able to obtain things faster and faster, but the quality of goods and services we receive suffers with every increase in speed and efficiency. The Slow Food movement offers an alternative to this that equates "slow food" with "high-quality food." It should be pointed out, however, that speed does not necessarily bring with it poor quality.

Starbucks is an example of a chain that serves a high-quality product (coffee) and it is able to deliver that product quickly. Indeed, while the fast food industry has been dominated by mediocre products, I think that the future will bring more and more efforts to apply the principles of McDonaldization to the provision of higher-quality goods and services. That being said, it remains the case that high speed will, in the main, continue to be associated with mediocrity.

Slowness and quality

Does the Slow Food movement represent a threat to the increasing McDonaldization of the food industry? While there are some exceptions, slow and quality do represent the alternatives to fast and junk. There is a population throughout the world that is repulsed by McDonaldization and craves leisurely produced, high-quality goods and services. These are the people who are likely to be drawn to the movement and reject the McDonaldization's model.

However, a major problem facing the Slow Food movement is the power that McDonald's and its clones wield over young people in the United States and increasingly throughout the rest of the world. Advertisements, especially on television, are aimed at very young children and are designed to "hook" them at a very early age on fast food and its simple salty-sweet tastes. As the child matures, the nature of the advertisements may change, but they are continually designed to maintain the fast food industry's hold over young people. This hold is buttressed by the fact that, in an increasing number of American communities, there are fewer alternatives to McDonaldized settings. Even if young people didn't want to eat in such settings (and they usually do!), they are increasingly forced to by the absence of alternatives. The result is that by the time they reach adulthood, a growing number of Americans have experienced relatively few non-McDonaldized settings. The fast food restaurant and its products are the standards by which younger Americans judge the alternatives. Thus, to many of them, a home-cooked gourmet hamburger is not likely to taste as good as the McDonald's hamburger they have eaten all their lives. The McDonald's hamburger has become the standard of quality, and against that all alternatives are likely to be judged negatively. If there is hope among young people, it is among those outside the United States who have not as yet been as profoundly affected by McDonaldization. They can still see that there are slower, better alternatives, and they can be appealed to on that basis. However, time is short given the massive international expansion of all sorts of McDonaldized systems, many of which are emanating from the United States. McDonald's itself is now opening more outlets overseas than in the United States, and the majority of its profits come from its overseas operations. Furthermore, most nations are not only eager to accept these American exports, but they are aggressively building their own indigenous businesses based on the principles of McDonaldization. Unless opposition is mobilized quickly, the young people in many other societies will be confronted with what their American peers already face—increasingly ubiquitous advertising of McDonaldized products and the disappearance of the non-McDonaldized alternatives.

Let us assume that the Slow Food movement is able to act fast enough and "save" large numbers of the world's youth from McDonaldization. These young people, in combination with the natural constituency for the movement (those from less- or non-McDonaldized societies who know the glories of unhurriedly produced, high-quality products), then serve to create a massive international community. The problem, almost immediately, will be the difficulties involved in resisting the pressures to

McDonaldize such a movement. There have been many efforts to escape from McDonaldization (back-to-nature camping, mountain climbing, and so on), but as soon as they become successful, they have attracted entrepreneurs who have rationalized them in order to reach larger audiences and reap higher profits. If quality can be McDonaldized (as Starbucks has dem-onstrated), then a massively successful Slow Food movement would not be immune to McDonaldization. Money could be made and power attained by McDonaldizing that movement as well as its various elements (that is, businesses specializing in the ingredients, technologies, and recipes needed to create high-quality food).

Eluding the iron cage

Is there any hope of resisting the McDonaldization of food and every other sector of our lives? There is, but it is a slim hope given the seemingly inexorable expansion of McDonaldization. The Slow Food movement might find grounds for hope in the recent so-called McLibel trial in London. McDonald's sued two activists for slandering it in a pamphlet they were distributing, and while McDonald's won the case, the judge sided with the defendants on several issues. More importantly, the negative publicity surrounding the case has made McDonald's the lightning rod for a variety of dissident groups such as those concerned with environmental, health, and economic issues. McDon-

ald's is on the defensive vis-à-vis these groups, since the McLibel trial proved to be such a public relations debacle, and it is not likely to undertake similar legal action any time soon. The Slow Food movement might find natural allies in the groups that have been brought together and mobilized by the McLibel case.

McDonald's, with its over 20,000 outlets throughout the world (to say nothing of the other fast food chains and their outlets), makes for easy and visible targets for those interested in protesting against McDonaldization. There are other collective undertakings that can help stem the tide of McDonaldization. For example, there is the need for more people to found non-McDonaldized businesses and institutions of all types. And, more people need to overlook the allure of McDonaldized systems, and patronize these alternative businesses.

One difficult problem facing the Slow Food movement is the possibility that it might become an elite movement that attracts mainly members of the upper classes. After all, it is that group that can most easily afford the higher prices that are generally associated with quality goods and services. In fact, the upper classes already find themselves best able to avoid or resist McDonaldization. The Slow Food movement needs to find a way to attract middle and lower class supporters. This will not be easy, but it can be done by, for example, emphasizing the importance of home cooking using readily available recipes and high-quality, perhaps homegrown, ingredients. It also can be done by pointing out that fast food is not nearly as inexpensive as it seems: that one actually pays a lot for what one gets. It is often far cheaper, and sometimes, given travel time, even easier to cook the same kinds of foods at home.

I have focused mainly on fast food restaurants and the Slow Food movement, but I want to make it clear that the problem is a far broader one. It is not just food that has been McDonaldized, but also schools and universities, health care providers, businesses of all types, the mass media, tourism, sports, and more. Ongoing trends within these settings need to be resisted in the same way they are being opposed within the food industry. If we do not resist these trends, or if we are not successful, we will find ourselves, paraphrasing the great German social theorist Max Weber, in an iron cage of McDonaldization.

Efforts to resist the McDonaldization of food cannot succeed on their own; they need parallel efforts in all other settings. There is little prospect of successfully resisting the McDonaldization of food if all other sectors of society are highly McDonaldized. To be successful, this must be an effort that is undertaken in every sector of society.

A BROKEN HEART

Tom Bruce-Gardyne

Westerners have become a parody of their own self-indulgence. As they waddle into the new century, they have grown fatter, more toothless, and more constipated than ever before. While the Third World struggles with malnutrition, the West is plagued by the so-called diseases of affluence.

Of these, coronary heart disease (CHD) is one of the worst, and Scotland is in a league of its own. The country has the highest death rate from CHD in the world, with Scots five times more likely to die prematurely from its effects than their cousins in southern Europe. There is now overwhelming evidence linking this to Scotland's poor diet—a diet of saturated fats, fags (cigarettes), too much salt and sugar, and, worst of all, precious little in the way of fiber, fruit, and vegetables.

The evidence is there at your feet, where the empty cigarette packets, tin cans, and shards of polystyrene scutter across the concrete. Here amidst the bleaker housing estates in Scotland's inner cities where CHD is so rife, an excess of affluence hardly seems the point. And yet in some way perhaps it is when compared to the past. Had today's junk food been available two hundred years ago, it would have been well beyond the means of most. In those days, the rural poor who made up the great bulk of the population had no choice but to survive on oats, kale, milk, and increasingly, potatoes. It was a frugal, unremitting diet, but it was undeniably healthy. In her fascinating book *The Good Scots Diet,* Maisie Steven quotes the parish records from the 1790s for Fortingall in Perthshire: "In general the people are long-lived. Many are between 80 and 90: some between 90 and 100, a few live beyond that age." Such statistics are by no means atypical, and the prospect for those who had survived the fevers of youth (and childbearing for the women) had never been so good.

Within a hundred years, things had deteriorated badly. The drift to the cities to work in the shipyards to the Clyde and the jute mills of Dundee had been turned to a stampede by the Highland clearances and the periodic bouts of potato blight. It was a time of crushing urban poverty: by 1861, the homes of a third of the population consisted of one room. It was at this time that the foundations of Scotland's poor diet were laid. As wheat became cheaper than oats, bread took the place of porridge, and once steel-roller mills were introduced in the 1870s, white bread began to replace whole meal. Scotland's love affair with processed food began in the 1860s, with the arrival of cheap canned meat, first from Chicago and then Buenos Aires and Montevideo. Within sixty years, meat consumption had risen 40 percent and with it people's intake of saturated fat, though much was being burnt off in heavy physical labor rather than left to clog up the arteries. Meanwhile, consumption of sugar rose a staggering 500 percent in the hundred years leading up to 1936.

It took the Boer War at the end of the last century to cause indignant public concern: half the Scots recruits, who had been such good cannon fodder in the past, had to be rejected on grounds of size and health. Gradually, improvements in living conditions helped reduce such ills of the poor as infant mortality and rickets, while dietary advice was aimed at combating under-nourishment. For nutritionists it was the outbreak of War World Two that heralded the golden age of healthy eating. In 1949, the Scottish dietitian Dr. Passmore was able to conclude: "Probably never before in history, and certainly not within living memory, have the children of Scotland been so healthy."

The wartime diet was abandoned with glee by the Scots, who indulged in a serious eating binge once the last shackles of rationing were removed in 1954. Meat pies, burgers, and loads of candies were washed down with Irn-Bru—Scotland's national fizzy drink, "made from girders" and as sweet at Coke. Producing enough meat, milk, and dairy produce to make them affordable to all seemed desirable, and after the centuries of want, who would deny the Scots the chance to enjoy their newfound wealth and buy what they felt like?

Causes

By the 1970s, an increasingly sophisticated food industry was there to hook people onto an expanding array of easily stored and transported goods.

For the industry and the big retailers there were obvious attractions in moving from bulky, perishable commodities into processed foods with added value that could be turned into major brands through advertising. By 1991, a mere 4.5 million pounds was spent on advertising for fresh fruit and vegetables, compared with 28 million for crisps (potato chips) and 83 million for

Massimo Cavallini

According to reliable data collected in 1993 by the Centers for Disease Control and Prevention, the percentage of fatties—or "large people," as the National Association to Advance Fat Acceptance (NAAFA) insists they should be called—had risen from 25 to 33 percent over the previous ten years. Just one year later, a study published by the *Journal of the American Medical Association* mercilessly calculated that no less than 58 million—30 percent more than in 1985—American adults were clinically "at risk" because of their excess weight. As the *JAMA* data revealed, the number of fat teenagers, which had remained stable at 15 percent in the 1960s and 1970s, had risen to 21 percent.

In July of 1998, the parameters defining obesity were lowered and the National Institute of Health added another 29 million people, and on the eve of the third millennium, official figures for fat people in the United States topped 97 million—55 percent of the adult population. This fact was featured on one of the placards borne aloft on the "one million pound march" between Santa Monica and Venice, California, that concluded the NAAFA conference at the end of September 1998. "55 and counting" read the triumphant message flaunted before the beautiful bodies of "Muscle Beach."

However, Fat City is not just a statistical majority. More than in numbers, the real strength of this overweight constituency rests in the ways that the culture, which despises and fights fatness, can be identified with radical health-consciousness, itself a facet of that "shared feeling for excess" known as consumerism, an integral part of the U.S. philosophy and economy. According to psychologist Kelly Brownell, manager of the Center of Eating and Weight Disorders at Yale University:

> Americans get fat for many reasons. And many of those reasons are to be found in that fast-food culture they've spread all over the world. But perhaps the most blatant reason of all is the huge, well-oiled, heavily advertised presence of the food industry on TV. The average child watches 10,000 food ads a year. And they are not seeing commercials for Brussels sprouts. They are seeing soft drinks, candy bars, sugar-coated cereals, and fast food, all of them eagerly swallowed by extremely thin guys. Put the two things together and you can have only one result—obesity.

TWO TRADITION AND CONSUMERISM

Statistics show that Fat City may be a product of plenty, but it is certainly not a rich city. The highest percentages of overweight people are to be found among the most marginalized segments of the population—for example, over 80 percent of the Native Americans on the Indian reservations. And a recent study carried out jointly by the National Research Council and the Institute of Medicine has proved—by examining a large sample of Mexican immigrants in Fresno County, California—that obesity is one of the most typical and widespread "diseases of Americanization." As Professor William Vega of the University of California at Berkeley points out: "Newcomers put on weight because the double message that they receive from the new culture is 'consume and stay thin,' and they generally only grasp the first part." In other words, belonging to Fat City is a way of "feeling American," or rather of becoming part of a nation that has invented thousands of diets but has never acquired the ancient virtue of moderation.

chocolate. And having converted the consumers to convenience, there was little risk of losing them back to the kitchen.

Handing over the cooking to others is not always such a good idea, however, especially when the food is being laced with sugar, fat, and salt—the cheapest flavorings around. When it comes to salt, the British eat five times more than they need, and two-thirds is reckoned to be from processed food. A recent study claims that reducing the daily salt intake by as little as 3 grams would lower blood pressure enough to cut premature deaths from strokes and heart disease by 15 percent.

In the mid-1950s, the correlation between heart disease and diet began to cause deep concern. The mountain of research grew and grew, contradictory advice multiplied, more and more

Scots continued to die young. With half a million of them currently suffering from some form of heart disease such as angina, we are talking of an epidemic.

Yet it is only comparatively recently that there has been real consensus on the probable causes. Apart from a patient's family history, smoking, high blood pressure, and high levels of blood cholesterol are the main suspects, and it's when two or more factors are high that things start to look dangerous. Having all three high places you in the top 5 percent of those at risk.

A diet heavy in saturated fats without the antioxidants that come from fruit and vegetables boosts the level of cholesterol in the blood. As the arteries clog up, the supply to the heart is restricted, and if the heart is under strain through high blood pressure, stress, and obesity, the chances of a fatal clot increase.

If it doesn't kill you, a heart attack is still a pretty serious indictment of your state of health. And yet in Scotland, a third of all those who survive are unable or unwilling to change their diet, and in a recent survey, despite all the evidence to the contrary, 69 percent of Scots consider themselves healthy eaters. Such complacency reflects the way the message of health and diet has been confused and often discredited. The State telling people what they should eat tends to backfire, just as when preaching on morals. People are sensitive and attach value to their own behavior, and anything that smacks of Puritanism— of nanny State wagging her finger and saying "Don't!"—is treated with contempt. Thankfully, there's a greater awareness now that changes must involve the community and be from the bottom up, but it will inevitably take time. The twenty-five-year campaign to lower Finland's chronic levels of heart disease made no impact at all for the first ten years. It will not be easy in Scotland, with the constant pressure for results to justify every aspect of health spending.

Supermarket diet

The supermarkets are part of the solution and part of the problem. They control over two-thirds of the food bought in Scotland and have clearly increased the available varieties of fruit and vegetables dramatically. But whether their prices are fair, and whether they haven't helped create the so-called food deserts in the inner cities is another matter. It would be hard to say there's a cartel in operation, but prices on fruit and vegetables are notably similar among the big five supermarket groups, and margins are by all accounts pretty fat. More serious is the lack of access to healthy food at reasonable prices for those stranded without wheels or public transport deep in the country or down in the urban wasteland. Having killed off the competition, the modern British supermarket tends to sit out of town, offering one-stop shopping for those with cars. In some of the poorer parts of Dundee, the only reliable source of vitamin C is chips (french fries).

Heart disease in Scotland is closely linked to social class—the poorer the population, the greater the number affected. Ironically, for many people a healthier diet could be cheaper and certainly a better value than processed food, whose high price helps fund the flash packaging and advertising. The good Scottish diet of the past is long gone, and the idea that people will abandon the pot noodle for gruel is a little fanciful. Yet it is nonetheless tragic that so much of Scotland's fish, beef, and soft fruit is bundled into lorries and dispatched south. Some of it comes back heavily processed with its origins hidden, and few Scots seem to care.

Much of the efforts to wean the country onto a healthier diet for the sake of its heart have been aimed at the very young. Small babies born to smoking mothers are quickly put onto formula, a nonmilk substitute, and then weaned onto packaged and processed baby food. Preferences in taste are fixed early on, and there's evidence that Scotland's notorious sweet tooth stems from the nursery. A taste for vegetables never develops. Among the most exciting of the many community projects are efforts at teaching the basics of cooking. People need to gain confidence: if they can learn to cook vegetables with real crunch and flavor, they may overcome the years of damage by school lunchrooms and their evil ways with cabbage and sprouts. Today, fruit and vegetables are often given free at school mealtimes, and mobile fruit shops visit during recess, though some teachers complain of banana skins on the playground. Presumably they would rather have candy wrappers.

At last things are starting to improve and the ambitious targets set for Scotland's diet look like they are being met. For example, on the east coast, where the raspberries grow with such ease, there are plans to copy Finland's berry project, which encouraged many Finns to fill their freezers with fruit.

By the year 2005, due to this and other programs, the proportion of energy derived from fats, especially saturated fats, should fall below 35 percent, while fruit and vegetable consumption should double and the intake of salt should be cut by over a half. The tragedy is how long it has taken to make progress amidst the maelstrom of conflicting interests from industry, politicians, and scientists and pure misinformation from the media.

Meanwhile, how many Scots have gone early to the grave with a broken heart?

Author's note: I would like to thank Anne Woodcock, Dr. James Dunbar, Professor C. Bolton-Smith, Belinda Linden, and Bill Gray.

TWO : 3

UNNATURAL COOKING

Massimo Montanari

The words "fresh and in season" immediately conjure up images of the good old days when flavors were strong and genuine, and industry had not yet made all food taste pretty much the same, regardless of ingredients.

Nothing could be further from the truth. In the "good old days," the universe of food had little to do with the concepts of "fresh" or "in season." To understand just why this is so, we should take a separate look at the history of "poor" cooking and elite cuisine, the culinary culture of the low classes and that of those who ruled over them.

Since the dawn of civilization, hunger has been the main feature of poor cooking. Perhaps not so much hunger itself as the fear of hunger. The fear that there might be no food, that abundance would be followed—as it invariably was—by want and famine. Hence the desire to store, accumulate, and preserve food: to defeat the seasons and their whims. Why else would humans have invented so many techniques for protecting themselves from hunger? Choosing foodstuffs that last over time: grains, pulses, chestnuts. Processing those that cannot be kept: milk into cheese, meats into preserved meats, fruit into jam

and marmalade. Corning (preserving with salt) fish and vegetables. Smoking or drying in the heat of the sun. Pickling or preserving in oil. The agents involved were sugar, oil, vinegar, smoke . . . all of them capable of chemically modifying the products in different ways, of drying them, changing their nature in order to preserve them. Only thus was it possible to guarantee a uniform diet for as much of the year as possible. No farmer has ever been able to base his diet entirely on fresh foods that were "in season."

The situation was different for those in power, for the social and financial elite. Unlike the poor, they could display seasonal produce at their tables as symbols of their privileged condition. In the Middle Ages, for example, fresh fruit appears to have been a typical feature of "aristocratic gluttony"; similarly, fresh meat and fish replaced cold meats and dried products. However, until recently the cuisine of the rich showed little real interest in "natural" products and tastes. Indeed, Roman, medieval, and Renaissance cooking styles appear to have focused on culinary artifice, transformation, and distortion, perceived as evidence of power over nature. It was fashionable to mix flavors: sweet and sour, salty and acidic. Plenty of spices were used, and there was a particular predilection for pies, pastries, and other dishes in which the single ingredients lost their individuality. The cuisine was a show in itself, prone to creating astonishing effects: meat with the shape and texture of fish; fish with the shape and texture of meat. Colorful cooking of this sort made use of all sorts of products, both natural and artificial, to turn dishes into works of art. It was deliberately ostentatious, distinguishing itself from popular cooking by its systematic use of fresh products. Yet "territory" and "season" were not perceived as intrinsic limitations: offering foods from different regions and fruits out of season was for centuries a sought after luxury and a sign of privilege. Bartolomeo Stefani, the great Bologna-born chef who worked at the court of the Gonzagas in Mantua, was one of the foremost experts in culinary art of the 17th century. As he pointed out, strictly speaking, there are no products "in seasons" as such, since there is nearly always a place where they grow, and to get them all you need is "full purse" and "fast horses." Roman emperors and medieval lords boasted that they could always find all sorts of products out of season. The 18th-century abbot Pietro Chiari explained that nobles disliked cheap food, "fruits, herbs pertaining to the season," preferring "foreign and very rare things," like strawberries in January, grapes in April, artichokes in September. It is thus reasonable to suggest that in our own century the love of exotic foods and produce out of season

is only indirectly a product of the revolution in transport and preservation systems. For such improvements have simply made available to many people what was for a long time a privilege of the few. The overall attitude has substantially remained the same.

So the taste for natural cooking and products "in season" does not belong to the good old days. It was an unattractive concept to both the poor and the rich, albeit for different reasons. In their atavic fear of starvation, the former basically ate preserved foods whose original flavors were drowned by the predominant salty, sour, or sweet taste. As for the rich, they enjoyed showing off their wealth at the table by offering unnatural dishes that were also opposed to the seasons.

That cabbage should taste of cabbage and turnip of turnip is a simple but revolutionary idea that took root very slowly in European culture. It was launched by French chefs between the 17th and 18th centuries as part of the cultural rationalism that characterized the Enlightenment. One of the main tenets of this school of thought was the rediscovery of "natural simplicity." As a concept, this may have been ambiguous, but it was certainly also culturally stimulating. In today's advanced industrial societies, the threat of hunger is no longer a reality and society is finally much more receptive to the idea of "natural" food.

Modern industrial methods of food preservation include canning, refrigeration, freeze-drying, and the most advanced techniques for preserving the quality of products. Paradoxical though it may seem, these are much more compatible with natural and seasonal foods than the traditional methods used to be despite the claims of the preserved food industry during the 19th century.

So we should welcome the fresh food revolution, but beware of passing it off as a war against industrial food and a return to tradition. "Fresh" belongs to the culture of the future, not to that of the past.

FRESH—FOR A PRICE · "Those with fast horses and a full purse in every season will find all things that I suggest to them and at the same time that I speak of. . . . During the cold season, Naples and Sicily along their rivieras produce citrons, lemons, oranges, artichokes, asparagus, cauliflower, fresh broad beans, lettuce and charming flowers, all things which are sold all over their kingdom."

Bartolomeo Stefani, *L'Arte di Ben Cucinare (The Art of Fine Cooking)*

ARTIFICIAL NATURAL · "The plate covered with green grass made of sugar and gracefully laid out. . . . At the center of the plate there was a Statue made in the manner of a countrywoman, in marzipan paste with a basket on her head, with two doves, male and female, whose bodies were made of marzipan paste, but with real feathers."

Bartolomeo Stefani, *L'Arte di Ben Cucinare (The Art of Fine Cooking)*

Chapter THREE

Probably Good for You

ON FATS

Uda Pollmer

Food pontiffs see the cuisines of the world as a continual provocation. A typical example is the Mediterranean diet, which doctors believe to be good for the heart. What a shame that it includes almost everything that the most intransigent health gurus attempt to exclude from their clients' eating habits. A couple of glasses of Pastis or Ouzo as an apéritif, followed by the first course: instead of a bowl of raw salad, have an onion soup, possibly topped with high-cholesterol cheese *au gratin*. As a main course perhaps succulent fatty grilled meat. The vegetables served in Greek tavernas ooze olive oil, are well salted, and flavored with garlic. Moreover, gastronomy would be a non-event around these parts without a good glass of Retsina, Rioja, or Beaujolais.

North of the Alps, where there are no olive trees glittering in the hot summer sun, but in their stead dew glistening on the lush grass of pasture land, butter is the time-honored basic ingredient. At least this was the case until the margarine factories declared that such ancient customs were responsible for the rise in heart attacks: butter contains cholesterol, which, according to the latest research, attacks the heart and cardio-circulatory system. It remains a mystery why experts did not warn us against the dangers of breastfeeding, since breast milk is particularly rich in this insidious substance that newborn babies cannot produce themselves, but that they need for the development of the brain.

For all that advertising would have us believe, cholesterol is a dangerous external substance that enters our bodies through what we eat. On the contrary, it's a fundamental element in all the cells of our organism and is of vital importance for our metabolism. Leaving aside water content, about half the content of adrenal glands is pure cholesterol, which also accounts for about 10 to 20 percent of the brain. In a healthy person, even the heart, the organ considered to be most at risk from this selfsame substance, is made

up of roughly 10 percent cholesterol. Not that this is really so surprising: the body needs cholesterol to produce sexual and stress hormones, vitamin D, and bilious acids; without it, the nervous and immune systems could not function.

Not even vitamins play such a significant and multifarious role. The very fact that cholesterol is so important explains why the body does not rely on a sufficient supply from diet: the body must be, and is, able to produce its own. In a healthy person, the body produces from one to one and a half grams a day, according to need. If diet does not provide enough cholesterol, the body produces more. This is the reason why, for most people, a low-cholesterol diet is not successful in reducing levels of the substance in the blood.

Statistics

Where does the cholesterol theory spring from? The answer is simple: from statistical figures. In countries where greater quantities of animal fats are eaten, myocardium heart attacks are more frequent than elsewhere. If one delves further, the artifice becomes clear: in developing countries people have less to eat and die from diseases that differ from those afflicting the well-fed populations of industrialized countries. This, however, means nothing. Developing countries differ from rich Western societies in many other ways: suffice it to mention the number of cars, sales of dog food, or television ownership.

Juggling numbers has long been a specialty of marketing experts, whose power to scare has even infected a number of doctors. As a result, there are plenty of members of the medical profession who make up for what they lose through cuts in the national health system by "treating" those hitherto considered healthy and now deemed subject to excessive cholesterol levels.

Yet the cholesterol theory is essentially so shaky that sooner or later it was bound to be modified. The focus has now moved from the quantity of cholesterol in food to fatty acids. It has been said that only unsaturated fats, such as those in margarine, can protect the heart. Saturated fats, found for example in butter and animal suet, are thought to be the main causes of the "diseases of prosperity."

What appeared to be decisive proof of the fact that the right diet lowers cholesterol and guards against heart attack was provided by the famous study carried out in the northern Finnish province of Karelia. Finland has one of the highest levels of heart disease anywhere, and the statistics for Karelia used to break all records. A widespread campaign succeeded in stopping the region's inhabitants from smoking, introducing dietary margarine, and eliminating butter. Comparisons were then made with the inhabitants of the nearby province of Kuopio, which also had similar levels of heart disease.

Over the years, a decrease in cholesterol levels was noticed alongside a reduction in deaths from heart attack. The success was widely celebrated. It was a shame that doctors were not shown the results of studies conducted on the inhabitants of Kuopio, where the number of deaths due to cardio-circulatory diseases decreased more than in northern Karelia despite the fact that people continued to smoke, eat, and drink in peace. The results of a study carried out in Great Britain were even more clear: a conspicuous number of people who died from heart attacks were found to have eaten more margarine and less animal fats than those who died in road accidents.

Margarine

So how can all this be explained? New types of fatty acids, which do not occur naturally, are used in the production of margarine. The nub of the matter is the so-called partial hardening, during which only part of the unsaturated fatty acids are transformed into saturated fats, while those that remain change their structure. It is still not known how many new substances develop during this process or what biological effects they may have, yet a link between arteriosclerosis and heart attack has often been observed. Margarine manufacturers obviously assure the public that their products no longer contain transfatty acids, yet independent tests have shown that the fats used in the food industry, particularly by bakeries, are rich in them.

It wouldn't actually be difficult to obtain solid scientific proof of the truth of the cholesterol theory. A long-term study, for example over a ten-year period, would soon reveal whether lovers of butter were at greater risk of heart attack than margarine enthusiasts. No biochemical theory, however sophisticated, could be more convincing. So why have proponents of the theory resisted this kind of testing to date? Perhaps because the results

would be "wrong"? The large-scale independent survey known as the Nurse-Health Study involved 80,000 American nurses on the project and demonstrated that the risk of heart attack is higher among margarine eaters than among those who eat butter.

Even Ancel Keys, the mind behind the famous fats theory had to admit that his studies had not shown "a significant relationship between diet and cholesterol levels in the blood on the one hand and the appearance of coronary heart disease on the other." Some years ago, the *Süddeutsche Zeitung* wrote: "The margarine industry is today suspected of having simply bought many of the leading dietary scientists."

How is it possible that even those who read the specialist medical literature failed to see these links? In addressing this question, the Swedish scientist Uffe Ravnskov discovered that the majority of studies refute the fats theory. However, since such papers were at odds with doctors' preconceived ideas, they were simply not cited. Ravnskov concluded: "It is probable that human diet contains important substances for the blood vessels and heart, but there is almost no proof that the group of saturated fatty acids is harmful whereas the polyunsaturated group has beneficial effects."

Olive oil

At this point, another theory looms into focus. Perhaps it is not fatty acids that are responsible for the effects of fats, but some complementary substances. Let us take olive oil as an example. Until just a few years ago, public opinion north of the Alps considered olive oil to be pure poison for the heart; indeed, like butter, it contains few polyunsaturated fatty acids. However, a series of epidemiological studies in the Mediterranean proved the exact opposite: the more olive oil is consumed, the lower the death toll from heart attack. This finding spawned a new theory: the beneficial effects were attributed precisely to those hitherto denigrated simple unsaturated fatty acids found in olive oil.

However, perhaps the most plausible explanation is as follows: besides "fats," olive oil contains other complementary substances with pharmacological effects, for example, oleuropein. This belongs to the group of iridoids, which are found in many medicinal plants such as valerian, veronica, and gentian. Experiments on animals have shown that even small quantities (10 milligrams per kilo of body weight) of oleurpein reduce blood pressure by 60 percent. It also stimulates blood flow in the heart, increases the coronary flow, has an anti-arhythmic action on the heart, and has anti-spastic properties. It is a highly reactive substance that can be transformed into a wide range of other powerful active substances, such as dihydroxyphenylethanol. How come this pharmacological treasure was not discovered earlier? Perhaps lack of interest in the subject is a result of the fact that the medicinal substances in olives cannot be used commercially; the heart-protecting qualities of olive oil are so well-known that no patents can be issued, and besides, oleuropein can be found in supermarkets and pizzerias. Pills containing oleuropein would therefore have no market.

In the end, the heated debate about the right fats, the constant changes in theories, the hideous consequences threatening anyone silly enough to ignore these theories, and the millions that are made from the fear thus engendered all boil down to one simple truth: our traditional fats are as tolerable and healthy as any typical ingredient pertaining to local traditions, whether these be bread, wine, or pomegranates. However, this only holds true if the fats are not refined. The products that satisfy this condition are only two to date: butter and olive oil. Clearly every cultural environment is fully justified in developing its own cuisine, and this will have its devotees regardless of the dictates of passing theories.

NUTRACEUTICAL FOOD

Marco Riva

The names are enticing: "functional food," "nutraceutical products," "designer food." In Japan and the United States, the homelands of these new food philosophies, business is booming (20 billion dollars in the United States and 3.5 billion in Japan), but Europe is also showing interest (the current market estimate is 2 billion dollars). Clearly the trend is exponential, since functional food was only conceived and developed a decade ago. The market is still wide open; functional food is the structured answer to the variously formulated demands clearly reflected in the choices of consumers in post-industrial societies over the last twenty years. The trend is toward balance with a focus on health, often undermined to date by a different dietary view of traditional food.

Pharmafoods

The term "functional food" was coined in the mid-1980s in Japan, when the phenomenon of a rapidly aging population drew public attention to the role of food in preventing dysmetabolic disorders and chronic disease. The great tradition of dietary philosophical prescriptions typical of Eastern civilization was "reworked" in a modern pragmatic key, much as that

tradition was reworked in the fields of economics, culture, and social custom. The outcome was the debatable concept that there are "determinate" foods for each age group, according to its exposure to health risks. This in its turn led to product definition in line with the dictates of engineered food. The vast range of products that ensued were duly assigned to the following categories:

• foods to lower the risk of the onset of cardiovascular disease;
• foods to fight hypertension;
• products that control the level of cholesterol;
• products that reduce the tendency toward osteoporosis;
• products that provide elements that block free radicals, considered to cause aging and the formation of tumors;
• foods that protect intestinal flora;
• products that provide energy that can be readily metabolized.

It was like an improved and enriched version of the dialectical *yin-yang* principle.

Unlike old-fashioned dietary products, functional food promises prevention and it is therefore attractive to people whose lives could be at risk, even only psychologically. These products are still in fairly surreptitious circulation on the European market, although two sectors (sports drinks, and milk and yogurt with bioregulating microbic flora) are already well-represented on supermarket shelves.

While we await the miracles of genetic engineering that will provide us with products endowed with the properties listed above, "nutraceuticals" or "pharmafoods" comprise ingredients, formulae, and suppliments based on bioregulating principles such as vitamins, mineral salts, antioxidants, microbic flora, amino acids, and vegetable extracts (especially garlic and ginseng). In Japanese and American nutraceutical stores, this marketing has focused on the usual products: whole meal or non-allergenic cereals (with selected fiber), juice fortified with calcium and antioxidants, carrots containing higher levels of beta-carotene, drinks with added fiber, high-protein spreads, milk enriched with vitamin C and oligosaccharides, and so on. The lack of precise regulation (at least in Europe and the United States) has made it easier to use the term "functional" to promote products that are high on promises but rather lower on actual bioregulating elements.

On the other hand, many traditional foods have potentially "functional" properties that have not been widely acknowledged. For our amusement, we have described some in the accompanying table (see next page).

Food as medicine

Much research is involved in the nutraceutical food business, and it is conducted along somewhat repetitive lines: demonstration of the protective action of a typical food, definition of the "functional" ingredient, indication of the development potential of this activity. To wit: the discussion of the protective activity of flavonoids contained in purple grape juice and wine that I found in a recent page of CNN's interactive "Health and Foods" Web site (see the sidebar on page 42).

In the meantime, before the celebrated Tuscan red wine

TRADITIONAL MEDITERRANEAN PRODUCTS
WITH FUNCTIONAL PROPERTIES

FOOD	COMPONENT	PROPERTY ACTIVITY	FUNCTIONAL
Concentrated tomato paste	carotenoid	antioxidant	More bio-available than in fresh tomatoes
Purple grape juice	flavonoid	antioxidant	Flavonoids are highly concentrated, and there is no alcohol in the product
Hazelnut chocolate	monounsaturated fats	energetic	Monounsaturated fats regulate cholesterol levels
Pasta cooked "al dente"	carbohydrates (starch)	energetic	Low post-meal glycemic levels
Low-fat yogurt	calcium	hypoenergetic	Anti-allergenic (little lactose), mineralizer (calcium), favors bioregulating intestinal flora
Zaziki	microbic flora, microbic probiotics, garlic	modulation	Bioregulating, hypotensive
Taramasalada	fats	energetic	Fish roe are rich in triglyceride omega-3-unsaturates, which fluidify the blood and deter the deposition of cholesterol platelets

Brunello di Montalcino gains ground among the masses as a "nutraceutical," a little investment in image and some targeted research (for example into the increased availability of calcium as a prevention against osteoporosis) would suffice to make a "pharmafood" of Gorgonzola. This is not gratuitous irony; of the many "codified" properties of functional food, no mention is ever made of sensory qualities. The underlying message seems to be that a foodstuff has to be unpleasant in order to be "active." Rather like purges, or those hydro-alcoholic infusions that friends ply on us: the residual jetsam of popular pharmacopoeia.

Something that occurred in connection to my research confirmed this conviction. I am working on retrogradation; that is, the process of becoming stale that affects cooked pasta and rice. This is a problem for many dishes (especially starch based first courses) that are cooked and then have to be heated up on request. Retrogradation is the transformation of cooked (or gelatinized) starch that recrystallizes into structures that are more coriaceous and resistant to digestion. My research suggests that retrogradation is accelerated by the conservation and refrigeration temperatures dictated by hygiene. One of my colleagues, a physiologist, experimented with my artfully retrograded rice and demonstrated that it has a positive effect on post-prandial glycemia and provides a good quantity of "resistant" starch, useful in the balanced development of microbic intestinal flora. While I insisted on finding out how foods could be formulated or preserved after cooking so as to avoid the formation of retrograde structures, he suggested I should propose "aged" pasta and rice as a pharmafood. He attributed little importance to the unappetizing taste of "aged" pasta and rice. Indeed, according to the "functional" philosophy, food is consumed as a medicine and is prescribed as such. I couldn't help thinking of my father, who worked in a factory and delighted in the day when, after years of trade union battles, he was finally able to eat in the canteen and abandon his mess-tin of cold, "retrograde" pasta. If the factory owner had known then about the beneficial effects of precooked pasta, he would have found it easier to argue against the need for a canteen!

Drinks, rice, eggs

Let's take a closer look at some of these pharmafoods. Japan is currently awash with probiotic drinks (Pocari Sweat, Yakult, Bifiel) enriched with "live" microbes that balance intestinal flora. The qualities ascribed to probiotics include lowering the level of cholesterol, chemopreventive action on the growth of tumors, and increased immune protection. There is also a boom in the market for drinks containing "prebiotics," short-chain oligosaccharides that promote the growth of intestinal microbic flora; the commercial brands include Suntory Asasui and Nichirei One Day's Vitamin, maple juice fortified with lacto-fructo-oligosaccharides and high levels of vitamin C. There is also a wide range of drinks with added fiber (Fiber Mini Be Can). However, if you think such drinks smack too much of medicine, you can console yourself with bread or tofu fortified with DHA (docosahexaenoic acid), a substance that is good for the retina and brain and the hematic level of cholesterol.

In the United States, the main issue seems to be fortification with calcium. Here, too, drink-form prevails; thus we have Tropicana's Pure Premium Orange Juice, with added calcium citrate (this form is more bio-available than the mineral). Prune Juice (if you prefer your calcium with prunes) and Sunboost (calcium plus various vitamins). Uncle Ben's Calcium Plus Rice adds the mineral to fast-cooking rice, and there is also a pasta enriched with bio-available calcium, as well as, naturally, calcium supplement gum! Campbell's answer is more complex: the Intelligent Quisine program was developed with the American Heart Association and the American Diabetes Association, and involves a veritable therapeutic system based on

ATLANTA (Reuters), March 30, 1998—An aspirin a day may keep the doctor away, but it may do the job better if downed with purple grape juice or a mug of dark beer, a research said Monday.

John Folts, director of the Coronary Thrombosis Research Laboratory at the University of Wisconsin Medical School, said studies of flavonoids—substances that cause dark colors in some beers, red wines, and purple grape juice—suggest those beverages may keep heart-damaging blood clots from forming.

"People should take their aspirin with a glass of juice or one or two beers, not eight or ten," Folts told Reuters. He said aspirin is "very good at turning platelets down," making them less sticky so they do not form clots.

The effect of aspirin, however, is negated when adrenalin kicks in while exercising or under stress, he said. "The adrenalin overcomes the effects of aspirin," Folts said, "but with flavonoids the adrenalin has no effect so the flavonoids keep on working."

The study involved only ten people who repeated earlier tests on laboratory mice, and Folts said patients on aspirin should not discontinue that treatment.

"I do recommend no one stop their aspirin and go to something else, because so far this is unproven. It may be twenty years from now doctors will recommend flavonoids instead of aspirin, but we're not there yet," he said.

Folts said flavonoids are found "in dark beer but not light beer, in tea but not in coffee, in purple grape juice but not in lighter grape juices that people give to babies, in red wines but not in white wines."

The study, presented to doctors attending an American College of Cardiology meeting in Atlanta, was funded by the Oscar Rennenbohm Foundation, the Nutricia Research Foundation, and Welch Foods Inc., one of the leading producers of grape juice. Folts said the Welch money had no bearing on the test results.

"I just picked up a can out of my refrigerator at home," he said. "My wife does the shopping and that just happens to be the brand she bought, but it would work the same with any other brand."

—http//cnn.com/HEALTH/9803/30/heart.juice.reut/index.html

functional food. Americans love eggs, which are not great for the health, so we have Eggstasy Eggs, which have reduced fat (25 percent), and added vitamin E and antioxidants, or Egg-Plus, also with added vitamin E and also essential fatty acids omega-3 and omega-6. Hypertension is another problem. Salt is the main culprit and thus we have Cardia containing potassium chloride, magnesium sulfate, and L-lysin. The United States also boasts Splash, the rather obvious name for a tropical fruit and carrot drink with added vitamins A and E. Power Bar (another imaginative name) is a high energy biscuit for sports enthusiasts. Arthraffect and Nutra-Joint are drinks for the elderly.

Other functional substances being marketed are extracts of *ginkgo* (improves memory), *ginseng*, and *guarana* (energizers): they can be imbibed in a Josta (Pepsi Cola group) or extracted while chewing gum. There are also gums enriched with echinacea, grape flavonoids (ActiVin), creatine, carnitine, and taurine (amino acids that favor the deposition of lean muscle)—veritable legal doping. Maybe worst of all: Yummi Bears, a range of spreads containing broccoli, Brussels sprouts, carrots, tomatoes, parsley, alfalfa, papaya, and apples.

The European market is less imaginative. The functional foods available include the usual sports drinks, milk and yogurt with added probiotic flora or prebiotic substances, a few margarines that promise to lower hematic cholesterol (The Finnish brand, Benccol), and some spreads enriched with the by now familiar essential fatty acids omega-3 and omega-6 (Gaio Spread in Denmark, Life in Great Britain). There is even a bread (Burgen Bread) enriched with soya flour and linseed oil containing phytoestrogens that can alleviate some symptoms of menopause! In France, the Pernod group has recently launched three new drinks: 220, containing an extract of *anamalahobe* (from Madagascar) with "electric" and "warming" properties; Gong, based on ginseng; and Devil, containing black pepper. The most amusing European product is a fruit juice named Bio-Solan, based on "medicinal" mineral water enriched with vitamins A, C, and E. The purported nutritional properties are often no more than advertising claims. Although Japan has specific regulations that apply, there is a worrisome lack of standards in Europe and America. It is therefore possible to describe any component as "functional" without any scientific back-up or proven reports on the quantity-benefit ratios.

What conclusions should be drawn? In societies moved by the cinematic *Titanic* and that listen rapturously to New Age music, these products (which often really do have preventive properties) are seen in the same way as the elixirs of the last century that promised velvet-smooth skin and eternal youth. Their popularity reveals a dangerous propensity: that of

43

entrusting the consumption of food to an idea or piece of information rather than to experience or curiosity filtered by intelligence. This is a troubling development that will no doubt sooner or later lead to the rejection of "free" pleasure as a sin.

THE CONVICT'S DIET

Annie Hubert

We are living in a historical period when food has become a major issue for the Western world, at times almost an obsession. While presently most people are blessed by abundance, we are more preoccupied with food, its quality, and its effects than we ever were in the past in times of poverty and famine. All Westerners are now aware of the close link between food and health, a truth already established a few millennia ago by the peoples of the Middle East and Far East as well as by our direct ancestor Hippocrates and his medical theories. And here we are, two thousand years later, reasserting the same principles, especially the postulates referring to climate, lifestyle, food, and its preparation, which notoriously have a great impact on our health. At the same time, we have become increasingly convinced that food produced and cooked according to the traditional methods of our forebears is much better from a gastronomic point of view, since it is not "contaminated" by synthetic chemical substances. This explains the current rage for culturally "typical" products, prepared according to so-called ancestral methods.

A purely biomedical concept with considerable traditional appeal has become a nutritional model that all Western peoples consider ideal, in terms of both gastronomy and health.

Epidemiologists and nutritionists have carried out numerous studies of eating habits in different parts of the globe, especially since World War Two. These surveys have revealed the close link between eating habits and certain diseases, in particular cardiovascular disorders and tumors. At the same time, epidemiological studies have shown that the populations of certain regions of the world appear to be less prone than others to developing such diseases. Nutritionists have concluded that the traditional eating habits of these peoples were "better." For example, the geographical area comprising the southern regions of the Western world, along the Mediterranean coast, was inhabited by peoples whose eating habits yielded a low ratio of heart disorders and tumors, peoples who lived longer than their northern counterparts. Let us acknowledge that poor rural populations obviously could not possibly develop the so-called "plethoric" diseases associated with an excessively abundant diet. In any case, these populations have largely upheld local ways of producing and cooking their food, so Greece, Italy, Spain, Portugal, and southern France have stood out as privileged regions due to the good health and longevity of their inhabitants.

Thanks to the recent focus on these studies by the media in Western countries, we now have a new and remarkably widespread nutritional concept: the so-called "Mediterranean diet." That this concept is somewhat hazy in no way detracts from its almost magical reputation. The Mediterranean diet has become a gastronomic ideal, presumed to be an endless source of goodness and health. The same goes for the underlying ancestral traditions, which are perceived as being closer to nature and therefore better.

With scientific data adopted and adapted by non-scientists, we see a credo treated as a valid model both by the original scientific community and by the ordinary person in the street. Let's take a look at the origins and development of what is now perceived as ideal traditional gastronomy.

The origins

As far as I know, the concept of "Mediterranean diet" first surfaced in 1824. According to an account in B. Santich's book, *What the Doctors Ordered* (Melbourne: Hyland, 1995), a young British Navy surgeon named Peter Cunningham had been entrusted in 1821 with the task of escorting a group of convicts deported from England to Australia. Like his Hippocratic predecessors of ancient times, as he described in his own book, *Two Years in Southwales Colburn* (1827), he was convinced that the human diet should be strictly associated with the climate and seasons. Considering the fact that convicts were heading south, where the climate would be hot and dry, Cunningham came to the conclusion that the men in his custody should eat less meat than they were wont to do in England. Conversely, their diet should largely consist of cereals, fruit, and vegetables. The assumption underlying this conviction was a pillar of early medical theory according to which certain types of food—especially vegetables—were considered "cold," and therefore refreshing, whereas meat and other products were "hot," and thus warming.

Doctor Cunningham was in charge of three deportation voyages and managed to complete them without any loss of life among the male or female convicts. Later on, he published two works in which he recommended a "Mediterranean diet" to all those who intended to colonize Australia. This would enable them to be healthy even in a hot climate, comparable to that of the Mediterranean. By "Mediterranean diet," Cunningham simply intended more fruit and vegetables and less meat. He never mentioned the fats that only much later, as we shall see, were to become in our time a fundamental component of so-called Mediterranean cuisine. Being the sort of physician that he was, it is strange that he never wondered what the native peoples of Australia actually ate—healthy Aborigines who had a very balanced relationship with their habitat. Never underestimate ethnocentrism!

After Cunningham, the subject was dropped and did not turn up again until the 1970s, when the expression "Mediterranean diet" was revived by a couple of American physiologists, Ancel and Margaret Keys, who published a book entitled *How to Eat Well and Stay Well: The Mediterranean Way* (Doubleday, 1975). In their work, the Keys suggested that there is a close link between the eating habits of northern and southern Europeans and their health, especially as far as cardiovascular diseases are concerned.

Tasty well-being

So what did those eminent scholars mean by "Mediterranean diet"? They were essentially referring to a diet that was poor in saturated fats but much tastier than the typical low-fat menus inflicted on patients suffering from heart disease.

A few years earlier, exhaustive information about the quality and quantity of food consumption had become available thanks to a number of studies carried out in Europe, in particular the 1960 survey promoted by Euratom. The Euratom study had highlighted the differences among the countries under investigation, especially with reference to the consumption of fresh fruit and vegetables, cereals, and meat. People ate less meat and more cereals in Italy, where the quantity of absorbed fats was the same as in the other countries, but the quality was different: Italians used more olive oil. Other studies followed, one conducted by the Italian Ferro Luzzi and another by the American Gene Spiller (*The Mediterranean Diet on Health and Disease*, van Nostrand Reinhold, 1991), but even these failed to provide a more precise definition of what a traditional Mediterranean diet was. They proved that Italians did not eat more vegetables than northern peoples, yet their rate of cardiovascular diseases was lower, so there had to be something else apart from vegetables. Further studies provided evidence that there was a close link between the long and healthy life of the Cretans and local eating habits. It was only then that researchers started to investigate the role of fats and take olive oil into consideration. They began to speak about a "Cretan model" in a general theory that the scientific community, and subsequently the media, identified with the attribute "Mediterranean."

An epidemiological study revealed that improved socioeconomic conditions in Italy had progressively encouraged southern populations to abandon their "traditional" poor diet and adopt a model known as "Northern European," which was rich in animal fats, meat, and dairy products. They were thus losing their "natural" or historical protection against heart disease and cancer.

An artificial image

At this point I cannot help but make the following observations: first of all, the concept of "Mediterranean diet" was developed in the Anglo-Saxon world; the Americans and the British were the first to coin the phrase. The concept is a haphazard collection of conclusions reached by various physicians and researchers, and the conclusions were approximate and general, since they did not take into account the wide range of cuisines and eating habits in the different regions concerned. This representation of a healthy diet was subsequently adopted by the "Mediterraneans" themselves, especially the Italians, who did not hesitate to ignore all aspects of diet that did not perfectly fit the scientific definition. The mass media seized these concepts and transferred them from the realms of science (not that they were very scientific in the first place) to those of everyday life. Hence the glorification of the "traditional Mediterranean" model and the myth of a healthy traditional cuisine.

The most illuminating recent work on the advantages of the "Mediterranean" diet derives from exhaustive studies carried out in Crete, discussed in M. Renaud's book *Le Régime Santé* (Paris: Odile Jacob, 1995). A comparative study of French patients who had suffered heart attacks was set up in the region of Lyon and involved two control groups. The first group was prescribed the so-called "Cretan" diet, while the second one stuck to a more typical low-fat diet. A triumph! Results proved that the patients belonging to the "traditionally Cretan" control group (as the researchers called it) had no relapses, whereas the others had relapses and a few of them died. I was curious to find out which characteristics of the diet had been defined as "traditionally Cretan" by the nutritionists. The answer I obtained was surprising, to say the least:

• Olive oil was not used, because its taste was not appreciated by all the patients included in the research protocol. It had been replaced by an olive oil–like type of margarine specially produced by a large food company.

• Cretan fruit and vegetables (including walnuts and purslane—*Portulaca oleracea*, a wild herb eaten as salad—considered by nutritionists to be decisive elements) had been replaced by French fruit and vegetables, ordinary produce from the region around Lyon, where the study was carried out.

• The "Cretan" model was therefore just a diet in which the consumption of bread, noodles, and vegetables was encouraged while proteins and animal fats were drastically reduced. So here we are, back to the theories of our good Doctor Cunningham!

For an anthropologist specializing in dietary problems and an ethnographer of food such as myself, this generalization was disconcerting. So I wondered:

• Do the Cretans have a monopoly on the definition of "Mediterranean"? Remember that the media usually refer to this diet as "the Cretan miracle."

• Why are the big countries of the southern Mediterranean area not included in this model? Nobody has ever recommended eating *couscous, kefta* (Arab-style meatballs), oriental sweetmeats, or other delicious traditional dishes from that area.

• Why are there no epidemiological studies analyzing the big differences between diets and cuisines? The fact is that cuisines that failed to serve as a panacea, a remedy against all evils like a sort of magic potion, had been completely eliminated from the research.

Magic

I'm not suggesting that this Mediterranean model should be condemned. In truth it is a diet that provides all sorts of benefits to our body. Nevertheless, as a model it has been artificially constructed by researchers referring to the data they collected in specific, circumscribed places, according to carefully defined nutritional criteria. So, where is the truth? Wouldn't it be more scientifically correct to point out that the health of a specific individual depends on the interaction of several different factors: lifestyle, bio-rhythms, profession, physical exercise, general conditions, afternoon nap (why not?), a certain attitude toward life? And that we are dealing with a series of broader cultural and biological tendencies that make some populations of the Mediterranean area healthier in certain ways than others?

There is no harm in exporting this model, but we should not consider it as traditional, since it is not really deep-rooted at an ethnographic level. Have we ever wondered if a Mediterranean diet would have equally positive results in northern countries? Can the experience proving that a Mediterranean diet is beneficial to individual patients with cardiovascular disorders be applied to a whole population? And may I also point out that for those accustomed to a dull, traditional, low-fat diet, the Mediterranean diet will necessarily produce a positive effect on their general conditions, by simple contrast!

Thanks to the influence of physicians and the impact of mass media, certain segments of society in northwestern Europe are now emulating the "Mediterranean" model. For example, in England the "Mediterranean diet" is beginning to affect daily eating habits, as plenty of cookbooks and TV programs sing the praises of the South. However, brief perusal of the recipes proposed will reveal a sort of transformation and adaptation to British culinary culture. Quite an interesting mutation! Just add a bittersweet flavor here, some sugar there, less garlic in general. . . . There is no doubt that the well-educated people of the British Isles are eating differently from the past, that Mediterranean products are having a heyday: tomatoes, olive oil, aromatic herbs, peppers, noodles. According to my British colleagues, a real culinary revolution is taking place, yet this has still not trickled down to the lower rungs of the social ladder.

Are we not constantly looking for a potion to solve all our problems of body and mind? Might we not find solace for our suffering in an ideal diet—gastronomic, ancestral, and immutable—and its underlying magic?

THREE : 4

FRYING

Françoise Aubaile-Sallenave

An excellent definition was worked out in 1932 by Edouard de Pomiane, a famous cuisine physiologist: *Frying is the operation which modifies animal or vegetable tissues in boiling fat, such that food is tasty, crispy and cooked to perfection.*

The two earliest cooking techniques are barbecuing on charcoal or stones and roasting in the oven. These were followed by boiling and stewing, known since the Neolithic Age and the invention of terra cotta. Frying was something of a latecomer, bringing up the rear in culinary practice.

Nowadays fried food is considered so commonplace and popular that we tend to forget that it used to be a dish for special festivities. Once a rarity, it now features in the daily diet of Mediterranean towns no less than those cities of the Western world, where fast-food chains and German *imbiss* call the gastronomic shots. Apart from the legendary *steak-frites* eaten in Paris, there is also the typical Anglo-Saxon *fish and chips,* the Belgian *moules-frites* (mussels and chips), and the universally known hamburgers and chips of American McDonald's restaurants. Fried food still mainly belongs to eating out and festive occasions, however, and this explains its presence at all manner of popular events, festivals, pilgrimages, exhibitions, and meetings. Even though its organoleptic charms usually get the upper hand, fried food is condemned by modern Western dietetics. It is no coincidence that in the French language, words such as *friand* (greedy) and *friandise* (gluttony) come from the very *frire* (to fry).

Two things are fundamental for frying:

• a metal or terra-cotta frying pan. In Spain, this kitchen implement is called a *sarten,* from the Latin term *sartago,* and *frutas de sartén* (fruits of the frying pan) is a way of defining all that can be fried. Another word, the Spanish *paella* (from the Latin *padella,* frying pan, from which the French *poêle* and the Italian *padella* are derived), designates both the container and the food cooked in it. You can also fry or brown food—that is, fry wok   or   frying   pan?

Frying means cooking by dipping food into hot oil or fat and leaving it there until cooked. Everything must be as quick as possible, just until the food is crisp and has a nice golden color. The two ways of frying are stir frying and deep frying.

In the former, the cooking oil or fat only covers the bottom of the pan, and it is necessary to turn the food to cook it, while in the latter the food is completely covered by the frying fat. Among the various frying implements, the two most typical ones are the frying pan—in the Western world—and the wok—in Asia.

The frying pan is a round container with low, curved sides and one handle that is generally as long as the diameter of the pan, in order to keep it perfectly balanced when on the cooker. The iron "skillet" we now know probably dates back to the 17th century, when it was made of forged and hammered black iron. Similar implements were evidently used much earlier, since one came to light during excavations at Pompeii.

"Black" iron—that is, not tin-plated—is the most suitable metal for all types of frying since it is not a good conductor of heat (60°C, compared to 392°C for copper). When particularly thick (2–3 millimeters), black iron automatically adjusts the heat produced by the flame, thereby protecting food from any sudden increase in heat that might burn it. The slope of the sides is essential for certain types of frying: for folding omelets, for example, and for some sautéed recipes with potatoes, diced vegetables, cutlets, or stews.

A wok is a large, slightly conical, iron or cast-iron, bowl-shaped pan with two handles, widely used in the Eastern world to prepare stir-fried dishes but also roasted or fried foods, and soups. A wok can be as much as 2 meters wide, but its diameter is usually 80 centimeters. The main advantage of this pan is that ingredients can be stirred rapidly, so they do not absorb too much fat. This "fast cooking" procedure is actually reduced to a mere twenty seconds in some Chinese recipes, and is the most widespread Chinese cooking method for finely chopped foods. Thanks to its form, the small pieces of food can be constantly moved around without burning. The wok is highly practical, since both small and large quantities of food can be fried in it. Because of its shape, it can cook 100 grams of shrimps with 2 tablespoons of oil, or 1 kilogram with 1 liter.

51

it on low heat with little oil—in a terra-cotta dish. In Greece, the *tebsi* is a plate with a low rim used for frying eggs with fat and maize.

• a good quantity of fat, heated well beyond the temperature of boiling water. In western Mediterranean countries, olive oil and sometimes walnut oil are frequently used, whereas northern European countries make use of butter and lard. In the Caucasus, preference is given to hazelnut oil; in the Middle East to mutton fat, melted butter, or sesame oil; while from India to southern China and Africa, palm oil is widely used. Nowadays we also have cheaper products: sunflower oil, grape-seed oil, colza oil, and margarine made of palm oil.

Meat, fish, vegetables, and fruit can all be fried, though only substances rich in starch are suitable, while the others never get crispy. This difficulty can be eluded by covering the food to be fried with a layer rich in starch: bread crumbs with egg to cover meat and meatballs, flour for fish and offal, batter for watery foods (zucchinis, apples) and fragile foods (zucchini flowers, acacia flowers). Potatoes have a very high starch content, which explains why they fry so well. Mediterranean peoples have been bread-crumbing poultry, sausages, brain, veal, tongue, and cutlets to fry them for a long time; likewise they also have deep-rooted experience in frying fish, eggplant, peppers, and other vegetables.

Yet frying was virtually unknown in ancient times in the Western world. The Romans used it very little, since they did not appreciate the crispy texture of fried food, which they covered with sauce. Although today fried food is present in nearly all the cuisines of the world, in many regions it has made a relatively recent appearance. Frying is unknown in the traditional cuisines of inner Asia, northern and central Europe, America, Africa, Australia or, generally speaking, in peasant cuisine. It is very widespread in Southeast Asia, southern China, Vietnam, Cambodia, Laos, Indonesia, Malaysia, India, and the towns of the Mediterranean area, where it was apparently introduced by the Arabs. In the 10th century C.E. frying pans were made of many different metals: gold or silver for the rich, or tin, lead, and copper. Frying spread quickly to France from the Mediterranean coast, where evidence of the first *paeles* (*poéles*, frying pans) and *roussoles* (*rissoles*, meat or fish pies) dates back to 1170, and *buignes* (*beignets*, pancakes) appeared for the first time in around 1250. By contrast, in northern European countries frying was introduced only fairly recently.

From a European viewpoint, frying seems a typically Mediterranean cooking method. However, it is less widespread than many believe, except as a pre-cooking method for a meat sauce or dishes with sauces. One of the features common to all the Mediterranean cuisines is the habit of flavoring oil before frying fish, seafood, poultry, offal, charcuterie, and also vegetables, though oil is never flavored when frying pancakes. To get the best out of their aroma, the ingredients used to flavor oil are treated according to their special properties. First of all, they are finely chopped. Of the four most commonly used seasonings, first comes garlic, which is usually associated with olive oil and is often removed after gentle frying. At this point comes the remaining three, which brown more slowly: onion and peppers and lastly parsley. In Tuscany, as in the Middle East, garlic, onion, parsley, celery, and carrot are the most commonly used ingredients for a good mixed fry.

Outdoor cuisine

Those who lived an outdoor life always used to fry their meals. In Spain, the *migas del pastor* (shepherds' "crumbs") vary according to the region they come from: La Mancha, Extremadura, the Algarve, or Valencia. The typical ingredients of the popular *migas* of the 18th century in Valencia are meat chops, oil or tallow, garlic and peppers. It is a mixture that bears witness to the sobriety of Mediterranean peoples. Fried food is also produced in specialized shops. The so-called *friteras* selling fried fish, crustaceans, and shellfish are very popular along the coast of Andalusia. Like grilled food, fried food also features in the cuisine of social and religious celebrations, especially pilgrimages, when the whole day is spent outdoors. It contrasts with everyday boiled food, and is frequently prepared by the men, thereby emphasizing its exceptional character.

Fried food is also associated with religious fasting, for instance Ramadan and the Catholic Lent. Cooked with oil, it is considered an acceptable Lenten "lean food" as opposed to "fat food" cooked with lard or butter. At Carnival time, the period preceding Lent and ending on Shrove Tuesday, pancakes are to be found under different names in practically all countries: *oreilletes* in Languedoc, flavored with lemon or orange in Montpellier; *frittelle* in Italy; *merveilles* in the Midi of France, and *bugnes* in Franche-Comté; *fritos, buños, churros* in Spain; and *crêpes* at Candlemas to celebrate the purification of the Virgin Mary. To add to which there are also the *shbâkiyyâ* of Ramadan and the gazelle horns of Maghreb, as well as pastries such as the Tunisian *brek*. One of these fried specialties traveled a great distance and gained worldwide renown. The *sambûsak*, of Persian origin, was spread by the Arabs in the Mediterranean area and was imported by the Spanish to Latin America where it has become a Mexican dish known as *samosas*. It also met with great success around the Indian Ocean. Another example of traveling fried food is the Japanese *tempura*, delicious pancakes of vegetables and shellfish covered by a very thin layer of dough. The Japanese adopted both the term and the technique from what was originally a reference to periods of Catholic fasting when the Jesuits used to eat plenty of pancakes.

Escabeche

This sort of preserve of very ancient origin is still found in Spain, Italy, southern France, and Corsica. Fish (in Andalusia) or partridge (in Toledo) is fried with the necessary seasonings and then placed on a soup plate where it is sprinkled with aromatic vinegar while it is still hot. It is then left to cool. The *scabecciu* is a Corsican fried fish with boiling oil, lemon-flavored vinegar, and myrtle berries or capers poured over it. This French name comes from Spanish, which borrowed it—through Arabic—from the Persian *al-sikbâj*. Curiously enough, the word is now to be found only in the languages that imported it. It is no longer present in modern Arabic, Maghrebi, Egyptian, or any Middle Eastern language.

Chapter FOUR

ʃtreet Food

FOUR:1

FALAFEL

Philip Sinsheimer

The origins of the falafel are obscure, even controversial. Taking issue with an article on the popularity of falafel in Israel published in the Tel Aviv daily *Ha'aretz*,[*] an angry reader wrote that "Falafel only have one real homeland: . . . Lebanon." Unabashed, the editor answered back that "falafel is to be found throughout the Middle East. It is Lebanese as much as it is Egyptian or Palestinian, and the Israelis have adopted it as their national dish."

My purpose here is not so much to establish once and for all the true origin of falafel as to recount what I managed to find out about the identity of this specialty in Israel during a stay there. It is worth pointing out that the controversy is partly the result of a

---

[*] *"Au pays du falafel, les estomacs voraces s'affichent gourmets,"* Courrier International section, *Ha'aretz*, 29 July 1999.

linguistic muddle due to metonymy. The word falafel is used to refer to two distinct entities: a round fritter of mashed chickpeas or other pulses (in Egypt they use butter beans), and the Arab bread sandwich (the round, flat kind that opens like a pocket) filled with those fritters and miscellaneous garnishes. In Israel, the second usage prevails, whereas in the Lebanon, the word falafel is used to refer almost exclusively to the fritter, which combines with other dishes to form the traditional *mezzé*.

In Israel, you find falafels all over the place. The chickpea fritter is for sale all across the country, in big cities and small villages, and even at gas stations in the middle of the desert. Israeli as opposed to Jewish, it is loved by all the different communities that live together in the country, irrespective of religion. The Palestinians of Jerusalem and those of the Arab quarter of Jaffa, south of Tel Aviv, serve and eat falafel just as Israelis of Jewish origin do. The kosher precepts governing the eating and preparation of meat and dairy foods consider the all-vegetable falafel neutral, so whether you are Jewish or not, you can eat falafel at any time of day. Nutritious and cheap, it is ideal for eating in the street and it also happens to fit in very nicely with a certain image of Israeli civil society as hard-working, united, always on the move, and ready to fight.

The spirit of the place

One may wonder whether this vegetable fritter is made the same way throughout Israel. In other words, is one falafel worth another? In Jerusalem, I heard talk of an exceptional falafel—the Shlomo—"the best in town, possibly the best in the country." After walking round the new town for ages, I eventually came across the district they had told me about, Mea Shearim. It's a place inhabited by orthodox Jews; the men dress in black and woman cover their heads. I kept getting lost, and the people I asked for directions all replied with a hasty wave of the hand that I found hard to interpret. I moved out of narrow streets into wide avenues and got lost again. It was more by good luck than good management that I found myself on Shlomo Mosayof Street, the one I'd been looking for. About a hundred meters away I could see a tiny shop with a queue of six people standing in front of the counter, patiently waiting their turn. I joined the queue. I had come to the right place. In front of me was a Jerusalem Israeli with two American friends he had brought to try what he considered the "best" falafel in Israel.

As I waited, I observed. There were two men working behind the counter. One, a plump little guy of thirty or so, was preparing the chickpea fritters and tossing them into a vat of boiling oil. When they were golden brown, he would dry them off on an old iron draining board. Beside him, a man with a white beard (I later discovered he was the uncle) would pick up fritters and stuff them into Arab bread rolls, garnishing them with a mixture of diced cucumber, tomato and onion and a tablespoonful of tahini (sesame paste), plus a hint of red pepper paste, for those who asked for it. This was a rigorous version of falafel, without any frills.

As I waited for them to prepare my order, I told the two men behind the counter about my falafel survey. Without looking up from their work, they simply pointed up at the prize they had received for the best falafel in Israel. I paid my 9 shekels (the standard price), and popped a few discs of cucumber in brine and a long pickled yellow pepper into my falafel.

The moment of truth had arrived. I opened my mouth and bit off a lump of the giant sandwich. The fritters combined crunchiness and softness and blended to perfection with the garnish and the sauces. Neither too dry nor too moist, the sandwich was a model of equilibrium. No flavor prevailed over the others, and the taste buds were not overworked or overpowered. I asked one of the other guys in the queue what he found outstanding about this particular falafel. "It's clean," he replied. By that, he was referring not so much to hygiene as to a sort of purity. This is a simple straightforward falafel—the genuine article.

That is the benchmark for a dish now made in the most wild and wonderful variants. Apart from the cucumbers in brine and the pepper, which you can add at will, the Shlomo falafel is unalterable and unique, always produced the same way. It is light years away from the stuff served in restaurants, where punters are fobbed off with a pocket of Arab bread filled with falafel and can add all the ingredients and sauces they want. The widest choice of ingredients and garnishes I found was at the Elat Mixed Grill at Elat. There the falafel sandwich can be filled with red cabbage, white cabbage, sauerkraut, cabbage in mayonnaise, beetroot, carrots in brine, cucumbers, olives, fried eggplant, pickled peppers, fried peppers, and *shug* (Yemenite pepper purée), and can be dressed with tahini or curry and mango sauce! In this case, the chickpea fritter becomes a sort of symbol of the plurality of the Israeli people. In the confined space of a pocket of Arab bread open to the Mediterranean, the garnish evokes all the various communities. The variety of ingredients and the total freedom in combining them reflect the spirit of the place. Elat, a pretty seaside resort, is famous for its liberalism. Here sauerkraut and fried peppers are free to party and dance together at any time of the day or night in the dancehall of your choice!

At Mea Shearim, the *genius loci* is altogether different. The search for origin and respect for tradition are key values in this quarter of Jerusalem. Here the political and religious environment is reflected in the local falafel, with its claim to purity and immutability. The Shlomo falafel is designed to reassure. Prepared "in the family," the same unchanging recipe excludes excess and incongruous mixing. Books of ritual prayer are set out on the counter for customers to read. This "elect" falafel participates in the sphere of the sacred, though you don't have to be an orthodox or practicing Jew to appreciate it!

With culinary preparations that come in a thousand different variations, it is only natural for aficionados to seek out and promulgate the "authentic original." Take pizza, for example: since it is now available on any continent and garnished with any sort of sauce and ingredient (in California, even with Thai chicken), it becomes a sort of gastronomic ritual to taste a *pizza margherita* or a *pizza marinara* in a back street in Naples. Likewise, the simple, straightforward Shlomo falafel has now adapted to all sorts of mutations. Such objects of cult as these can whet the appetite of even the most secular gastronome.

Falafel
(Recipe found on a postcard)

INGREDIENTS:

600 grams dried chickpeas soaked overnight

1 teaspoon powdered cumin

1 teaspoon powdered coriander

1–2 tablespoons cayenne pepper

50 grams plain white flour

1 clove of garlic, crushed

salt, oil for frying

METHOD:

Drain the chickpeas and combine with the spices in an electric blender. Add the flour and mix well. Shape into balls with a diameter of about 3 centimeters, and fry all over in hot oil (190° C) for two to three minutes until they are golden brown. Stuff into a pita bread, and garnish using lots of imagination.

FOUR : 2

SQUID AND SWEET POTATOES

Sylvie Guichard-Anguis

On cold winter nights in Japan, the cry of the sweet-potato vendor pushing a cart along the street reminds those at home that they only need to endure a few seconds of freezing cold to be sure of warming up afterward with a hot potato—that is, if they manage to skin it with due haste.

Japanese delicacies are becoming increasingly familiar to Western readers. Nevertheless there are still plenty of popular foods relating to the Japanese way of life that are as yet unknown beyond those shores. Most are eaten using chopsticks or a sort of skewer. However, when no sauces are involved, people don't hesitate to use their fingers.

On leaving their offices or the bar to which they often repair after work, many Japanese white-collar workers head for one of these stalls sheltered by a fly-over (overpass) or a railway bridge. A tent fluttering in the wind barely conceals the camp-kitchen. A glass of saké is served with sizzling chicken kebabs, typical stand-up fare that requires no advertising beyond the enticing smells that pervade the neighboring streets.

The Japanese eat around the clock, and all sorts of establishments can satisfy a sudden pang of hunger at any time. In the morning, it is not uncommon to see a stall selling noodles on the platform of suburban railway stations. Served in a bowl with hot broth, they are quickly downed by people waiting for the train. Some of these popular "street foods" are readily available at the festivals of the Shintoist sanctuaries or Buddhist monasteries. On such occasions, a plethora of stalls are set up along the main road or within the perimeter of the sacred place, offering foods such as sugar-glazed apples, which can be eaten while walking or while sitting at rough tables under a canopy.

One of the foremost delicacies of the coldest months of the year is *oden*, a mixture of winter vegetables and fish pâté in various shapes. Then there are the ubiquitous hardboiled eggs and grilled *tofu*, cooked on a low heat in a rice-wine soup. Connoisseurs carefully select the products heaped on the plate and dip them one by one in mustard before tasting them.

Other foods are cooked on request and served immediately, like squid grilled and brushed with the eternal soy sauce, which gives them a slightly sweet flavor. The *takoyaki* rissoles made with a *crêpe* batter and mixed with tiny pieces of vegetables and octopus are cooked in special molds and are very popular in the Kansai region (Osaka, Kyoto, and Kobe). The secret

59

lies in turning them quickly so that they cook on both sides. They are then heaped into a throwaway cup and dressed with whatever ingredients (seaweed, dried and grated bonita, etc.) the customer chooses. Here again, this is food that can be consumed on foot.

Many of these snacks are sweet, for instance *taiyaki*. Greatly appreciated in winter, this is a sort of piping-hot wafer tart filled with bean paste and shaped like a gilthead. And in summer, cups of ground ice with syrup or green tea are still very popular, despite the success of ice cream.

Takoyaki

INGREDIENTS:

2¹/2 cups of flour

1 egg

a pinch of salt

2 cups of water

ingredients of your own choice, finely chopped:

cooked octopus,

cabbage, fried squid, tuna, anchovies, parsley

METHOD:

Grease and heat the little molds and then fill them up to a sixth of their depth with the batter, adding two or three of the ingredients. When the batter begins to come away, quickly turn the rissoles with a large fork to cook on the other side.

Once they are nice and round and done, remove them from the molds and sprinkle with soy sauce. Eat while hot with seaweed and grated bonito.

FOUR:3

TACOS

Jorge De'Angeli

One of the most astonishing phenomena in contemporary gastronomic history is unquestionably the worldwide expansion of Mexican cuisine. And the *taco* is its universal symbol, the popular Mexican food *par excellence*. The word basically means wrapping something tasty in a couple of *tortillas* heated on a *comal* (grill) and adding some sauce. You then grab the thing with two fingers and eat it standing up without bothering about cutlery. The appropriate stance involves leaning forward from the waist, to avoid dripping sauce on your clothes. *Tacos* sometimes feature on restaurant menus, largely to pander to tourists who often make fools of themselves by using knives and forks for food no Mexican would dream of eating otherwise than with fingers. The very suggestion! As bad as cutting up spaghetti for the Italians.

The Aztecs were big eaters of all sorts of corn *tortillas*, which took the place of bread. They used to roll them up, or break them in four and use them as spoons, dressing them in thousands of different ways. That time-honored tradition is still going strong. A *taco* can be dressed with just a pinch of salt, but there's nothing to stop you from filling it with *foie gras* or caviar. Traditional *tacos*, however, the ones that ordinary Mexicans eat every day, are quite unlike those consumed by tourists or the condescending well-to-do.

So although *tacos* as such are unquestionably the national food, the choice of *taco* is a clear indicator of status. In other words, a particular social class tends to favor a certain kind of *taco*. The middle and upper classes eat beefsteak or charcoal-grilled pork *tacos* dressed with sauces containing tomato, onion, chili, and hot spices. They also go for *tacos* filled with kid *barbacoa* and *borracha* sauce (made with *pulque* and *chile pasilla*). Or *tacos* with pork *carnitas*, using only prime cuts.

The poor, whose main sustenance is basically *tacos*, have a much wider and tastier choice. They know what they're doing when the ask for *tacos de cabeza* (cow or beef) and specify that they want tongue, palate, soft bone, brain, ears, face, or eye. Fussy and ignorant people miss one of the delicacies of the cuisine if they do not try *tacos* filled with *nana* (udder), *tripa gorda* (large intestine), or *repelados* (small intestine). In these cases, the meat is not stir fried but boiled, and therefore healthier and lighter.

And while we're on the subject of fried food, mention should also be made of lamb *machitos* (testicles, previously boiled), pork *longaniza* (sausage), and pork *cecina* (dry meat), fried in a big pot filled with lard, which sends delicious smells throughout the neighborhood and provides some unrivaled *tacos*. Between 11 a.m. and noon, bicycles laden with *tacos sudados* appear. These have been prepared at home and are carried to where they are sold on the bike's parcel rack, wrapped in a thick cloth lined with layers of paper to keep them warm. The choice ranges from *mole verde* (pumpkin seed sauce) with pork, to potatoes and sausage, *refritos* beans, and *chicharrón* (fried and crunchy pig's skin) with red sauce. The variations are endless. Every Mexican region boasts its own *tacos*, filled with all sorts of ingredients, from insects to seafood, tortoise meat to *tamales*, fresh cream to cheese and onion, always dressed with fantastic sauces, rich with the aromas and flavors of chiles, occasionally but not always spicy hot.

Streets, squares, and markets all over Mexico are a massive display of culinary imagination. The purveyors of such marvels are the housewives sitting at their front doors in small villages preparing local specialties, or the owners of immaculate stalls in crowded city streets and markets, the hawkers who work from 6 a.m. to noon or 5 to 11 p.m., and the *taquerías* that can be so big that they're managed like restaurants. *Tacos* can be a snack or a banquet, a staple diet or an occasional indulgence.

FOUR : 4

KHAO SOY AND OTHER NOODLES

Annie Hubert

Southeast Asia is a heaven for street food. In every town and village, food stalls appear at street corners. They are in fact portable kitchens of two kinds: a two-wheeled cart containing a charcoal stove, utensils, pots, ingredients, and crockery, or in its simplest version, two baskets carried on each end of a bamboo pole, one containing the stove, cooking pot or wok, and the other ingredients and bowls. Men, women, and sometimes children operate these small trades characteristic of urban life, and the majority of such tradespeople are of Chinese ancestry. The street food culture may in fact have come to Southeast Asia from China over a century ago, with the first great migrations of coolies from the south encouraged by various colonial governments in search of cheap labor.

In Southeast Asian towns, one can eat at any time of day or night, a light snack or a heavier dish, in the middle of a busy street, sitting on the curb, standing or squatting on a low stool. Most urbanites, including children, eat in this manner at least once a day, the very low prices making it affordable even for the poor; indeed, for the destitute this might be the only form of meal.

But the triumph of street food occurs in the evening markets. Each city has its street or area reserved for merchants of all kinds who operate at night and mostly provide local food specialties. The stalls are set up at sunset, with rough tables and benches scattered around them, and kerosene or electric lanterns to provide the necessary light. In the refreshing coolness, families or groups of friends stroll around and can share food, which is the traditional way of expressing conviviality. Smoke fills the air, and delicious smells entice customers from one stall to the other: sounds of sizzling, frying, sautéing are barely heard above the din of loudspeakers diffusing syrupy love songs sung by the local stars of the moment. Wide-eyed children conscientiously eat their syrup-flavored ice lollies, fried bananas, and

other such treats, while their fathers or mothers inspect the various stalls. Each one has a specialty, and a night market can offer a good sample of all the types of street food typical of the country or province.

Street food should not be confused with home food. Only what is cooked in a home kitchen and consumed with a rice base corresponds to the concept of "meal." Street food consists mainly of snacks or foods that are not prepared at home. Thus, at a night market, a family can enjoy a series of dishes that will replace the evening meal, but with a totally different content, since rice will not be the staple base. Sitting at one of the tables shared with other customers, everyone can create his own menu.

Chiengrai

One interesting area for street food is northern Thailand, and particularly the town of Chiengrai: a crossways of Shan, Chinese, and Thai cultures, along with some ethnic minorities. The food stalls offer a wide choice of dishes: grilled chicken or pork served with fresh herbs and chili peppers, rice gruel, glutinous rice in coconut cream with fresh ripe mangoes or *durion,* glutinous rice cooked in bamboo with black mung beans, grilled beef in a savory sauce typical of the Muslin Han (the Hui) from the Yunnan . . .

But the main, all-important fare is the noodles. These were probably introduced by the Chinese centuries ago. They are of two types: made of rice flour—white, slightly transparent,

63

of every width; or of wheat flour—yellow, and thinner than the rice variety. There are endless ways of preparing them; the most common being as soup. In a chicken, pork, or beef broth, they can be mixed with fish or meat balls, beef slices, chopped vegetables, pieces of chicken, or tofu, and are often accompanied by fresh aromatic herbs such as Asian basil, coriander, dill, mint, green onions, hot sauces, or fresh chilies, and always a slice of lime. The taste is hot, salty-sweet-sour and aromatic, a delight for nose and eyes as well as for the palate.

The characteristic and most popular noodle soup of Chiengrai is *Khao soy*, thought to be of Shan origin. It consists of a thick, spicy, brown, curried sauce with minced beef or chicken and a touch of peanut paste for additional taste. Thick wheat noodles of a bright yellow color sprinkled with fried onions and fresh herbs complete the dish. This soup somewhat resembles the Laotian *Khao Pun* (Laos is not far away, across the Mekong), which consists of rice noodles served with a spicy peanut sauce. *Khao Soy* is a favorite with children and often acts as a snack lunch.

But noodles can also be sautéed, and the possibilities there are as varied as for soups. Rice noodles may be sautéed with vegetables, onions, chilies, and the fragments of roasted peanuts that are a Thai classic. They can also be fried crisp with a sweet-sour sauce and bits of pork. Wheat noodles can be fried or sautéed, with or without sauce, with chicken, fish, or pork, with any variety of fresh herbs and juice of a lime. Each cook at his stall develops his particular blend of flavors, and this becomes a trademark. Reminiscent of their Chinese origin is the way these soups and most noodle dishes are eaten, with chopsticks and a spoon, which is not otherwise common in Southeast Asia, except for in Vietnam. Such consumption is a noisy business involving sucking in the noodles while pushing them in with the chopsticks.

Until the advent of mass tourism in the region, street food was the only cheap food outside the home. Restaurants were either Chinese or European. But street food remains, resisting the invasion of fast food, which is too expensive and tasteless for cultures that take a major interest in cooking and flavor and manage to achieve the best with a bare minimum of ingredients and effort.

Khao Soy

INGREDIENTS (for 4 people) :

1 clove garlic

1 teaspoon ground coriander seed

1 teaspoon ground cumin seed

1/2 teaspoon chili power

1/2 teaspoon ground cloves

1 teaspoon turmeric

2 cups chicken stock

1 large onion, chopped

2 cups cooked chicken meat, chopped

1 teaspoon sugar

2 tablespoon soy sauce

2 cups coconut milk

2 tablespoons chopped onion, deep fried so as to be crisp

4 "nests" of Chinese egg noodles

METHOD:

In large pan, sauté the chopped onion in some oil; when transparent, add all the spices and sauté for a minute. Add the pieces of meat (bite-sized). Add the stock, sugar, and soy sauce and bring to a boil, then add coconut milk at the last minute (it should not boil).

Cook the noodles one minute in boiling water, and put in soup bowls. Pour the liquid over and sprinkle with crisp fried onion. Serve on the side some chopped green onion and wedges of lime. If not salty enough, add a few drops of fish sauce (naam plaa).

FOUR:5

WITHOUT A TABLECLOTH: TAPAS

Carlos Delgado

When the gastronomically oriented customer enters a Spanish bar or *taberna*, he may initially be a little bewildered by the noise, high spirits, and impudence. However, what will astound him far more is the immense repertoire of tapas displayed there to temp the regulars, or described in white chalk on a blackboard. This amazing parade of culinary gems owes its being to a wide variety of ingredients and origins: here come the ineffable Spanish *tortilla*, the grilled *chorizos*, the *salpicón de mariscos*, the *cazuelita de callos,* the amazing Spanish cured ham, the voluminous *empanadillas*, the silvery *sardina en escabeche*, the symbolic whelks, the pinky *polpo alla gallega*, and so forth. The fundamentals: good bread, olive oil, pork, anchovies, sardines and mackerel, pulses and vegetables.

Those who are unacquainted with the Spanish *tapeo* ceremony (if the habit has not yet caught on universally, it should be encouraged to do so) are missing one of the world's great gastronomic adventures. Far from being a mere quick lunch to be downed in a hurry, a sort of typically noisy Spanish fast food, *tapas* is an almost ritual meal that can last for hours as participants wend their way from taverns to bars and *tabernas,* enjoying all the house specialties and washing them down with wine. It was probably this particular combination of wining and dining that gave the big restaurants the idea for their rather pretentious "tasting menus." Except that they misunderstood the whole essence of tapas: inexpensive, unrestricted, unsung.

Tapas offer a winning mixture of tradition and modernity. Though they can provide a quick snack, they are really a way of eating slowly. Customers forsake the pomp and ceremony of tablecloth, dining room, and waiters for the bar, the hot pan, a stool (when lucky), and really quick service. The food itself is ready to be served. That's the nature of it. Interestingly enough, some of the tastiest and most significant products of the Spanish culinary tradition have survived in the form of *tapas:* the rich *callos a la madrileña*, for example; strong, plebeian and irresistibly spicy. Other *tapas* such as the *berza jerezana* (a chickpea *cocido*) are like wonderful "miniature dishes." Moreover, in towns like Seville and San Sebastián, where *tapas* pierced with toothpicks are also called *banderillas,* this form of food has practically become an art in its own right.

Slow food without a tablecloth: this is the *tapa*; a never-ending parade of Spanish gastronomic ingenuity; a playful concept unconstrained by time; the quintessence of social eating; a perfect balance of regional cooking and wines. More than a mere quick lunch for people under no stress, *tapas* can become a unique experience, to be enjoyed with a glass of *cosechero* (a young red wine obtained with the carbonic maceration system) in the Basque Provinces, *Fino* in Andalusia, or a young red wine in the other regions. Relax and enjoy a form of eating that transcends time and reaches the very heart of friendship.

EN SEVILLA · "There's an anecdote that explains the origin of this word. The people of Seville have always enjoyed drinking and chatting in the open, where hosts of insects and butterflies tend to commit suicide in the nearest glass, thereby spoiling its original contents. That is, until one day somebody asked the landlord for a slice of ham or salami, or a piece of cheese, to cover *(tapar)* the glass and protect it from the buzzing hordes. This sort of edible lid subsequently took the name of *tapa* and became a common practice that gave rise to a rich Andalusian culinary tradition.

'Going for *tapas*' means savoring rich and varied tastes in an alcoholic and gastronomic crawl through bars and *tabernas*; socializing during a pilgrimage from squares to taverns; and talking for hours of matters human and divine. *Tapeo* is a baroque, sybaritic game which delights the five senses with the flavors, conversations, smells, handshakes, and beauty of the streets of Seville."

Enrique Bellver

Rules

Like any serious ceremony, *tapeo* has its own rules. First of all, there should not be too many people taking part if you want to find a "place" at the counter or a small table to sit at. Moreover, small groups are more conducive to good conversation than larger numbers, and can move more easily from one bar to the next. Secondly, *tapeo* lovers must appreciate that the virtue of *tapa* consists in its being a mouthwatering appetizer, not a loaded plate. Lastly, *tapeo* must be well organized: no repeating *tapas* at the different "stations"; and plenty of discernment in selecting cold or hot, stewed or fried, fish or meat *tapas*, eating everything in the correct sequence so that you will have had a full meal by the end.

Varieties

The range of *tapas* is extremely wide. It includes simple cold snacks with olives, cold meats or cheese as well as many vegetable, meat, and fish dishes cooked in different ways (stewed, fried, marinated).

What follows is a map of the most common *tapas* that you can find in the *tabernas* of Seville.

Vegetarian

Olives can be offered aliñadas (marinated with herbs) or stuffed (these are called *rellenas*). Both the fruit *(alcaparrón)* and the bud *(alcaparra)* of the caper are eaten.

Vegetables

Spinach *esparragadas* (cooked with asparagus) and chickpeas. Asparagus *trigueros* (a variety cultivated together with wheat) and bitter grilled *amargosos*. Broad beans with ham. Russian salad. Tomatoes marinated with green peppers and onion. Anchovies in *vinaigrette* sauce. Eggplant.

Pulses

Chickpea soup. *Cocido* (boiled meat and vegetables) with lard.

Preserves

Tuna in oil and *en escabeche* (marinated with vinegar and herbs), salted anchovies, mussels *escabochados*.

Cheese and *chacinas* (dried meat)

Mature cheese, Spanish ham. Cold meats. Pork loin *en adobo* (that is, preserved with herbs or spices) and pork loin *caña*. Ham *serranitos* (mouthfuls) with fried green peppers.

Fish

Fried: cod or salt cod *pavia* (breaded and fried fish pieces). Hake. Plaice. Mullet. Sardines. Squid. Anchovies. Salt cod omelets.

Grilled: cuttlefish. Swordfish.

Stewed: dogfish (shark-like fish also called "seadog") with potatoes. Cuttlefish with broad beans. Tuna with onions. Salt cod in tomato sauce.

Aliñados. Aliñada is a marinade used to flavor fish (anchovies, octopus) and eggs.

Seafood: stewed, grilled, and breaded shrimps. *Bigaros* (whelks from the Cantabrian sea). Boiled scampi and squills. Squill omelet. Clams with garlic sauce. Mussels steamed and with a spicy sauce.

Meat

Stewed meat or meat with tomato, potatoes, or wrapped in lard. Stewed pork loin. Breaded chicken breasts.

Tripe and offal

Bull's tail. Black pudding with onions. Mixed offal with onions. Stew. Fried chicken livers. Kidneys with sherry and grilled kidneys. Marinated spare ribs.

FOUR:6

FISH & CHIPS

Lesley Chamberlain

Fish and chips sits happily in the top league of English food, beside the more refined pleasures of roast beef on Sunday, scones and jam for tea, and bread, cheddar cheese, and chutney for a pub lunch. But fish and chips is not a street snack, like hotdogs or the traditional roasted chestnuts you still see in London in winter. It is a hearty whole meal, although with the peculiarity that it is usually "taken away" to eat—in good weather on a park bench or at the seashore perhaps, but generally at home.

Fish and chips seems to have originated in northern England, where women employed in the cotton mills hadn't time to make a daily hot family meal. Alan Davidson in *North Atlantic Seafood* dates the habit from the middle of the Industrial Revolution, with vendors "frying [their fish] in open cauldrons fired by coal" and offering baked potatoes alongside. Fish and chips was always urban food, appetizing despite being malodorous, and invariably attracted a noisy and colorful public. The habit spread from Lancashire and Yorkshire all over the British Isles, where fish bars sprang up for over-the-counter purchases.

Fish and chips is fast food, but speed of preparation is the only thing it has in common with modern burgers. The fish is fresh, the potatoes vitamin-packed, and the optional side portion of mushy peas adds fiber and energy. Deep-frying seals in the flavor, while the richness of the whole is offset by the traditional acidic accompaniment of brown malt vinegar and pickles (onions or cucumbers). An old penchant for sweet-and-sour dressings on savory food, which the English share with the Germans across the North Sea and the Chinese on the other side of the world, shows up in the final sprinkling of tomato ketchup.

Now you may be able to hold all this complexity of dressed fish and chips in a greasy bag, wrapped in newspaper and held close to your heart like a hot-water bottle in bed, but it's easier to sit down, open the paper, and spread your feast on a table or your knee. The "chippie" will always ask you: "Eat now or take away?" and will give you the option of adding your own seasoning at home. Personally, I wouldn't miss the sensation of a real take-away. I remember as a child clutching that warm, double-wrapped packet in the back of the car, especially looking forward to supper because my temperamental mother would be pleased not to have to shop, cook, or wash up. For me, more than a century after the Industrial Revolution, the feminist revolution of the 1960s gave fish and chips a new *raison d'être* in ensuring some family togetherness. The other great social merit of fish and chips, I would say now, in our wretchedly stratified Great

Britain, is that unlike most eating habits it cuts right across class barriers.

The batter is refined white flour and water, thickly mixed, into which the cook dips already skinned and boned fillets of cod, plaice, skate, haddock, or rockfish (huss) before tossing them into a stainless-steel trough of bubbling fat. The northern tradition is to fry in beef dripping, which gives a dark, crisp coating. More common everywhere these days is vegetable oil. Chips, borrowed from France, replaced baked potatoes around 1870.

Yet English chips were happily never those all-crunch *allumettes* or matchsticks McDonald's has copied. They were plump white fingers that steamed with real substance when you bit into them.

Today's chippies in the south are often owned by Chinese immigrants. The Yorkshire chain Harry Ramsden's and various London venues have had success in relaunching fish and chips "up-market," with in-house tables, and appetizers and desserts to swell the menu. Meanwhile local chippies have added vegetarian and ethnic alternatives to the blackboard, like "Jamaican patties in batter." But the traditional item retains its great and broad appeal, the more so as the fish shop queue is a friendly place. The only ponderable is what to drink. Chippies sell sweet fizzy drinks, and maybe lightness and sweetness are the clue. A wine from the Rhine or the Mosel was a pre-war British favorite. Sweet cider is another possibility. In any case, bubbles aerate the hefty plateful. On special occasions we should probably do the eccentric English thing and choose nothing less than champagne to accompany this classless and timeless instant feast.

FOUR:7

FARINATA

Maurizio Maggiani

Were I to look back at what I have sown during my life; were I to contemplate the quality and quantity of everything I have left on the road as a sign of my existence; were I suddenly to succumb to the insidious desire to summarize what I have been and from whence I came; should I, like Thumbelina, pine to leave the darkest forest of middle age to find my way back home, then surely I would have to lower my eyes. For my gaze would be met by the sight of a large path of greasy papers, strips of butcher's paper, bits of thick and porous paper, soaked in the oil of all the *farinata* of my long and tormented mortal toil.

Ah, how sweet the daily "shots" of *farinata* seem, even in retrospect; how exquisite their intake whether hungry or not. Leaning against the grimy wall of a steaming hot bakery, sitting beside the piles of firewood, with paper in my hands and a glass of white wine between my knees: such is true joy. Indeed, as I look back, the only coherence that I can discern in an otherwise inconstant life is that of the regular exercise of jaws and stomach while propped up against a pitted marble bar whose greasy smears are occasionally spread by a lopsided old waitress armed with a cloth.

I started when I was a boy at school. Our paradise was "La Pia," a *farinata* shop that opened at seven, just for us. Incidentally, the earliest hot food pushers were the tripe sellers, whose cups of tripe soup were ready for the dockers at 5:30 a.m.; people swore that tripe soup was just what dockers needed—with a chunk of stale bread soaked in it and half a bottle of white wine, or course. Tripe sellers are now dead and buried, whereas "La Pia" is still there. When I was young, for the price of a doughnut we got half a piece of round *focaccia* with 200 grams of *farinata*. We kept it in our schoolbag until break time, and schoolbooks and exercise books got soaked with oil and took on the sweet-spicy smell of chickpea flour fired in the cauldron of hell. At ten, it was still lukewarm. Eventually we learned to play truant to go and buy *farinata* whenever we felt like it, and then we would eat it right there, in front of the shop sprawled out on the sidewalk, one beer shared between two of us. Lukewarm, because there was no fridge there. I have never stopped eating *farinata* since.

And sometimes when I wonder why I have never left this shit hole of a town, the only reasonable answer I have is that a *farinata* like you get in Spezia is not to be found anywhere else. Hot at all hours of the day and night, thin and crunchy, soft with a soul and an oily body. Go to Genoa, go to Savona, and maybe you get stuff

1-inch thick, cold as a dead corpse, cooked in the oil of Multedo warehouses. At present, I go to Faina de l'Orso in Pegazzano, a dirty place where none of the posh people who came here to see me want to enter, because even when they are brave enough to cross the threshold, the owner—Orso (the Bear), who else?—scares them off with a single look. I think this is the best *farinata* of all, especially because of the olive oil. The dough of water and flour must float as it fries in the oil: the zinc-plated copper pan must be burning hot, and olive oil is the only oil that remains healthy at such a temperature. Cooked this way, the *farinata* comes out firm and soft, and when Orso cuts you a large piece and lays it on the paper, you have in your hands a perfumed wafer just waiting to be inserted into the correct opening, where it melts on the palate without any crumbling, or indigestible raw pieces, or the stench of burnt oily deposits.

Between you and me, I believe that all this *farinata* has shortened my life expectancy to medieval levels. Good as it may be, it is definitely neither light, nor biotic, nor homeopathic, nor phytotherapic, and sooner or later—but let's allow me a few more years—I will pass away with that beautiful greasy paper in my hands. After all, this is what I deserve, this is what history has reserved for me, and I am not complaining. The two pieces—half a pound if the *farinata* is perfect—will be the barricade on which I have fought to the very last an admirable but desperate battle against the contemporary world.

Against the first-past-the-post system, against first and second *nouvelle cuisine*, against California wine and Internet sites, against the increase in the price of bread and liberal-democratic thought. In the name of worthless stuff, almost impossible to digest. Like eating in the streets, laughing and joking with your mate, and proving yet again that what could have been a base porridge of chickpea flour is actually transformed in your hands and mouth into a truly noble substance. Such is alchemists' gold, clear evidence of how it is possible for man to transform the nature of things.

Farinata

INGREDIENTS:

300 grams chickpea flour

1 liter lukewarm water

extra virgin olive oil

salt

black pepper

METHOD:

Pour the lukewarm water in a terra-cotta bowl and slowly add chickpea flour, stirring with a whisk. Add salt, but remember that the batter is always insipid upon tasting. Continue to stir carefully trying to avoid lumps.

Let the batter rest for at least two hours (ideally four hours!), then skim the froth from the surface, add a (medium-sized) glass of oil, and stir. Grease a 38- to 40-cm copper pan and pour the batter so that it covers the pan with a layer no more than 1 centimeter thick (less would be better). Stir once again.

Bake in hot oven (260°C) until the surface forms a thin golden crust. It would be ideal to use a wood oven: high temperature (300°C) and quick cooking (ten minutes).

Farinata must be eaten warm and dusted with black pepper. You may top it with rosemary leaves, thinly cut fresh onions, or fresh whitebaits. Add the toppings just after stirring the oil and before putting the batter into the oven. Serves 4.

—Recipe from Trattoria U Papa,
piazza Andrea Dorie, La Spezia, Italy

FOUR : 8

THE SMOKE MARKET

Bernard Rosenberger

In his "meticulous and diligent description of the city of Fez" in Morocco, which was published at the beginning of the 16th century, Giovanni-Leone l'Africano explained that part of the population was accustomed to breakfasting out, early in the morning, before going to work. Close to the vegetable market, they could find vermicelli and well-spiced meat-balls fried in oil. However, even more popular were the so-called "smoke markets," where more than a dozen shops were busy all day cooking fritters in oil, roasting meat, or preparing a "strange red soup," the recipe for which was readily provided. Roast meat was not skewered, the author pointed out; and a whole lamb would be cooked in the oven all night long. In fact, this is how they make *méchoui* in Morocco to this day. Fried meat and fish were also sold, as well as "a sort of bread as light as a broad flat noodle," which used to be eaten with butter and honey.

Those who travel through Morocco today can still watch similar scenes, and find in the narrow and densely populated streets of the medinas the smell as they would in the smoke market in Fez. There are fritters, meat, or grilled sardines for sale, and the travel-er can have a quick snack while stand-ing in the street or at the bus stop: meat *kebabs*, lamb giblets or minced meat-balls—*kefta*—are eaten in a round bun—a *kesra*. For those with time at their disposal, it is pleasant to sit out-side at one of the tables covered with an oilcloth. Along comes the waiter armed with a sponge for wiping the table between customers. On it he places a *tajine*, a meat stew cooked over low heat on a surface of enameled terra cotta, or possibly *couscous*, or an egg and tomato salad. The same occurs in the countryside, in the *suks*, the mar-kets where rural people gather. Here you can also find other dishes—for

instance, the *sikouk*, a sort of coarse-grained *couscous* moistened with milk, highly appreciated in summer.

In Khemisset, on either side of the road from Rabat to Fez, there are a number of small stalls where delicious *kebabs* are prepared at almost any time of day and night. The smoke alone would draw the attention of the most distracted passer-by. In Mar-rakech, in the famous Jama'a al-Fna square, apart from the usual *kebabs* or meatballs, the hungry may also opt for *tajines* or a simple bowl of *harira*, a rich soup made of flour and dried legumes, scented with fresh coriander. During the blessed month of Ra-madan, just before the siren an-nounces the breaking of the fast, people wait with steaming bowls of soup in their hands, smacking the liq-uid surface with the back of a wooden spoon to cool it. In the same square, they also sell fresh fruit and sweets. Many food lovers go for a portion of snails cooked in an aromatic broth that they gulp down after emptying the shells. At the top end of the main road of the *suk*, chickpeas are grilled in very small premises, and lamb heads cooked in the oven, much to the enjoy-ment of peasants and city inhabitants. I heard one exclaim that this was the smell of heaven itself. In the port of Essaouira, in the ancient city of Mogador, fresh sardines are grilled and served with lemon and half a *kesra*, still hot from the oven.

Anywhere in the city, outside cinemas, schools, hospitals, offices, countless peddlers display their

75

merchandise on unbelievable vehicles—loads of salted pumpkin seeds, boiled lupines, chickpeas, peanuts, candies, and brightly colored confectionery and sweets that both children and adults can crunch for a few coins. Other vendors sell boiled eggs or, depending on the season, sweet acorn (which tastes slightly like chestnuts), *leben*, a kind of fermented milk, or *raib*, a sort of yogurt that can also be bought in small shops. Then there are ice creams, a symbol of modernity.

The cries of street vendors blend with the braying of donkeys, the honk of car horns, and the noise of the crowd. This is the ultimate synesthetic street symphony.

FOUR:9

SOUVLAKI

Dimitris Antonopoulos

Walking along the main streets of Athens, especially in summertime, you are likely to find tourists eating a *souvlaki*. According to Greek and Mediterranean custom, they should "bite" it well enveloped in the *pitta*, a circular flour dough seasoned with oil and pre-cooked in the oven, then slightly fried in oil before being served. Correctly prepared, the *pitta* becomes slightly crunchy and its taste recalls that of a non-sugared doughnut.

Inside, the *souvlaki* hosts some of the gems of Greek gastronomic tradition. First of all, roasted meat, with salt and red pepper; tomato slices, to give a hint of natural sweetness; finely chopped onion, mixed with parsley to make it more desirable; and, if you want it, a little *tzatziki*—a mixture of yogurt, cucumber, dill, and a bit of garlic, which counters the meat's fattiness with its acidity. The result is a mixture of intense scents and strong flavors whose combined tastiness never fails to appeal.

The Greeks are crazy about it. When they feel slightly hungry, they follow their noses and eyes to the nearest *souvlaki,* which they eat while walking or sitting in a *souvlatzidiko,* sipping a cool beer, or in front of television with some friends, watching a football match or a game of basketball.

The birthplace of *souvlaki* is Monastiraki, a traditional district of Athens, where the antique market is currently held, warmly patronized by Athenians and tourists alike. The first *souvlatzidiko* was opened in 1924 by an Armenian, Misak Anispikian, who used to make a *souvlaki* with minced mutton served in a roasted *pitta* with tomato and onion. Misak had learned his craft in Egypt, where he lived before moving to Athens. In due course, *gyros* were introduced and became the most popular form of *souvlaki.* With Greek immigration, it also made a name for itself abroad: in the United States as *gyros,* and in Europe as *souvlaki.*

Gyros means tour. The meat piece is skewered in an upright position and made to rotate beside the fire. The meat—the most commonly used is pork—is first marinated in lemon juice and oregano, then cut up and fitted onto the skewer in the shape of a cone. A crunchy meat crust forms on the outer surface, and the juices withdraw inward. The skewered meat is then cut in thin slices and placed in the *pitta.* The combination of the outer crunchiness and the juicy softness on the inside is delicious. The simplest form of *souvlaki* consists of meat pieces fitted onto a wooden skewer and then roasted on coal, seasoned with a bit of lemon juice, and eaten with toasted bread slices.

There is a variation of the theme to be found in Cyprus. The *pitta* is different, resembling Arab bread, elliptical in shape. Pork meat, minced and enveloped in a net, loses its protective layer on the outside, which melts and impregnates with fat when coming into contact with heat from the burning coals. Seasoned with aromatic herbs (such as basil and thyme), the Cypric version comes with vegetables (cucumber and cauliflower) and pickles.

Chapter **FIVE**

Beer

THE POST-INDUSTRIAL PINT

Michael Jackson

Crush fruit (usually grapes), run off the juice, ferment it, and you have wine. Steep grains (usually barley) in water until they begin to sprout; arrest this at the optimum point by drying them in a kiln. The grain has now become malt. Make an infusion or decoction of this malt in water; ferment that. Now you have beer.

Wine is in some respects a simpler drink than beer. Both are products of equal antiquity, dating at least from the first civilizations of the fertile crescent. Wine may have spread west through the temperate but warm grape-growing climes of Turkey, the Balkans, Italy, France, and Iberia. Beer may have followed a cooler, grainier path through Armenia, Georgia, and southern Russia to brewing regions like Bohemia, Germany, Belgium, and the British Isles.

Why is the simpler drink the more readily revered?

Perhaps southern Europe's soft, fleshy, voluptuous grape and colorful meal-time companions like tomatoes, eggplant, and peppers make for a more sensuous tableau. The north's tougher grain and underground foods like potatoes and turnips are less obviously exciting.

Some people argue that wine was the drink of the imperial ruling classes: the Romans, Burgundians, Normans, and Napoleonic French. Although Tacitus was rude about beer, my feeling is that the snobbistic distinction between the two drinks came later, when northern Europe was first to industrialize, especially in the mid-1800s. Breweries took up steam power and produced beer on an industrial scale; railroads distributed beer far and wide; coal miners and steelworkers, dehydrated from their labors, drank it in vast quantities.

The wine grape, nearly wiped out by the aphid phylloxera, was vulnerable and valued. With its dusting of local wild yeast, it was reluctant to travel. Grain was hardier, a staple, and commonplace.

Imported wine was the luxury of the bosses; beer was ever-present, less expensive, the drink of the working man.

Beer, sweet and sustaining when accented toward barley, is rendered tart and quenching by the use of wheat;

silky-smooth by oatmeal; spicy by rye; nutty, toasty, roasty, or smoky by the style of kilning . . . but these variations began to diminish as artisans gave way to industrial brewers.

Like ancient wine makers, brewers had once used a wide variety of tree barks, leaves, herbs, spices, berries, and fruits to flavor their product. In the industrial era, most restricted themselves to the conelike flower of the hop vine.

After the work of Pasteur, beers fermented with wild yeasts survived only in very traditionalist regions (Belgium's Lambic family is an obvious example). After the invention of refrigeration, fermentation at warm temperatures became less common, though the technique did survive in ales, stouts, wheat beers, and German styles like the Alt of Düsseldorf and Kölsch of Cologne.

Cloudy and golden

All beer had been either cloudy or dark before the technology was developed to use indirect heat in kilning the malt, and to precipitate yeast. In the days of stoneware, metal, or wooden drinking vessels, color and clarity were not an issue, but mass-produced glass was becoming available when the world's first golden beer was launched in Pilsen, Bohemia, in 1842. This beer, Pilsner Urquell, is still produced. It is noted for its flowery, herbal, and dry hops aromas and flavors, balancing a deliciously sweet maltiness. Pilsner Urquell has lost some character in recent years, but is still a fine beer.

Elsewhere today, the great majority of the world's beers are very distant—blander—imitations of that Pilsner style. These international brews are designed for easy consumption rather than character or complexity. In that respect (though not necessarily in production methods), they are the "fast foods" of the beer world.

Golden beers first spread through Europe and were then exported by breweries like Beck's (in Bremen, on Germany's short coastline) as well as Carlsberg and Heineken (both in countries with small local markets, lots of sea, and a consequent trading tradition). In the 1870s, the American brewers Anheuser-Busch introduced Budweiser, named after a great Bohemian brewing city, as the first nationally marketed beer in the U.S. At the time, every immigrant community in the U.S. brewed its own native styles of beer, but these would largely be wiped out, especially by Prohibition.

On both sides of the Atlantic, the two World Wars closed small breweries and left a conflict-weary public seeking unity and sameness. In the English-speaking world, it was the era of white sliced bread, television dinners, processed cheese, and instant coffee. But the bland 1950s, with their peak of mass-marketing, were followed by the "alternative" 1960s and the rise of the first post-war teenagers. When the Woodstock generation got their hands on the levers of power in the 1970s, a century of mass-market growth faced its first challenge. Urban modernization gave way to conservation, the unquestioned power of the car was challenged by concern over the environment . . . and people began to care about what they ate and drank. A consumer society became also a consumerist society.

In Britain, a spontaneous consumerist movement called the Campaign for Real Ale formed in 1971, fought against the filtered and pasteurized beer made by ever-larger national brewers, and favored the cask-conditioned products of smaller producers. In 1973, the German-born economist E. F. Schumacher, who spent most of his life in Britain, published his book *Small is Beautiful*. It was a major influence in his adoptive country.

Revivalist brewers like Peter Maxwell Stuart at Traquair House, a castle in Scotland, and Fritz Maytag at Anchor Steam in California proved that Schumacher had a point. At a nuclear submarine base in Scotland, a young American, Jack McAuliffe, made the decision to go home to the United States and start a small brewery in California. He called this first new-generation brewery, New Albion, in recognition of its British roots. It was founded in 1976–1977, and began what came to be known as the micro-brewery movement.

Other young Americans who had traveled in the military, as students, or on vacation tried in the U.S. to create British, Belgian, German, and Czech styles of beer. In doing their utmost to be authentic, they often made beer more traditional in character than their European models, and still do. They also evolved new American styles, counter-pointing the blandness of the mass-market brews by featuring the intense aromas and flavors of hops from the Pacific Northwest. Many of the new beer makers began as amateurs, often inspired by Charlie Papazian, a schoolteacher who founded the American Homebrewers' Association. He later added an organization for micro-brewers. These amateurs-turned-professionals were like lovers of good food who open their own restaurants. When I began writing about beer, there were fewer than fifty breweries in the United States and only a handful of (hard-to-find) specialty beers. There are now about 1,300, each producing anything from

three or four styles to a dozen or more.

An early source of information on traditional styles was my book *The World Guide to Beer*, first published in 1977, with an extensive update ten years later. As the influence of revivalist American brewers has spread worldwide, this has been reflected in a newer work, *Michael Jackson's Beer Companion*, first published in 1994, with an update in 1997.

In researching my early books, I felt like a musicologist traveling the Mississippi Delta to record elderly blues singers before they died. I wanted to describe traditional beers before they vanished. I discussed not only their flavors (often using wine comparisons) but also the ways in which they were served, and the moments at which they were (or might be) best enjoyed.

New drinkers

The appreciation of beer requires a diversity of styles (not just taste-alike golden Pilsener derivatives) and an understanding that each has its uses. In almost every economically developed nation, there is a growing diversity, though only Japan approaches the United States in the number of varieties available.

In the opposite direction, the polarization toward blander brews reached its extreme in the U.S. four or five years ago with "clear beer." This colorless, virtually tasteless product was a failure.

When I began writing about beer, the world's largest single brewery, Coors of Colorado, had only one product. The biggest producer, Anheuser-Busch, with a dozen breweries, had four beers, notably including Budweiser. Each now has thirty or more, and their introductions in recent years have ranged from hoppy Pilseners and malty Bocks to Belgian-style spiced or fruited beers, English-accented Porters, sweetish "Irish" brews, and far drier, aromatic new American styles. The mighty Miller company now controls three smaller breweries, making good examples of lagers, ales, and wheat beers, respectively.

These giants have no shortage of brewing skills, but it is difficult for them to make small specialties economically worthwhile. They are trying to do so because they are sophisticated marketers. They know that, while they can sell huge quantities of their mainstream beers, the days of a largely uniform American culture are gone. So is the era when millions of thirsty steelworkers emerged from shifts in cities like Pittsburgh. This is the post-industrial period. Once, Budweiser could send every prospective (male) consumer to the refrigerator at an appointed moment by advertising on three national TV networks during the breaks in football games. Today, viewers tape programs and watch them when they feel inclined, often fast-forwarding through the commercials. The networks are losing audience to cable and satellite stations, rented videotapes, and the Internet (which is full of talk about specialty beers).

Today's workers labor at computer screens. They are not dehydrated at the end of their working day, but they still fancy the reward of a drink, perhaps one that is less quenching but more satisfying in flavors. For reasons also of health, or simply the need to drive, people are drinking less—but tasting more.

Older drinkers may not change their habits, but a new generation is doing so. A majority of the beer-lovers who attend my seminars in the big American cities are young professionals, a good number of them women.

The new American beer lover may choose (for example) a wheat beer in a vase-shaped glass as a quencher; a Belgian ale in a Burgundy sampler as an aperitif; a whole range of beers with meals or in cooking; and a snifter of barley wine after dinner or with a book at bedtime. These are choosy, critical consumers. They want real information on the beer they are drinking.

They are more knowledgeable than their counterparts in Britain or Belgium, and far more questioning than those in Germany or the Czech Republic. German beers are becoming blander, and those in the Czech Republic even more so.

The United States has long been a global influence, but never more than now, in the post-Communist era. We Europeans may find ourselves being reintroduced to our tastiest traditions by the Americans. If not, we could succumb to the blandest products of Coors, Anheuser Busch, and Miller.

In a world as free as we have ever known, do we want real diversity or an endless "choice" of samey, bland beers? That will be determined not by the marketer but by the consumer. It is for us to decide.

FIVE : 2

DRINKABLE BREAD

Luigi Wanner

The first time I had beer, my very first intoxication—was when I was two. I actually have no memory of it, but my mother told me.

At that time we lived in Africa, it was quite a hot day, and I was all alone and very thirsty. There was a big bottle of beer sitting on our porch. It allegedly put me to sleep for twenty-four hours. For the same number of years afterward I did not touch any beer. This does not mean I turned into a teetotaler. In the Ticino, my second home country, Bacchus in the guise of my grandfather managed to seduce me with a *boccalino* full of wine. In my grandfather's words, "Boccaline di vino/succo genuino/di miele divino": "A measure of wine/if the product is fine/is honey divine."

The image of Grandpa with his *boccalino* quarter jug and, by his side with a giant stein of beer, Beatrice Barbaforte (meaning "horse-radish") as he called Grandmother, who came from southern Germany and whose real name was Elsa, née Rettich ("radish")—this image has stayed fixed in my mind. Grandmother never drank wine, she was always sober, of portly stature (grandpa's "fuzzy" head just about reached to her shoulder), and a mug of beer obviously went well with her merry and sociable

nature. Her eyes looked tender but firm, and besides she had a magnificent bosom. As Grandfather said: "Occhi teneri e severi, sul davante abbondante": "Sweet but firm eyes, and a bosom of generous size." She loved him, and she honored and adored him even in the end, when he remained befuddled by drunkenness, somber, with his mind obfuscated. He died in a state of inebriety, as he had lived. Pursuing intoxication and the Muses, susceptible to the joys of the flesh, he wrote poems for her. She, in return, cooked for him divinely. So utterly different were their devotions—and yet so kindred!

Thinking of beer brings memories back to me. Memories of a culture that had felt strange to me for a long time, and yet somehow must have been present in the figure of Grandmother. Grandma's recipes, the savor of her meals, her solid cuisine—like the fritters of beer dough, her roast beef marinated in beer and onions (served with horseradish, of course)—are unforgettable elements of it. She used beer not only in the kitchen; when I was a child she told me to use it as a shampoo. She said, "It makes your hair strong and keeps it healthy, it's an ideal rub-in tonic." Proof of this was Grandfather's mop of curly hair. I have tried it but once, and I cannot recommend it.

"Even the pharaohs used it for their braid and beard care," she declared. Today I know that she may have been right. As it happens, I am supposed to tell you something about the first beer in history, and with the pharaohs already mentioned, it's only a step back to the Sumerians.

Before the beginning of time

Beer was already known in Babylonian times. A kind of "drinkable bread" must therefore have existed earlier than that.

Nobody has found out yet. It cannot be attributed to Osiris or to any other god or goddess in antiquity. We might as well go right back to the Stone Age. There must have been something with a resemblance to our beer as early as the Neolithic Period, a sort of "archetype" beer made of fermented, wild, primeval cereals. In olden times, people even imbibed the swig by means of giant straws—Babylonian reliefs bear witness to this. Nowadays this is a barbarian custom that should be limited to milkshakes. The *Gilgamesh* tale (circa 3000 B.C.E.) says: "Eat the bread, Enkidú, it belongs to life, drink the beer, as is the custom in this country!" The story tells how the demiurge Gilgamesh turned the fuzzy animal-man Enkidú, into a real man. To do so he had to convince Enkidú that this would be an advantage. Nothing was to be more persuasive to this wild animal-man than a beautiful woman. She said

to him: "Enkidú does not know how to eat bread, he is not acquainted with drinking beer." In the end, Enkidú drank seven mugs of beer, and "his innards relaxed and he turned merry. His heart rejoiced, and his face shone. He washed his shaggy body with water and anointed himself with oil—and became a man. . . ."

Apart from this *Gilgamesh* episode, far-reaching research undertaken by historians on the subject of beer has yielded no results. Neither a mythologically well-founded trace nor an inventor of beer has come to light. No Dionysus or Bacchus, no Noah who have cultivated hops and subsequently become inebriated, no beer of Caanan, no alchemist who would have revealed the mysteries of a primordial recipe. Like all good discoveries, we also owe this one to "sheer accident" that brought to us the "drinkable bread" of primeval man via the beer of the Babylonians and ancient Egyptians.

From the monks in the monasteries of the Middle Ages to today's breweries with their huge brewing pans and sophisticated technologies, beer-brewing has grown increasingly refined. But for thousands of years, beer has quenched the thirst and need for sociality of both slaves and kings. In ancient Egypt, beer was considered liquid "power food" for the slaves employed in the construction of the pyramids. There were even regulations on how much beer each inhabitant was entitled to. The higher the rank, the greater the options. The daughter of a pharaoh was entitled to have up to five mugs of beer daily.

The Babylonian beer laws of King Ünik Hammurapi can be viewed as forerunners of the purity law of 1516, which has prevailed practically unchanged in Germany ever since, despite the laws of the European Union. They regulated everything—from the content of seasoning used in the production of beer to its

BIERKRUGMUSEUM · For the Germans, beer tankards are objects of daily use, whereas for tourists visiting Germany they are probably the most popular and precious souvenir. Be they big or small, with or without a handle, in ceramic or pewter, beer tankards are increasingly becoming collectors' items. Many German antique shops now display in their windows very valuable examples dating back to different periods. Some are decorated with the coats of arms of old aristocratic families, others with landscapes, miniatures, dedications, and proverbs. Tankards with finely chiseled silver lids fetch high prices, as do those made of porcelain or decorated with small sculptures. Visitors wishing to make off with the best of them may have to fork over several thousand marks for the privilege.

A few years ago, the world's only beer tankard museum was set up in Bad Schussenried, Germany, a small spa resort in Swabia between Lake Constance and Ulm. The Bierkrugmuseum is attached to an old brewery and displays over a thousand tankards of all types in its three-floor exhibition space. The oldest dates back to 1470, and the many curios include wedding and firemen's tankards, as well as a number of items in unusual materials, such as coconut or ostrich egg. Small children's tankards are also on display, along with those that the society ladies of the 1930s used for drinking beer instead of their customary afternoon tea.

—Dario Bragaglia

Bierkrugmuseum Wilhelm-Schussen Strasse 12
Bad Schussenried, Germany
Tel. ++49/7583/40411
Closed on Mondays.

selling price. Anyone adulterating beer or charging too high a price for it was punished by drowning (not in beer, however).

What did beer taste like in those times? Definitely not as dry and bitter as today; it was a sweet-sour, mellow beverage because (until a good five hundred years ago) it used to be brewed without hops.

Aristotle and beer

I ought to confess something: I am not a connoisseur and no real aficionado of beer. Since I started living in Berlin I have been asked now and then why I—as a wine drinker—would order beer when meeting with friends in a restaurant. First of all, I prefer drinking wine at home; that is the right place for enjoying a good bottle of wine alone or in company. Secondly, a good bottle of wine costs a fortune in a restaurant, and one cannot get good table wine outside the area where it is produced. Thirdly, in memory of my grandmother's virtues, I feel as big, strong, and merry as she was when I have a glass of beer. Dionysian inspiration and the pursuit of inebriation (in the broad sense of the word) remain grandfather's legacy—but that's a story I should rather tell some other time. A last world of advice: to get drunk on beer has consequences that have already been described by Aristotle. Along with discovering that beer is an agreeable nightcap, he noted that people intoxicated by beer fall on their backs, whereas excessive indulgence in wine causes them to fall on their faces or sideways.

Years ago, I was invited with some friends to partake of a Sunday morning "pint." In keeping with a north German custom, we had a shot glass of wheat liquor with each glass of beer. I do not remember how many glasses of beer and wheat liquor I downed. When finally I did struggle to my feet I fell, stiff as a board, on my back . . . Aristotle was right.

—Translated by Miriam Maimouni

Sandro Sangiorgi

A creamy, uneven froth that leaves an embroidered pattern on the sides of the glass is the first sign of a good beer. Yet the visual impression transcends mere appearances to suggest the substance and quality of a drink as old as bread itself. So this is as good a starting point as an other for an organoleptic analysis of the beverage. Unlike wine, beer lacks a specific tasting method. Enthusiastic writers have outlined the main features of quality beers, but balked at taking the analysis any further. As a result, there is no tasting card and underlying methodology that all experts agree on. It is not our intention to provide one here, but rather to summarize the quality aspects by means of which a beer is judged to be good, without forgetting that the choice is inevitably personal. As with champagne and cognac, consumer taste is the basis for production: the final quality of beer is not dependent upon the fruit of a particular harvest, but rather on a process in which the quality of the raw materials goes hand in hand with sophisticated manufacturing techniques. It is possible to undertake a comparative tasting of the finest red wines in the world—such as Bordeaux, Langhe, Rioja, and California—whereas a similar comparison of the finest German, Belgian, and British beers would be pointless, given the fact that each one has been developed with a particular consumer in mind. Breweries—be they small-scale or industrial—meet their customers' expectations, guaranteeing the color, aroma, and taste they cherish. An enthusiast may well appreciate a new beer and examine it thoroughly, but in the end he is likely to stick to his favorite. This is why beers such as the light Berliner Weisse and the overwhelming and alcoholic Kulminators are consistently ranked among the finest in the world.

froth, bubbles, bouquet

A well-made beer reveals a number of qualities that are easily visible. We have already mentioned the structure of the *froth,* and should add that the quantity of froth tends to depend on the habits of drinkers (and those who serve the beer), thus whether it is plentiful or scarce is unimportant for assessment purposes. What is essential are the *bubbles*, which must be fine and persistent, as in top-quality sparkling wines; if this is not the case, it means that natural fermentation has been adulterated by the addition of carbon dioxide.

The central elements in the quality of the *bouquet* are harmony and richness; the scent of the hops, whose shades range from pungent to mentholated; the intense malt overtones in the Helles from

Bavaria; the fruity aromas of apple and pear of the Lagers; the aroma of toast and melted butter of the Ales; the flowers and spices of the Trappists' beers are characteristic features of various types. Those characteristics are negative elements when they seem like an aromatic monotone, the one-sidedness of a raw material falling short of expectations, or the result of a careless production process. Moreover, an uninviting flavor may result from inadequate preservation, since beer—like all living drinks—suffers from oxidation and light: overtones of cardboard, stale biscuits, and cauliflower are fairly typical of spoiled beer.

The *taste* of beer is relatively complex, depending on a subtle balance among the sweetness of the malt, the freshness of the carbon dioxide, strength of the extracts, warmth of the alcohol, and—last but not least—bitter finish of the hops. Sweetness must be sharp and immediate, proving that good quality malt has been used without additions of sugar or other concentrates that tend to leave an unnatural sweet aftertaste. The alcohol content and body are not qualitative features in themselves, but become so if they are part of the development of the overall taste. Even the strongest beers should leave a clean sensation in the mouth. A bitter aftertaste is an advantage since it encourages further tasting. Just as with wine, persistence of aroma and depth of taste are important for a final judgment; nevertheless, the pleasant fleetingness of a Weizen remains the most attractive feature of this beer.

FIVE:3

5,000 VARIETIES

Manfred Kriener

Suckling pig with vinaigrette sauce and mustard grains— it goes without saying, you should drink a tasty Kölsch with it. *Rollmops* of red mullet on a bed of hop shoots go very well with a light, low-alcohol ale. Smoked cod with large beans and chanterelles? Nothing better than a stout Bock. A duck stew cooked in the oven with three different types of cabbage is just fine with a bitter, sour Pils, whereas goat's cheese from Baden wrapped in bacon requires a full-bodied Altbier. As a dessert, a beer timbale with plums sprinkled with a Weizen, rich in yeast. Six dishes, six different types of beer—and six audacious gastronomic feats. This menu has been created by the chef of the Taube of Grevenbroich, Dieter Kaufmann, and his sommelier Oliver Rasper, with a view to demonstrating that in Germany—the land of beer *par excellence*—beer can be something more than the drink that usually accompanies a shank of pork or roast of chicken. They wanted to demonstrate that, to a certain extent, beer can even hold its own beside sophisticated cuisine.

Oliver Rasper has summed up the basis for a successful marriage: "The food must have strong aromas." Sweet, soft, and subtle flavors clash with the tannic acid contained in beer. "I cannot drink beer with a *poché* fish, but I certainly can with smoked fish."

Nevertheless, menus including beer still tend to be an exception, even in Germany. True, many sophisticated restaurants utilize beer froth in their preparations, making beer soups or zabaglione with Altbier, but they invariably suggest wine to go with their dishes. For instance, renowned Berlin chef Sigfried Rockendort has drawn up a drinks list comprising over a hundred wines but no more than one beer, "mainly consumed by the kitchen staff." Sommeliers in the most famous restaurants tend to relegate beer culture to beer festivals. A dish that goes with beer is practically beyond their ken.

200 liters per year

Learned disquisitions are largely lost on the average German drinker, whose thirst last year alone was quenched by 132 hectoliters of beer. And since this estimate of per-capita consumption also includes teetotalers, newborn babies, and grannies, we could easily bring the figure up to 200 liters for the typical beer drinker. Germans traditionally compete with Czechs and Belgians in bearing the palm as the world's biggest beer drinkers. Certainly they are global champions as far as the number of breweries (1,254) and the different beer types they produce (over 5,000) are concerned. As Mark Twain said, "German beers are as different as hens in a yard: pale, dark, even black. . . ." In recent times, however, there has been a constant fall in the number of breweries, year after year. Big fish swallow small ones.

Yet those who actually take advantage of this almost endless range of products are relatively few. The delight of experimenting, the quest for the new, the parallel tasting of different beer types—all this is a real exception among beer drinkers. How sad it is to stick to the usual sour and bitter Pils (the most widely consumed beer in Germany) when there are so many varieties to discover. And speaking of Pils, in a parallel tasting session organized by the TV network ZDF, Pils brewery owners sampled fifteen different types of Pils and were largely unable to recognize their own products. Famous beers all evidently taste pretty much the same. At the end of this alcoholic marathon, by which time many participants were visibly drunk, Henninger owner Peter Lämmerhirdt drew the following conclusion: "Just like cars, beers are doctored to such an extent that it is impossible to tell one from another."

But beer connoisseur Dietrich Höllhuber maintains that "only the most narrow-minded people consider beer as a drink for narrow-minded people." In his opinion, "beer is much richer in shades, colors, and facets than its image as a popular drink would suggest. Moreover, beer embodies the same regional differences as wine. Hence the plain charm of a light Kölsch; the creamy froth of a stout Bock; the crimson-bronze reflection of Alt; the toasted aroma of black ale, reminiscent of coffee; the clove aroma of Weizen . . . the beer flavor may be fruity, sweet, bitter, yeasty, hop-like, fresh, sparkling, smoky, or bitterish, and each of these with any possible alcoholic content. Yet,

91

unfortunately, when beer is old or badly made, it may also taste of bread, paper, oxide, milk, or have a rotten or stale flavor.

Cold, in small tankards

Experts have traced over a thousand aromatic substances in beer, the most important of which are esters, aldehydes, and ketones. During the tests that are regularly carried out by DLG (the German society for agriculture), the examiners review the range of aromas through smelling and tasting. They analyze the porosity and stability of froth, the fineness of bubbles produced by carbon dioxide, the quality of bitterness, the effervescence, and the fullness of taste, smell, and flavor. For example, a Pils should have a bitter taste, but this bitterness should not be too tangy. It should be clearly felt as an aftertaste, yet without lingering too long in the mouth, and without leaving the throat dry.

More aromatic beers—that is, those with a higher extract and alcohol content—should have a fuller, stronger taste. A Weizen should be fizzier, thus containing a higher level of carbon dioxide. Carbon dioxide actually forms very fine bubbles in a good Weizen, and is therefore not excessively aggressive or predominant.

But what are the distinctive features of a good beer? "A beer is truly good," maintains Dietrich Höllhuber, "if its aspect, first sip, and aftertaste are distinct and complex. A monotonous beer suggesting no significant mix of aromatic elements is acceptable, but not good."

A good beer must be—first of all—fresh. Beer cannot grow old. A few months after bottling it already loses vigor, and is not as fizzy. This is why beer produced by small breweries and drunk locally has a fresher, more lively taste than some of the prestigious German ales exported overseas and stored for a few more months.

Beer often loses its freshness due to faulty tapping. It must be served chilled, at 8°C, and poured carefully. A good Pils does not last seven minutes—as many will insist it lasts no more than two. Those long taps that plunge into the tankard shoot shafts of air into the beer with disastrous consequences: the carbon dioxide comes out, and the beer loses its strength. Another common deadly sin among bartenders is to pour beer into various glasses to keep the froth down, and then mix two half-filled tankards to get a full one. If this is the case, customers should head for the exit, or content themselves with a glass of mineral water.

Another suggestion: even when extremely thirsty, you should drink beer in small tankards. The huge one-liter tankards of Bavaria, famous worldwide as the symbol of the Okto-berfest, are a complete denial of beer culture. Freshly tapped—and even at the third sip—a good beer maintains all its flavor. And at the fourth, the glass should be empty.

FIVE:4

NEW BREWS

Charlie Papazian

If you pass through the United States you cannot fail to notice that we have be-come a country impassioned with beer. Not just any beer. Not light, fizzy, cold, pale, charac-terless American lager beer. Seeing is believing. Throughout most of the world, American beer has been dismissed as a bland, homogenous, uninteresting commodity. Rightly so. Ninety-five percent of the 235 million hectoliters of beer annually consumed in America is a pale, highly carbon-ated, thirst-quenching beverage with little character.

Discovering that there are over 1,250 small micro- and pub-breweries in the United States therefore comes as something of a surprise. After all, this is the land of Budweiser, Miller, and Coors. How can such originality exist in a land so long monopolized by very large breweries? Yet it does, and how:

there are four new breweries opening every week.

If you walk into an American restaurant that respects the customers' desire for variety, character, and flavor in their food and beverages, you will be presented with both a wine and a beer list. The choice often involves more than twenty different beers. To have ten or more truly different beers on draft is not uncommon. In thousands of restaurants that take pride in presenting beer culture, the choice may exceed one hundred or even two hundred beers. Visit a shop or grocery store, and the choice may exceed four hundred different kinds of beer from all over the world.

Take note: there is not one American micro-brewery producing fizzy, light-tasting, American-style lager. The revolution is over. A new attitude and direction for American beer drinkers has been established. The challenge now for craft brewers and their supporters is to sustain this new awareness.

Ales and lagers; crisp, hoppy British-style pale ale; dark, bittersweet, chocolatelike porter; hop-floral and assertively bitter India pale ale; big, strong, slowly aged barley wine with hints of toffee and caramel; brown, well-balanced, and smooth English-style mild ale; Belgian-style Tripel, light-colored and fruity; brown and sumptuously malty, the sweet Belgian-style Dubbel with its hint of banana fruitiness; two-, three-, sometimes four-year-old matured, spontaneously fermented Belgian-style Kriek (cherry), Framboise (raspberry), and Cassis (black currant) flavored wheat-based Lambic; French-style strong, floral, bottle-conditioned, corked, and matured country ales and *bière de garde*; hearty, smooth, malty and strong German-style bock and double bock; yeasty, nutious, fruity, refreshing, spicy, and highly effervescent Bavarian-style Weizenbier (wheat beer); Irish-style stout; American rye beer and oat beer; Swedish juniper berry beer; American colonial-style pumpkin beer; maple-syrup-flavored ales; hot and spicy chili-pepper-flavored beer; Aztec honey, chocolate, corn, and chili ale; German, Alaskan, and Swedish smoked-malt-flavored beer . . .

Drawing pleasure

The products of American brewers continues to include perhaps seventy traditional styles of ales and lagers. Beers whose origins emerged half a world away, or perhaps a new creation to be regarded two hundred years from now as a classic worthy of protection. All being brewed one small 3-, 5-, 10-, 20-, or 50- hectoliter batch at a time in small rural towns, large cities, and countryside inns. The craft beers of America have captured 3 percent of the total beer market and are still growing strong. Americans have interpreted and embraced a respect for the brewing traditions of the world, while creating beers uniquely American in spirit. The art and science of crafting beer is well over five thousand years old. From barley, rye, wheat, rice, oats—malted, roasted, caramelized, torrified, milled, mashed, and boiled—artfully combined with hop flowers, herbs, fruit, and spices, then put to yeasts of a thousand sorts, aged and carefully conditioned through thirst to glass. Enjoyed, savored, sipped, contemplated like fine wine with an exquisitely prepared meal, or shared with a dear and genuine friend. We who have guzzled our insipid light lager for so many decades have reawakened to beverages crafted with care.

And interest in them is spreading. A new appreciation for crafted beer is evident in Japan, Thailand, China, Brazil, Argentina, Peru, South Africa, Zambia, Israel, Russia, Sweden—in fact, the world over. This change in attitude is developing slowly. It doesn't shriek from billboards like quick, mass produced commodities, but must be sought out and nurtured with respect. It is a quiet product of the American landscape. It is a joyous pursuit of pleasure and a tribute to the wonderful world of little things.

FIVE:5

FOR STOUT LOVERS

Michael Jackson

The dynamic businessman had made his money from the company that brews a famous golden beer, but he told me that his own first drink had been a *Schwarzbier* from Thuringia (the same beer that had nourished Goethe, Germany's greatest poet, in the 18th century). "When?" I asked the brewer. "As a baby at my mother's breast," he explained. The notion that dark beers are for women, especially nursing mothers, is typical in Central Europe. Is this perhaps an oedipal explanation for the idea that the blackest of brews are aphrodisiacs."

The black lagers of Central Europe are exceeded in intensity by the classic high-roast styles, porter and stout.

95

Again, the nourishing breast is evoked. Not quite mother's milk, perhaps, but lactose is used in some sweet stouts. The one made by the local brewery on the island of Malta adds vitamin B, too. Its label shows a trident-brandishing Neptune, king of the sea. Not Venus? Not amniotic fluid? We are luxuriating in deep waters here.

The depth of the blackness in these beers seems full of magic. The darkness of the unknown? The hidden threat—or promise—of black night? The "Decadent" writer J. K. Huysmans, in his novel *Against Nature*, described a quest for the rare and perverse in sensation. He imagined an all-black meal involving Russian rye bread, caviar, game "in sauces the color of boot-polish," plum puddings, kvass, porter, and stout. Catherine the Great, who was rumored to have made love to her horse, commanded that porter be brewed in her St. Petersburg, and it still is. In Finland, I have sweated naked in the sauna, jumped in a muddy lake, then consumed porter with smoked eggs. Unfortunately, given my sexual tastes, all my naked companions were male.

The Swedes, purported to be blonde sexual gods, have always had laws to inhibit their consumption of alcohol. For years, they required a doctor's prescription to buy one particular beer: a black porter now produced in Stock-holm but originally made in Gothenburg by a Scot called Carnegie.

Porter and stout were first brewed in London, and part of their truest character is the earthy aroma of two English hop varieties. Fuggles and Goldings (which take their names from the growers who first identified them). The smell of these hops reminds me of sex. I think we are talking about pheromones. Perhaps that is why women who pick hops are said to be untroubled by hormonal mood swings.

In its Georgian and Victorian heyday, porter was offered in London pubs with bar snacks of free oysters. The precious bivalves were inexpensive and plentiful in the days before the Thames estuary and the North Sea were polluted.

The black and the red

Off the shores of northern England, the Isle of Man has a tradition of producing stouts that actually contain oysters, boiled in the brew-kettle. Two aphrodisiacs in one? This Celtic island is said to have been torn by the gods from the soil of Northern Ireland, leaving the hole that is now filled by a lake called Lough Neagh. The Northern Irish, who have a passion for funerals, held one for the perilously drinkable Guinness porter when it was withdrawn from the market in 1973 in favor of the same company's heavier stout.

"When I die, I want to decompose in a barrel of Porter and have it served in all the pubs in Dublin," mused that chronicler of dissolute behavior, J. P. Donleavy. "I wonder, would they know me?" Even in the smoky, male ambiance of Dublin's famously sociable pubs, there is always hidden in the black brew the promise of an encounter with a redhead called Molly, whether Ms. Malone (with her cockles and mussels) or Ms. Bloom (with one hopes, her orgasm).

If fishy arousal is not for you, and your tastes are for a sweeter love, try a chocolate stout. I know of several, and one of my favorites is brewed in a former matzo bakery in Brooklyn, New York. In middle America, in Kalamazoo (where Glen Miller had a girl—or was it Tex Beneke?), a former disc jockey and professional baker runs a brewery making half a dozen porters or stouts. Flavors include snuff, a sometimes poisonous pod (rendered harmless by roasting), cherries, coffee, and double cream. One of his more extreme versions, Dr. Bell's Medicinal Stout, also known as Eccentric Ale, is served with pickled hot peppers and quail eggs. What does this do to one's sensibilities? The brewer once called me long after I had gone to bed at night, inviting me to sample his latest vintage.

Can black lightning strike thrice? At the risk of seeming to boast, I cherish one particular hotel in San Francisco because I have shared bedrooms there with three loves (I shall dilute the potency of this story by conceding that each was in a different decade). The most memorable of these encounters was after a meal that began with prawns marinated in smoked beer and served with Guinness, and ended with apple bread pudding and stout.

Had we been Chinese, we would have waited until the Eighth Moon . . . and bathed our newborn baby in Guinness's curiously named Foreign Extra Stout. It is all, I am assured, a question of *yin* and *yang*.

Chapter SIX

Markets

SUNDAY MORNING IN LIMOGNE

Annie Hubert

To feel the pulse of a village, district, or city, there is no better place than the market. It's a place of exchange for material goods and intangible realities, a space and time in which human dynamics can take shape and become manifest. Markets also often draw out the visual, olfactory, and auditory aesthetics of a given population. Moreover, they offer the inquisitive visitor a marvelous opportunity for "getting inside" a different world.

Our planet is full of markets, each different from the next. Though they may initially appear to be chaotic, they actually embody all the logic of specific social intercourse.

I have visited innumerable markets—some exotic, others ordinary, some far afield and others near at hand. I tend to use them as a way of getting to know the wider universe around them that transcends the immediate realms of sight and smell. And every time, even if the hundredth, the experience is all-embracing and intense. These are places of embryonic dishes, of food in its raw state, of vegetable, animal, and crafts products. They lead me into a world that I can slowly decode through its tastes, shapes, and techniques. And as I get to know it, I may also learn to love it.

In the south-west

The "markets of my heart" are those of southwest France, which I have elected as my homeland. They are the quintessence of this region, each one a stage for the food most representative of local production. And not only are they venues for the display and exchange of food, but also for the circulation of news, the narration of stories, and the celebration of a wide range of events. In such distinctly rural areas, the weekly markets in the main square of the village are also primary meeting places; in fact, nowadays they tend to replace the church square for the purposes of socialization.

Limogne is a case in point. A small village on the Causses du Quercy, it consists of around one hundred houses, a butcher's shop, a baker's shop, and a bazaar that sells practically everything. There is even a minute supermarket, which has survived over the years without getting bigger. Expansion has probably been thwarted by the vivacity

of the Sunday morning market. Whatever the season, the market in Limogne is what quickens the heartbeat of the local community. By seven in the morning, the farmers of the area are already to be seen with their vans setting up their stalls in the square facing the church and along the street leading into it. Not only the small producers meet up for the occasion, but also the pensioners who sell the produce of their vegetable gardens, orchards, and courtyards. The itinerant stall-holders usually turn up a bit later, their vans packed with work gear, aprons, clothes, and items of that sturdy underwear much favored by the elderly. There is also a pork butcher from the nearby Aveyron, a cheese maker from Cantal whose van turns into a stall, and a trader from the Maghreb whose olives, spices, fruit, and fried legumes fill the air with pungent smells. From ten o'clock onwards, the activity is in full swing. All the able-bodied oldies gather in their Sunday best, while men and women rally in small groups in the middle of the street to exchange views and news, their empty baskets still hanging from their arms. You have to elbow your way along the street and through the square to reach the stalls, and this is all part of the socializing. Young women pushing their prams stop in the middle of the crowd to admire their respective offspring. Younger men tend to gather on one side of the square, in front of the café, where coffees and glasses of *pastis* are served apace. And among the crowd, in

99

the tourist season, groups of vacationers stand out, particularly the "foreign strangers" who are not "from these parts," as opposed to the "domesticated" strangers who have houses in the area and have been coming back for many years.

In this restricted area—a few hundred square meters—stalls display pyramids of fruit and vegetables in their natural state. This produce doesn't look selected, washed, and polished as it would in supermarkets; instead there's plenty of color and pleasant smells that fill the air with a heady mixture of garlic, the spicy green magic of tomato leaves, and the pungent presence of potatoes still sheathed in a film of nourishing soil. Smallholders proffer a few boxes of fruit: apricots, peaches, apples or pears, cherries and strawberries, including the delicious *mara des bois*—a variety reminiscent of wild strawberries that I first came across in this very region. In front of the stalls, close to bunches of scallion, braids of pink garlic, and the piles of zucchini, tomatoes, and eggplant, the country women sell large bunches of flowers from metal buckets: iris, dahlias, daisies. The *habitués* queue in front of the cheese van, and conversation flows on and on, eased by the smooth, sonorous accent of the area.

The cheese maker is an important person because he "does" a number of markets in the region, and can thus convey information very quickly. Live conversation beats boring old phone calls any time for animation, taking on dramatic tones abetted by gesticulation and some responsive audience participation. The vendor is perfectly acquainted with his customers' tastes, successfully dealing out huge slices of a fresh, cream-colored Cantal and a tasty golden Salers. Impressive portions of Roquefort also find their way into shopping baskets: in this area, sheep's cheese is only ever eaten in industrial quantities. The small, round, locally produced Cabécous cheeses are particularly appreciated by "tourists," who consider them a cult-product of the Quercy plateaus. Then there are the few stalls reserved to *pastis* makers. This is not the anise drink of the same name, but a delicious cake made from very fine, transparent pastry, rather like Austrian *Strüdel:* toothsome proof of a Saracen legacy that is reminiscent of *baclava, pastillas,* and *briks.* These *pastis* are filled with apple slices soaked in plum brandy. To make them, pastry makers knead the dough on a large cloth-covered table. Further down, on small foldable tables, country women sell a couple of chickens, ducks, or rabbits gutted, cleaned, and wrapped in transparent plastic bags. Alas, plastic holds sway everywhere: all stall-holders have a stash of plastic bags for their products. Long gone is the age of the newspaper and paper bag, much to the disgust of the older people who complain more about the waste than the pollution.

Salami, confit, cucumbers

On the pork butcher's stall, the ever-present and emblematic pork sausage is accompanied by salami large and small, fresh and seasoned, along with large chunks of salted ham and salted and smoked duck breasts. Various pieces of *confit* (cooked meat preserved in fat) of duck and pork are heaped up in the enameled containers: they will enhance soups or be grilled and served with potatoes *sautéed* in lard. A bit further along, a wine seller displays a full range of bottles of a good Cahors and a few glasses for tasting—this for the "foreigners," those who are not from the area. Virtually all those who are have a vineyard on their land and produce wine for family consumption; it is certainly not Cahors DOC, but in good years these homemade wines can be delightful. In the appropriate season there are also mushroom gatherers who bring their baskets of scented *porcini* or orange chanterelles to market. In spring they also sell bunches of *respountchous*, young hop shoots that taste rather like small, wild asparagus, slightly bitter and aromatic. Connoisseurs boil them and serve them with a *vinaigrette* and boiled eggs. Then there is the herb and "organic" produce vendor. This is an elderly farmer who discovered one day to his considerable satisfaction that foreigners regarded the produce he grew without chemical fertilizers in his vegetable garden as being organic. He lost no time in making a nice cardboard poster claiming his role as a grower of natural products. And the tourists could not have been happier.

There is also a cucumber lady: on a foldable table she sells one or two jars of homemade pickled cucumbers, some small trays of raspberries, red currants, or blackberries toward the end of the summer, and a few jars of jam in winter. All this is a far cry from industry, from regulations and mass-consumption. The word "trade" is reductive for this kind of exchange. For these are products that mirror both the vendor and the customer, who are acquainted with all aspects of production, and find the time to chat and joke together. The word used in food and farm talk is "traceability," and there's plenty of it here. The provenance of these products is a known quantity, and this makes them effective, simple, and reassuring. The outcome in the kitchen will be dishes that hearten us as they nourish us.

The crowd is so thick that you can only move a few steps at a time, and very slowly. All around you hear the singsong local accent, and occasionally the notes played by a small band playing in a corner of the square. A white truck parked in front of the small supermarket draws many a customer. Pizza only made its appearance in the region fifteen years ago, but since then has never looked back. Not only among the tourists is it successful, but also among the country folk. Driven by curiosity, they must first have thought they were about to sample a sort of *quiche*. They now include it in their Sunday lunches as an element that lends a little extra color. Patrick the pizza maker has even invented a local version using Roquefort, Cabécou, and the ubiquitous salami.

People's shopping baskets fill up and the roads gradually empty. By about 1:30 the little village has returned to its usual quiet and sleepy ways. Everyone has gone home for Sunday lunch, and since this is a farming region where good food is still an essential part of the joy of living, the post-market repast continues to be an important family custom.

SIX:2

THE VALUE OF TIME

Gianni Vercellotti

Solitude calls for encounters; silence screams for voices; the monochrome needs color. This is maybe the reason why Africa is a land of markets. To grasp the truth of African life, you must be willing to surrender to them, devoting hours and days to aimless wandering amidst the music of voices and the endless display of products, smells, and colors. The market: a place for encounter and exchange, where everything and nothing may happen, a self-perpetuating nucleus of life. These markets are as ancient as the world, yet constantly new, always different. And they are endless. In Addis Ababa, Djenné, Antananarivo, you find miles and miles of wooden stalls, of multicolored awnings; people by the thousand, a constant thunderous rumbling of voices; endless, deafening queues of cars in a beeping frenzy, with exhaust-pipes spitting black poison, and rusty decrepit bodywork kept together by various layers of fancy paint. But elsewhere you also find four eggs and five bananas proffered in the shade of an acacia, stranded in the middle of nowhere. The vendor is an old woman who cannot get any older, her skin already mummified by the sun and the wind. She utters not a word, awaiting your offer with just a timid, trachoma-glazed glance, knowing all too well you may be the only person walking by the whole day. Then there are basketfuls of mangoes and vegetables waiting for a purchaser, abandoned at the foot of a tree in the forest, with no vendor, no owner to be seen; and bags of charcoal or bundles of dried twigs at the edge of the desert, placed there to remind you that further on you will find nothing else to light a fire and boil water for tea, thus quenching your thirst and celebrating the ancient sacred ritual of hospitality typical of the caravan routes.

It is impossible to list the items for sale in African markets: a thousand different vegetables and a thousand types of fruit, a thousand pancakes and a thousand meatballs, roasted iguanas and skewered chickens, snakes' skins and dried dromedary fetuses, colored minerals and gray powders, semiprecious and precious stones, suitcases and trunks, pepper and coffee, various kinds of teas, karkade, and shea butter. The market is a pool of knowledge and a well of curiosity. You can find the few survivors of dying tribes who have come out of the forest and are unable to face a journey back to silence and nothingness. There are also peddlers

with awful golden watches and leopardskin berets, mirror sunglasses, and warthog-teeth necklaces. And then women, women, by the thousand, everywhere—all with children clinging to their necks, on their shoulders, snoozing among the baskets, looked after by slightly older sisters just about able to walk. Women who have covered miles and miles along the tracks with their loads of fruit, vegetables, eggs, and chickens. They come from villages beyond the horizon and will return there after nightfall, still in time to take water from the well and prepare the *ugali* or the *posho* for the family meal.

There are children everywhere: serious-looking, pensive kids with eyes bigger than their faces, keen looks, and snotty noses; children who run trailing makeshift wire toys or who kick a rag ball along dusty spaces scattered with plastic bags captured by the wind.

Some of the men are playing cards, their leathery hands deftly dealing out the worn and greasy pack. Others are engaged in a complicated game of skittles involving a tray full of holes and a philosophy that is hard to grasp for those born outside this culture. Some of the men have assembled to listen to a *griot*, the last ballad-singer, who still sings of mythical tales and epic battles fought when the Sahel was the center of the universe, well before the time when the Arabs coined the motto: "God made the land of black men and then burst out laughing."

Mercedes and supermarkets

The market is timeless because it takes place throughout the day. It is born with the dawn, dies at sunset, and envisages no established times for meetings or appointments. The Arabs say: "Our time is Allah's time. . . ." and do not concern themselves with minutes. The sun rises, moves, and sets, while in the markets trash, empty baskets, waste paper, and cardboard boxes accumulate, raising the hopes of exhausted dogs and wild cats struggling with ravens and marabous. In one corner dice are tossed, in another goats' throats are cut and chickens are dipped in boiling water. Steadily buzzing flies swarm over the exposed chunks of meat, as the blood dries, giving it a curious bluish patina. The wasps, for their part, prefer the sugary sweetness of overripe bananas or rotten pineapples.

Voices and words create the sound, and the music is always dance, which informs the way people walk in Africa. Children dance at the beat of a spoon on an enameled bowl, boys sway in front of huge transistor radios that are the pride of the village, their cardboard boxes emblazoned with Chinese script.

A number of languages and dialects intermingle, striving for comprehension by using common words derived from the Swahili and Arabic, and the French and English learned at school or from the missionaries. All this in a whirl of gags and jokes, laughter and winking, calls and shouts. The market avenges itself on the long, silent hours and the days of solitude in empty places. People can forget the wind and the sun as they rediscover the pleasure of being a crowd—an opportunity for talk and dialogue, a store of news and information.

In the market people talk, tell tales, get supplied with things and ideas, returning to their villages with commodities and stories. Those who were unable to go keenly await their return. As they sit by the fire later that evening there will always be someone from another hut who draws close to find out what has happened, what there is to be learned, what can be passed on to the next person.

In Africa the market is like a newspaper that tells the truth despite despotic governments and regardless of corrupt journalists. It expresses all the rage, criticism, needs, and hope of the people, revealing what they require, lack, and await. It is no coincidence that there is brisk trade in the bags and bags of supplies sent by international relief organizations: goods that should be distributed for free and instead are sold to the higher bidder. How did the vendors get hold of them? And who is reaping the benefits? Perhaps the *wa-benzi*, a name coined in resigned humor by the poor Africans who attribute the nominal value of a new tribe to the owners of Mercedes-Benz. These are new rich, the new rulers, the new "managing" class, intent on getting rich and forgetting Africa.

Calls echo here and there among the smells of fruit and veg-etables, the rustle of clothes and fabrics, the tinkle of necklaces and bracelets. Many of the surrounding bodies are works of orna-mental art in themselves, with incised flesh, tattoos, and paint-ings revealing proud membership in a particular tribe. But in the cities, in the largest villages, shops are beginning to appear. Boxes and tins and plastic containers are stealing the thunder from local produce. Mysterious mixtures make the poultry and cattle swell, while billboards advertise the arrival of goods from afar, equal for everybody.

Worn, ripped bank notes impregnated with the smell of smoke are counted: products are exchanged for Maria Theresa thalers; six eggs can be purchased for a few thousand Zaire shillings; fetishes ready to become medicinal powders are fea-tured on a stall alongside tubes of aspirin some twenty years past their sell-by date. In a cubicle, an Indian man lends money at exorbitant interest rates while two Arabs heap the dollars in orderly packages; a quack offers dried lizards and an acrobat dances on a rope.

But the appeal of those shops is growing by the day. Supermarkets are arriving with their artificial colors, their artifi-cial goods, their artificial lights. And Africa without its markets will also lose the magic of their necessary counterpart: the soli-tude, the silence, the void. As it loses the solemnity of its spaces, Africa will also be divested of the magic of its words.

ALKMAAR: THE CHEESE MARKET

Grazia Solazzi

With its atmosphere of bygone times—the bearers wearing white uniforms and hats, and the cheese rounds on display in the square—the cheese market at Alkmaar is one of Holland's major tourist attractions, visited every year by more than three hundred thousand people from all over the world. To this day it is held with the utmost respect for tradition, and is well known for being the largest and oldest wholesale cheese market in the world. The first records of the market date back to 1622, but it would seem that the city of Alkmaar already had special scales in use for cheese-weighing in the 14th century. In any case, 1622 is the year in which the cheese bearers guild was founded; unlike other guilds, it had no patron saint or altars in the Church, but did have a credo taken from the Bible: "A false public scales is awful to the Lord, whereas a full weight is a pleasure for Him." At that time, the market was held on Fridays and Saturdays from May to All Saints' Day, but it gradually became so important that in the 19th century it was held four times a week. In the early 20th century Waagplein—the public scales square—was expanded to increase the trading area. In 1916, on every market day, approximately three hundred thousand tons of cheese were traded, and negotiations could well last until one o'clock in the morning. Today, the market is held against the beautiful backdrop of the medieval city of Alkmaar every Friday from mid-April to mid-September.

The procedures stick to the old ritual. Very early in the morning, under the eyes of the market supervisor, the rounds of cheese are unloaded and heaped in long rows on the square, but the real trading takes place from ten to noon. Transport and weighing are still carried out by the guild, which includes four groups (*veem*), each made up of seven cheese bearers. Each *veem* has a color of its own: red, yellow, green, and blue. The bearers wear a white uniform and a straw hat of the color of the *veem* to which they belong, as goes for the characteristic wooden stretchers. Called a *tasman*, the senior bearer of the group is entrusted with the task of putting the weights on the scales when the cheese is weighed. He wears a distinctive black leather bag around his waist, whereas the chief (called *overman*) sports a silver coat of arms with a ribbon in the color of his *veem*. When the market is held, both traders and supervisors taste the products, assess the quality of the cheese, and set its price. When negotiations are concluded, the purchaser and seller sanction the agreement with a typical gesture: slapping their right hands together.

Today, the volume of trade registered at each event, as compared with the early 20th century, is down to approximately one tenth: 30 tons—a large enough volume, yet a modest one in a country that produces some 688,000 tons of cheese per year and exports 400,000 tons. Nowadays the Alkmaar market is possibly more a matter of folklore than business. The vendors are not small producers. Indeed, supply is in the hands of no more than two companies: Campina Melkune and Cono Kaas-makers Midden Beemster, respectively selling two thirds and one third of the cheese traded. There are no more than five or six purchasers either, so that each trades in large quantities. In other words, the market is preserved as a tourist attraction and for the sake of tradition. It is regarded as a very interesting promotional event, backed up by the press and TV to help to promote Dutch dairy products in the world. It is sponsored by the municipality as well as being financed by the Noord-Hollandse cheese makers association.

Only NH-branded products are bought and sold in the Alkmaar market. These are all made with cow's milk from pastureland reclaimed from the sea in the northern region of Holland. This is high-quality milk, fatty and slightly salted, that confers a special taste to dairy products. In 1996 a denomination of protected origin was given to the Noord Hollandse Gouda, a medium-textured cheese whose taste goes from delicate to pronounced as it matures, and the Noord Hollandse Edammer. The former is yellow and comes in flattened, round forms that weigh from two to thirty kilograms, whereas the latter is smaller, plumper, and has the characteristic red waxy outer skin. At the market, 90 percent of trade concerns young, 4- to 8-week Gouda cheese (a cheese is considered when it has been seasoned for three months or less, mature with three to six months' seasoning, extra-mature up to 9 months, old from 9 months to one year, and extra-old over one year), while the remaining 10 percent involves Edam and herb cheeses (with cumin seeds added).

Those interested in the secrets and traditions of these cheeses should make a visit to the public scales office (*Waggebouw*) at the Kaas Museum in Alkmaar, which has a collection of old tools and old and new films showing the Gouda and Edam manufacturing processes.

SIX:4

NATIVE CHILES IN SANTA FE

Deborah Madison

Farmers' markets in the United States are virtually the only public places where one can find traditional foods grown and sold in a way that indicates a deep acquaintance with them rather than a passing fancy. Outside of these markets, you just about have to know a farmer personally if you want foods with integrity. Along with those comparatively few restaurants that make serving regional foods their mission, it is farmers' markets that give us the surest clue about what is unique to any region of this large country, the United States.

In Madison, Wisconsin, you'll find fresh-cracked hickory nuts at the farmers' market, but not almonds; in Birmingham, Alabama, you'll see that the okra is carefully sorted for size, depending on whether you plan to fry, stew, or pickle it. Sweet Muscadine grapes as large as wild plums can be found in the South, but not in the Southwest. Fragrant Meyer lemons grace only California's farmers' markets, and so forth. While chile peppers can be found in almost any farmers' market because they're popular at the moment, our market in Santa Fe, New Mexico, is the only place where you can find New Mexico's native chiles.

The Santa Fe farmers' market is twenty-five years old: old for most American markets, but younger than those of Philadelphia and St. Paul, which began in the 1800s. The market here nourishes our entire community, for it is an intensely social place where farmers and shoppers exchange conversation as well as food and money. But like all markets it began with a handful of farmers, mostly Hispanic, who sold little more than a few carrots, some onions and peas, and perhaps a jar of chokecherry jelly or some dried chile. Today, at the peak of summer, there are more than one hundred farmers selling produce, all of them from northern New Mexico. This is especially significant because in our market the farmers must grow what they sell, so they are truly farmers, all local to the region. Anyone suspected of selling corn from a cousin up in Colorado had better be prepared to defend himself against a fierce market manager and other angry farmers!

Santa Fe, which is one of the oldest cities in the United States, sits at the confluence of trade routes and cultures. The Old Santa Fe Trail, the Old Pecos Trail, and the Camino Real converge here, so a mix of plants, seeds, and food tastes have long made up the area's culinary history. The food culture of the indigenous peoples, the Pueblo Indians who still live here along the Rio Grande, was based on native plants and game, but they traded with the Plains Indians to the east and other tribes to the south, in Mexico. It's quite possible that chile was among the goods exchanged before the Spanish came, but usually the conquistador Don Juan de Oñate is given credit for having brought chile peppers with him from Mexico when he came north to Santa Fe in 1598. I don't think anyone knows for sure how chiles, our most emotionally significant food, came to New Mexico, but in a similar fashion, Spanish foods that arrived with the conquistadors were incorporated into the indigenous diet. Among these new imports were chickpeas, fava beans and peas; milk, cheese, and meat from goats and cows; apricots, peaches, and plums. Many of these foods are still in evidence at the Santa Fe farmers' market. In spring and again in the fall, tables are covered with bags of garbanzo beans, peas, pinto and bolita beans, favas, and jellies made of wild cherries, plums, and apricots. If you ask a farmer what kind of cherry or herb she is selling, she may well say, "It's a Spanish cherry, or Spanish basil." Cheese-making using goat's milk has been revived, and even meat is for sale at our market, including lamb from the Churro sheep, another Spanish import. Native American varieties of melons, squash, and corn along with chiles and wild foods such as *quelites* (a member of the goosefoot family) and *verdalagas* (purslane) are still gathered by the older Hispanic farmers who sell them at market. I might add that our younger Anglo farmers grow a plethora of vegetables from European

seeds, so any French or Italian slow foodist strolling the aisles would feel at home with *pain de sucre* or Biondissima Trieste chicory, Chioggia beets, Charentais and Cavillon melons, arugula selvatica, Violetta di Firenze eggplant, and so forth.

Española, Velarde, Dixon

The one food, though, that stands out most vividly to natives as well as visitors is the chile. New Mexico is a chile-eating and chile-growing state. In the south, hybrids developed by the university grow in fields hundreds and thousands of acres large. They are shipped all around the country, and some in their dried form go to Germany to season sausages. But here in the north, we grow what's called the "native" chile. Although it's not truly native to this place, it has been here a few hundred years, its seeds passed down from generation to generation, and that's native enough for most people. Varieties of this chile are often named for the place they're grown— Española, Velarde, Dixon, and Chimayo. They are basically the same plant, but conditions such as the availability of water and the sandiness of the soil cause subtle differences in their flavors and heat. The largest field of native chile I know of is 3 acres. Essentially, these chiles are grown in patches and gardens, the total acreage is very small, and they stay mostly in their neighboring communities.

Unlike the big, meaty hybrid chiles from southern New Mexico, the native chiles are about 5 inches long, thin-fleshed, and usually twisted. This makes them unsuitable for stuffing because the twisting means you can't get the skins off or the stuffing in, both of which are necessary for proper *chiles rellenos*. Their thin walls also make them more difficult than other chiles to roast, so for this purpose they are usually mixed with some fleshier local varieties.

There's quite a lot of excitement when the chiles come into the market in September. Generally, the customers know whether they want them extra-hot, hot, or mild, and they're already sorted as to their intensity. You take your chiles to one of the farmers who has a roasting set-up, which consists of a wire cage equipped with several gas jets. Your chiles are dropped into the cage, then turned slowly over the fires until the skins are blackened, a process that fills the air with an aroma that makes everyone very happy. When judged to be sufficiently roasted, a trap door is opened on the bottom of the cage and the chiles fall into a plastic sack. By the time you get them home, they've steamed enough that the skins slip off. People usually remove the skins, then repack the chiles along with their juices into smaller bags to freeze for use during the winter. In the days before freezers, fresh chiles were buried in sandy earth, then dug out and roasted as needed. Of course one should always pause and take a few of the warm chiles, set them on a fresh tortilla, then crumble over them the fresh goat's cheese you bought at the market just an hour before. This makes a most delicious *quesadilla* to savor for breakfast.

The other thing that's done with the native chile is to allow it to remain on the vines until it's red. Usually by then the night mountain air has become cold enough to make the chiles very sweet as well as hot. They are then picked and set aside to dry on rooftops or in attics. Once dried, the seeds, stems, and veins are removed, then they're ground into a *molido* or powder. The *molido* made from dried native chiles is thought to be the best of any *molido*, as all the native chile powders are characterized by a rich, deep pepper flavor that's well under-scored with heat. The *molido* made from Chimayo chile is particularly prized. This fragrant, highly coveted chile is used to make *chile colorado*, a brick-red sauce scarcely enhanced with any seasonings, which is served with regional foods such as *posole* (corn treated with lime), *chicos* (corn dried in the *horno*), beans, *enchiladas*, and so forth.

In the recent past, the whole chiles were tied into *ristras*, or strings, and hung to dry under the eaves of houses, much like they're draped over Tunisian houses in the Sahel. One *ristra* always stayed in the kitchen and when a chile was wanted, it was simply plucked from the string, then ground or cooked whole with beans or corn. *Ristras* are still made today, but more for decoration than for practical use. They seem to give us a feeling of connection to the old traditions of the region. Most families in Santa Fe have a *ristra* hanging somewhere in their home, and some use the chiles to season their food as well as to delight the eye.

Certainly our market is made more colorful with these long strings of chiles, the air more fragrant with their roasting, plain food more delicious with their presence. As long as we can support our farmers, I am confident that native chiles will continue to grow on this land.

THE MARKET AT ULAN BATOR

Cinzia Scaffidi

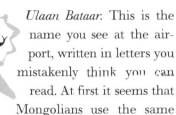

Ulaan Bataar. This is the name you see at the airport, written in letters you mistakenly think you can read. At first it seems that Mongolians use the same alphabet as ours, but following different rules: they read Ps as a Rs, Ys as Us, Cs as Ss, and so on.

On arriving at the airport you feel as if you are looking at yourself from above, walking on the righthand edge of a map depicting a stretch of land squashed beneath mighty Russia and practically strangled on all other sides by China. Tiny weenie, just an insect with its luggage, wandering helplessly in a remote corner of the planisphere. They have been telling us for five hundred years now that the world is round and has no corners. But here in Ulan Bator the world does have boundaries—it certainly does, and I feel close to them, far too close. How many kilometers separate me from my underwear drawer, from drinkable tap water, from the bar where I don't even have to say what I want to drink?

12,000. Twelve thousand. Once you say it, once you pronounce the figure or letters needed to name all those kilometers, you feel as if you could master them, as if you could give them some form.

Twelve thousand. Like traveling up and down Italy from one end to the other four times in a row, without so much as having a rest. Only four, not such a big deal really. Twelve thousand. I think I'm beginning to feel a bit better. Just a bit.

Smelling, touching

That odd planisphere feeling returns as soon as I reach Ulan Bator market. People elbow their way in and there are at least two gates to get through. As I approach, I find myself looking suspiciously at the crowd around me. I don't know what awaits me on the other side. I feel as if I am progressing far more slowly than all others, getting right in the way of everyone. People poke me, knock me about, push me to one side. With their hands and elbows, as if I were water and they were swimming. Men don't make way at all; if a woman reaches the gate at the same time as a man, he simply walks on—no thanks, they just don't see you. But here I am, finally inside huge tiled halls with very high ceilings, long rows of stalls in the middle and all along the walls. This is the market—and what about the square, the stall umbrellas, the bawling of vendors and customers? Well, forget it. Here the temperature is bearable for no more than a couple of months; for the rest of the year it falls dozens of degrees centigrade below zero, so you can forget open-air markets. Moreover, nobody talks loudly: there's a soft murmur, just like in any large department store; perhaps closed environments inspire whispering. The vendors just stand behind their stalls and wait. They don't try to capture your attention or promote their wares. People approach the stalls, ask questions, buy things, then walk on. Even in front of the stalls there are no queues, no waiting your turn; if you are not really buying, if you just wish to have a look, somebody will inevitably elbow his way in and push you aside. Again, I feel as if I'm caught on a narrow-gauge track. As if swallowed by an inexplicable silence. People are talking, yet I am incapable of decoding their sounds, of reducing them to something I can grasp. I try to concentrate on their body language and I soon realize that, when they count with their hands, they open them and fold their fingers one after the other. When I—*when we!*—count, we close our fist first and then gradually unfold our fingers. That's what it's like being on the other side of the world. But I'm here to play the game, even if I don't know the rules and wouldn't know how to ask about them. It makes me feel uncomfortable. Is this what the Western world comes down to—a need for rules? Or is it just the inevitable condition of any foreigner?

I pluck up courage and decide to approach the tomatoes. Aping the woman just in front, I start putting some on the scales. The vendor smiles at me. When I stop, she enters something on the small calculating machine and shows me the display—not for a moment does she think I might speak her language. Nor does she seem too worried about it. She can tell at a glance that gestures and figures are the only language we could have in common. I pay, I take the thin, transparent nylon bag she put my tomatoes in. I use my hands to ask for a bag, muttering "Can I have a bag, please?" so quietly that she wouldn't have heard even if she did speak English. I have learned the first rule: words are unimportant here. She writes 50 as an answer on the calculator. I pay fifty *tugrog* (a few cents), and I take my bag. I walk on, feeling that I'm beginning to get the hang of it. Now, let's try with the sugar. Just like salt, rice, and flour, it is sold from big sacks; those containing sugar and salt are close to each other. I point at one of the two and ask whether it is sugar (something inside me *knows* it is sugar—you can tell, salt is more humid and compact, finer; still, in another section of my brain, something else tells me that you never know, that I am not at home, so I'd better ask). They answer me in Russian, giving me a small scoop (made from a plastic bottle) with a bag to put it in, but without understanding my question. I can't translate it in gestures, so I start feeling out of the game again, my brain and hands in slow motion. They smile and shake their heads. So, still in slow motion, I take a pinch from the

bag and put it into my mouth. It is sugar. Now they all laugh, understanding what I'd just asked, and I finally get the information I needed. Rule number two: you can touch anything here, nobody gets angry; the sacred notion of hygiene I'm so proud of is totally useless here. I laugh too, somewhat soothed by the crystals on my tongue, because they are sweet, as sweet as the sugar back home, because the very taste of sugar takes me back to my childhood, and I didn't expect to relive these sensations here.

A few stalls further on I meet one of the few people I know in this city. How nice it is to meet somebody you know when you're feeling lost! She shakes my hand, formally holding her right elbow with the left hand, and approaches her face to mine, but without kissing me. I know the procedure by now, yet it never fails to surprise me slightly: instead of kissing me, she smells me. I always find this rather touching. I feel it expresses a different and more genuine interest in the other person. Kissing is a way of giving pleasure, but sniffing denotes an effort to understand who you are, what you smell of. In the measured and aseptic Western world, smelling each other is a sign of great intimacy—the gesture of lovers who wish to discover another way of recognizing each other, or of mothers wanting to understand if their children are well. It is a gesture of affection. And they—the Mongolians—smell me. I really feel part of the game.

For what these people and this land

113

reveal to those who can look without prejudice is sensuality. Food taken in the hands from a common dish expresses sensuality. So does the ritual cooking and cutting up of the goat for important celebrations. Likewise the way girls will stand out in the infrequent rains because they believe it is good for their hair. Even the children riding bareback is sensual, as is the pushing and shoving in the market, which denotes no fear of touching foreigners. Moreover, there is a certain intangible sort of sensuality in the fact that the unknown is an unfamiliar concept in this land of two million inhabitants in a territory five times that of Italy. There are so few of us, they often declare in sociological studies and historical explanations. And what we expect them to say next is that they all know one another. Instead, they just want to explain why this share of the market cannot be of much interest to large industries.

Nothing but space

We let Ulan Bator a few hours ago and are now heading south, toward the desert. The chimneys and brick buildings soon disappear and the city is easily forgotten. Stretching out ahead is the countryside, though the term is far too homely, too reassuring, too soft and rounded to convey the reality of what you find once you leave the capital. The Uaz—a Russian jeep which looks as if it were designed by a child and made with Lego, but which works wonders in this roadless country—suddenly stops, and the interpreter announces: "We are going to have a look at the horses." I did see some horses a few kilometers back; why didn't we stop then? But I am the one who's got it wrong: having a look at the horses is a common expression for going for a pee. "What if they really want to have a look at the horses?" I ask. "How can you tell?" If someone in the center of Milan said he was off to look at the horses everyone would understand what he was on about. But horses abound here, quietly grazing outside their owners' tents, and every so often someone goes out to check on them. The interpreter smiles. And then off he goes

I get out of the car too, and as soon as I set foot on the ground I become a tiny dot crawling on the planet once again. The sensation is devastating in this open sea of a desert. The immediate impulse is to sit on the ground to take shelter from so much space. Clouds loom above, peacefully hanging from the sky, so blue and so close. The ground beneath my feet—yes, my feet, on the Gobi desert!—seen from a height of roughly 160 centimeters, looks like the stony earth of any desert with sparse, bristly vegetation. But if I raise my eyes and look toward the horizon so distant, so very distant—I can see the land rolling on for kilometers on end. And what staggers me is precisely the fact that I can actually see all these kilometers. All of them. They tell me that the place we are going to is near, less than half an hour from here. How far is that in kilometers, I ask, since I am unable to calculate distances in minutes. Fifteen, I am told—but look, it's just there. And it's true. If I look, a few degrees to one side, I can see our destination. And I think of what there is fifteen kilometers from where I live. I can think of various things, depending on the direction. In any case, I could not turn and look at them, since they would be fifteen kilometers of villages, houses, roads, trees . . . Whereas here, this is a distance you feel you could cover on foot, or on horseback. Perhaps even swim there. Swimming in this endless sea of a desert that unites rather than separating. Because if you can immediately see the distance you have to cover, you can envelop it in a glance from the very first step, you can heed the summons of your new destination. Mongolians don't know the sea, and beyond the great mountains there is something that is not Mongolia, but China, or Russia. But in Mongolia

there are no barriers. And if there are mountains, all you have to do is follow the rivers step by step, from one valley to the next. Lake Huvskul to the north, 160 kilometers long and 40 wide, is the biggest mass of water most of them will ever see, and this is what they call an ocean. It's an ocean that freezes over in winter and can be crossed by cars, animals, and people. Thus it too becomes a distance to be calculated with time as the unit of measurement. The whole of Mongolia can be crossed, and time is a plentiful asset for this nomadic population. And as I crouch there in half a square meter (I ended up by having a look at the horses), I can cast my gaze across the surface of this huge marble called the Earth, and it seems to me that yes, it really does dip over there, it does slope down, and at a certain point I can no longer see it simply because it really is round. Finally I can put a name to the nagging feeling that has been with me ever since I set foot in this land at the airport: vertigo, because this is a country without a parapet, or protection. A country shamelessly unveiling itself before people's eyes and requesting full surrender. I take a few steps while the sky keeps sloping down. My trekking shoes on the dry earth are the only noise that moves the air, redolent with an herb I do not recognize. And I bless all those kilometers, all twelve thousand of them. Look at them all stretching out in a row: they are the thread connecting me to my roots.

Chapter SEVEN

Prohibitions and Prejudice

SEVEN:1

PURITANICAL PROSCRIPTIONS

Carol Nemeroff and Mary Davis

Food selection and consumption are clearly central concerns for human beings the world over. As such, they engage powerful emotional reactions. At least one major reason is that, as psychologist Paul Rozin has noted, the act of eating is both "necessary to sustain life and fraught with danger." Eating constitutes one of the two major incorporative activities of human beings, and involves taking substances into the body in the most complex way imaginable. Eating involves not only risking the ingestion of toxins, but also quite literally allowing the foodstuff to become part of oneself. So it is not surprising that food taboos are a universal phenomenon: cross-culturally, the vast majority of potentially edible items are in fact not eaten, particularly those of animal origin, and restrictions are common on even those foodstuffs considered "edible."

Generally, the types of negative outcome believed to result from the ingestion of prohibited foods are either a threat to physical health or a threat to spiritual health and the integrity of the self. A central theme running through most religion-based food rules is concern with purity and pollution. Thus certain foods are ingested to elevate the self to a higher spiritual level (e.g., the Catholic Eucharist), other foods are avoided because they are "unclean" (e.g., pork for Jewish and Muslim people), and fasting and purging are seen as ways of cleansing both the physical and spiritual selves.

Why is the act of ingestion so closely linked to notions of purity and pollution? We propose that the basis for many food prohibitions lies in a form of thinking called the "magical law of contagion." The law of contagion describes the transfer of properties—physical, moral, or behavioral—from a source to a recipient through contact. The derivative "you are what you eat" states that one takes on the properties of the things one eats (as eating is clearly the most potent contact possible). An example of the "you are what you eat" principle is the Hua belief, in Papua New Guinea, that eating fast-growing, leafy vegetables will make one grow fast, or alternatively, that young, male initiates should avoid food that are "female" in their appearance, for fear of stunting their still-fragile manhood. We have demonstrated that the "you are what you eat" principle operates to a covert level in the thinking of educated adults in the United States.* University students judged fictitious people as having different characteristics depending on the foods those people were described as eating; for example, boar-eaters were seen as being more boar-like (irritable, hairy, etc.) than turtle-eaters.

Although magical contagion and "you are what you eat" are probably universal forms of thought, their specific content (which trait is believed to be transmitted through contact) appears to be largely culturally determined. Thus rabbit might invest its eater with timidity, fertility, or the ability to run fast, depending upon which attributes of the rabbit are emphasized within a culture. This in turn determines whether the item is eagerly sought out, avoided, or even prohibited.

What are some food concerns specific to the mainstream culture of the modern United States? The popular media reveal a clear trend to refer to a subset of foods as "sinful" or "decadent" and related eating behavior as "bad." Other foods are presented in

---

* Nemeroff, C., and P. Rozin. 1989. "'You are what you eat': Applying the demand-free 'impressions' technique to unacknowledged belief." *Ethos: Journal of the Society for Psychological Anthropology* 17(1): 50–69.

advertising campaigns as "the right thing to do." Women are even shown hiding in closets to enjoy ice cream or, conversely, as reveling in their freedom to eat a dessert publicly if it is low in fat and therefore "allowed."

Good and bad

As described in a 1995 journal article,* university students were asked to identify foods that they considered to be "good" and "bad" and explain why they thought of them in this way. Explanations were uniformly cast in terms of how healthy or unhealthy and how fattening the foods were. Another group of students rated fictitious individuals who ate either good foods (fruit, chicken, salad, etc.) or "bad foods" (hamburgers, double-fudge ice cream sundaes) on a checklist of personality attributes. Students rated bad-food eaters as significantly less moral than good-food eaters. Was this an American version of the "you are what you eat" principle in action?

Exploration of the mechanism of this moral-food effect revealed two key ingredients: concerns about pollution, and a Puritan ethic. It was not surprising to us to see these two mechanisms working together to produce the effect: once a food is judged "sinful," ingesting it will of course result in moral taint. But it is the Puritan ethic, so fundamental to the historical origins of the United States, that appears to determine which foods are seen as sinful. Three aspects are key: first, sensuous pleasure of any sort was seen as suspect by the Puritans, so that a food—or other experience—that is highly pleasurable is considered decadent and sinful. Second, gluttony—associated with being fat—was sinful. Being fat is currently a source of extreme stigma in the U.S., and foods that contribute to it are clearly perceived as dangerous and evil. And third is a societal emphasis on productivity and performance. While this idea probably finds its origins in the Puritan notion of hard work as virtuous, it has taken on a new flavor recently with the body viewed increasingly as a tool to maximize performance. Fat is nonproductive, representing not

* Stein, R. I., and C. J. Nemeroff. 1995. "Moral overtones of food: Judging others by what they eat." *Personality and Social Psychology Bulletin* 21: 480–490.

only gluttony but also inactivity. Its historical benefit of protecting from famine is irrelevant in the abundance of modern America. On the other hand, sugar—wickedly sensual though it may be—finds some measure of redemption in its utility as a source of "quick energy," so that candy bars are sometimes marketed as quick snacks for active athletes.

The result is a culture that vilifies bacon, red meat, and rich, fatty desserts, and elevates homemade (labor-intensive), low-fat, low-sugar, health-enhancing foods to the status of moral prescriptions and magical panaceas. This is exemplified in the recent ad in a health food catalogue, describing the health benefits of red wine that "the French have known for years": now the reader can get these same benefits, without the negative effects of alcohol, by buying red wine capsules. We see this product as prototypically American: no calories, no fat, no alcohol, certainly no sensual pleasure involved; and furthermore, quick, easy, and ostensibly health-enhancing.

No smoking

Some of these same concerns seem to be playing themselves out in the anti-smoking sentiment and legislative policies currently sweeping the U.S. Cigarettes played an important role in colonial America, profiting the colonies as a product, and becoming thoroughly integrated into the cultural lifestyle. In 1964, at the time of the Surgeon General's shocking report

declaring that smoking was "hazardous to health," approximately 50 percent of the population were smokers (the proportion was somewhat higher for males and lower for females). Since that time, rates have dropped substantially so that, at present, only 25 to 30 percent of Americans smoke—touted as a major success for public health and prevention initiatives. Interestingly, the anti-smoking trend has taken on a dramatic moral value. Smoking has been transformed from a pleasurable, harmless, social activity that may even enhance productivity (with hard work symbolized in old movies by ashtrays full of cigarette butts), into a shameful, thoughtless, selfish, polluting behavior and—as an addiction—a sign of weakness, degradation, and loss of control. Smoking is now prohibited in airplanes, government buildings, and in some cities even public buildings and bars. Smokers huddle in pathetic clusters on outdoor staircases in all manner of bad weather to get their "fix." Passers-by give them a wide berth and pitying or disapproving looks. Smoke is seen as polluting and smokers as polluted (vividly depicted in the public health advertisements aimed at teenagers: "Tobacco: tumor-causing, teeth-staining, smelly, puking habit"). The taint is evident on teeth, fingers, hair, and clothing, in the breath and lungs, and in the cigarette butts that could once litter the ground with impunity. How did this once-beloved pastime become anathema? Several factors may have been involved: research indicating that second-hand smoke is harmful to non-smokers (as well as to infants *in utero*) turned smoking into a territorial issue (territorialism is, of course, fundamental to the American credo). Second, the crisis in health-care costs resulted in acute awareness of how much smoking was costing the public in tax dollars—again, a territorial issue, as well as invoking all the negativity associated with being "unhealthy." And third, and perhaps most important, was the campaign started in 1981 by Surgeon General C. Everett Koop to categorize alcohol and cigarettes as "drugs of addiction." This profound shift in perspective allowed all the moral baggage of "drugs" and devils of "addiction" to be applied to smokers. It is perhaps for this reason that lawsuits against the tobacco industry finally achieved a measure of success recently. The tobacco industry can now be portrayed as evil, corrupt, lying "pushers" who promote addiction and target our children. The line between tobacco executives and drug lords has blurred, and smoking has gone from a social activity that enhanced productivity to a sign of waste (of both health and money) and vice.

Pleasure and moderation

Interestingly, trends of smoking in the United States show that for the first time in history, smoking rates in young women are projected to rise above those of young men in the near future. How can this be? It is perhaps the ultimate irony that young women tell us they smoke to stay slim. With fattening foods off-limits to them and being fat seen as, quite literally, a fate worse than death, the appetite-suppressing effects of cigarettes are increasingly attractive to girls. This may also be one reason why, in spite of recent findings indicating that women are less physiologically addicted to nicotine than men, women have more difficulty quitting than do men.

There may be other links between attitudes about food and attitudes about smoking, particularly for women. Smoking is fundamentally an incorporative activity and a sensuous pleasure. Smokers report that drawing the smoke into the lungs is a particularly good feeling, as is the mild "buzz" that results from nicotine intake—perhaps acting in a fashion similar to the endogenous opiate release that can follow binge eating. Furthermore, smoking at this point in history usually requires taking a few

minutes out for oneself, taking a break from the situation to "go for a smoke." It can serve to keep others at bay, in that passers-by will generally go around the cloud of smoke that surrounds the smokers. Again analogously, obesity has been described by some theorists as a means of distancing from others and concretely enforcing one's "personal space."

Considering all the taboos associated with substances detrimental to health, and all our efforts to restrict intake of these substances (as evidenced, for example, by the truly astounding size of the diet industry), Americans are nevertheless eating over 40 percent fat in their diets as well as smoking and failing to exercise regularly. Obesity is on the rise and, at least among young women, so is smoking. In a tragic paradox, it seems that the more guilt people feel over eating and smoking, and the more they try to restrict these behaviors, the more they engage in them in unfulfilling ways that simply lead to more of the behavior in question—and without deriving any of the health-enhancing effects of pleasure itself. We wonder if attempting to focus more fully on *enjoying* our food, or if necessary, our cigarettes, might lead more successfully to moderation. At least this seems likely to lead to more happiness.

SEVEN : 2

VIETNAMESE SNAKE TAVERN

Barbara Santich

It seemed the easiest thing in the world. There was an edge of challenge to it, a display of bravado hidden under the pretense of professional duty. After all, I'd eaten chicken feet and *witjuti* grubs and lamb lights before, and enjoyed them. And part of the reason for going to Vietnam was to experience its food and culture.

I asked the hotel receptionist if she knew the village Lê Mât. "Of course," she replied, "it's just on the other side of Hanoi, fifteen minutes away." "Have you eaten there?" I pursued. "Ah yes, one time." "And you enjoyed it?" "Yes, yes, very good, very good, very healthy," she beamed at me. "So you want to go to Lê Mât?"

Organizing a car and a driver to take us to the best restaurant in Lê Mât was no problem. It might have been better had the driver spoken just a little English, so that I could have asked a few questions—but on the other hand, perhaps not. So there we were on a hot, sticky November morning, lording it along the three-lined avenues of Hanoi's colonial quarter, past the sparkling white Hotel Metropole with its deep green shutters, past the Parisian-domed opera house temporarily hidden by a frame of scaffolding and burlap, and finally across the Red River on Highway 1A.

No signs pointed to Lê Mât, nor even indicated we might be approaching it—but suddenly our car was surrounded by a squad of youths on motor scooters, all waving business cards and pressing them against the window, waving and gesticulating to us to follow: "Come to my restaurant!" They must have been jubilant, accompanying the car as we turned off the pavement and on to a muddy, potholed road barely wide enough for the car, strewn here and there with brown stalks of rice for threshing. We proceeded, and one by one they dropped away, having failed to entice us into their particular restaurant. Though they weren't really restaurants, as such, just houses with snake signs out in front, belonging to people who would temporarily vacate their living rooms for visitors who came to enjoy a feed of snake.

At the end of the lane we turned left, past a swampy patch of broad-leaved water plant, and came to the last sign; and here our driver turned in and stopped the car beneath the carport. We must have been expected, for as soon as the car stopped two men came to greet us. The younger one immediately opened the lid of a mesh fronted wooden box and, with a length of wire, gradually extracted a slithering, shimmying, slender, brown snake. As I got out of the car it was only a meter away and wriggling furiously.

All my worst cultural fears rose up

in me—the summer threats of sharks in the water, funnel webs in one's shoes, and death adders in the sand-hills. These were real, live, writhing snakes, coiling and twisting and baring their fangs. The idea of eating one suddenly became reality. Only just did my resolution overcome my instinctive impulse to take refuge inside the car.

The two men seemed to find it all quite amusing and, once I had regained my composure, agreed to photographs. They smiled and nonchalantly posed with their charges—until one reared up and bit the hand of the older man. He immediately dropped, but just as quickly retrieved, the creature, and that decided it: this was the one which, for his troubles, would be sacrificed. And the adventure began in earnest.

The ritual of slaughter is part of the experience. Holding the head firmly and the body of the snake bent back on itself, the man makes a gash along its belly and extracts, separately, the heart and the greenish-blue gall bladder. These two organs are carefully placed in two small glasses. Then the snake is bled, and the blood collected into a large glass half filled with rice wine. It's all over in two or three minutes.

As the snake was hurried off to the kitchen we were ushered to an upstairs tower room and invited to settle ourselves on the straw mat around a low black table. Our genial host, the older man, arrived with the first course, a plate of long cucumber quarters to be dipped in pepper, salt, and lime juice, and a pile of crisp, deep-fried rice wafers. So far, so good. Then came the cocktail, pale pink and frothy, and the special glasses with the inner organs. The gall bladder was, it seems, destined for me, and as the wine-blood mixture was poured over I took the glass with some trepidation. It was only blood, I told myself, and only rice wine, and I only needed to take a tiny sip—but as the rim of the glass neared my lips my insides rebelled. I took a stick of cucumber instead.

The kupruk-like crackers were meant to accompany the first snake dish, light brown, crumbly, and crunchy. Next was a gluggy, gelatinous soup with very fine shreds of snake flesh and dark fungus; snake fillet stir-fried and topped with crisp shallots; a plate of lightly battered and deep-fried spirals of skin, eaten with a hot dipping sauce; and some little rolls of pounded meat, wrapped in green leaves and grilled. The dishes arrived in ones and twos, always preceded by the tinkling of a little bell in the kitchen. After five courses a reverse Pavlovian response set in, and I was starting to dread that tinkle.

It wasn't that the flavors and textures made the dishes repulsive. Foreign, yes, and unappealing, but not so much so as to deter a professional palate. The surroundings had an influence, but what came between me and the food was the idea of snake, the association of snake, the deep-down knowledge that snake was not in my cultural realm of the edible. Even now I have no recollection of what snake tastes like.

But there were more courses to come: sautéed fillet of snake with crisp-fried shreds of ginger and chili; rice-paper rolls of finely minced snake meat, deep fried; another sauté with fresh lemon grass; and finally, a thick rice congee sprinkled with some of the crunchy first course. And throughout the meal, our host kept urging us to drink the blood cocktail (he'd always down his glass) of which, eventually, I managed a few minuscule sips.

Clearly we were a disappointment to this man who, a youthful sixty, was a living advertisement for a snake diet. He kept trying to tempt us to sample the various liquors on his shelf, large jars in which reposed coiled snakes and befeathered black cock. He told us (or rather, indicated with gestures, our only common word being "no") what parts of the snake we were eating, and what part of our bodies they would be good for (not surprisingly, the same parts). Snake is highly prized in Vietnam and is credited with many health-promoting qualities; both snake elixir and gall are prescribed for rheumatic pains, and recent research has confirmed their anti-inflammatory properties.

Jubilant to have reached the end, I even managed some of the lukewarm earthy-flavored green tea in the downstairs sitting room with the television and our chauffeur. And we departed, farewelled by even wider smiles—a result of the cocktail, in part, but also of

the fifty dollars I had forked out. I have to admit that, once back in Hanoi, we repaired to the Metropole and indulged in the all-you-can-eat afternoon tea with French-style pâtisseries and fresh coffee. And I almost obliterated the snake-eating experience.

Almost—but not quite. Soon after, on the Reunification Express, I bought a bowl of rice congee, topped with a crumbly beef mixture, which instantly recalled one of the snake dishes. A few days later, in a restaurant, I ordered chicken in wild betel *(la lot)* leaves and recognized, at first bite, the taste of snake. At another restaurant the crab and asparagus soup, with its threads of beaten egg, awakened memories of the gluggy snake soup. These dishes had nothing to do with snake, except in my mind, but I found it impossible to enjoy them.

From an intellectual viewpoint, it was interesting to realize that, in Vietnam, snake is treated in the same way as pork or beef or chicken; there is no special repertoire exclusive to snake. The more startling realization, however, was the extent to which mental association can influence perceptions of taste, even in a seasoned taster. The palate memories might be lacking, but I have the pictures to prove it: I have eaten snake.

SEVEN:3

LATTER-DAY RELIGION:
VEGETARIANISM

Lesley Chamberlain

Vegetarianism is an acceptable religion in Britain today. No one asks any longer why you hold this particular belief. Even though followers of the vegetarian faith are still technically in a minority, they are nowadays treated to equal rights wherever they go. What really matters in an acceptable religion is that no one asks or cares whether its members are true believers. Only a few modern-day vegetarians presume they have moral high ground, giving them the right to make themselves a social nuisance. In their case there is a faint tension about the land, in otherwise carnivorous restaurants and at similar dinner parties.

The television cameras recently went behind the scenes at one of Britain's largest hotels, the Adelphi in Liverpool, and it was amusing to watch the traditional-minded chef dealing with the vegetarian "problem." He was in the kitchen, preparing a banquet for 640 people, and the number of vegetarian reservations kept rising by the hour. The BBC bleeped out the besieged cook's comments as unsuitable for family viewing. His brief was originally 47 vegetarians, 8 vegans, and two people who don't eat food touched by other people. By the evening there seemed to be "a few hundred" who "had decided overnight or this afternoon" that they weren't going to eat meat. Had the chef been the owner of the restaurant, and able to afford a loss of business, he might have turned them away. In any case he suspected them of being somehow fake.

Well, vegans aren't fake. They don't eat meat, or fish, or any dairy produce, not even eggs, and if they're not careful they can leave their children malnourished. There have been some published cases. But some vegetarians eat fish, some not, and some even eat the occasional bacon sandwich. Plenty more people, less conceptually confused, describe themselves as "mostly vegetarian." The poor chef was right to feel there was something elusive about the opposition to his menu that night, but what he hadn't grasped was that purity of belief doesn't matter much to vegetarianism any more. Most people just want the option, without putting in a special advance order. And they expect to be able to do it in restaurants, if not at dinner parties.

The last time purity of belief mattered was before the war, when in the conventional British mind vegetarianism was definitely cranky and sectarian. The writer George Bernard Shaw epitomized it, though he was far too brilliant to be anything but his own

125

man. The popular idea of a vegetarian was a man with a beard and sandals, and queer ideas and peculiar relationships. He was almost certainly a Socialist or an anarchist and possibly homosexual. The late-Victorian dropout Edward Carpenter comes to mind. He abandoned a career as a Cambridge mathematician for a blissful Lawrentian life in the country with his male lover, a local laborer. Apart from eating only vegetables, he wrote books, sitting outside all year round. People used to drive out and look at him for something to do on a Sunday afternoon. Now, a hundred years on, both his vegetarianism and his homosexuality have become not only acceptable but fashionable. With the same word vegetarian we are talking about a quite different phenomenon, then and now.

If one were to take purity of modern vegetarian belief seriously it would be quite difficult to isolate. When Beatle George Harrison discovered the Lord Krishna in the early 1970s, a vast public found a reason for joining him in not eating meat. It would be interesting to know just how many fans followed suit because the vegetarian was Harrison. The Vedic wisdom is that any involvement with killing animals, including eating them perpetuates bad karma and engenders violence in human beings. Vegetarianism, despite Adolf Hitler's adherence, has this aura of pacifism, which appealed to post-Vietnam hippies and always appeals to the young. Similarly, if the rich and beautiful give up meat, many of us will copy them because we mainly want to be rich and beautiful too, not because we are converting to Buddhism.

According to Krishna

Perhaps you have to know the person well to detect real sincerity. I have one friend whose vegetarianism is so serious that, if I invite him to a culinary mixed dinner, I don't carve the meat in front of him. On the other hand I am deeply suspicious of vegetarians who proselytize their cause in the most aggressive and militant fashion: for instance Colin Spencer, the author of an otherwise splendid, 400-page book, *The Heretic's Feast: A History of Vegetarianism*, which was published a few years ago. Such people mostly want to feel righteous and to fight for a cause. The question remains whether any of these kinds of modern vegetarians can expect to be automatically catered to, privately or commercially. Publicly it is a matter of business. Privately, the etiquette is still uncertain. But my feeling, in terms of the dishes served, is no. Choose from what there is. There is always too much.

Part of Krishna's argument would logically compel many of us to be vegetarians, by the way. It is that if I eat meat, by implication I should be capable of killing the animal with my own hands. I agree. Anything else would be sheer bad faith. Except that, put to the test, I wouldn't kill the beast unless it were a matter of human life or death. In the end both this moral conundrum and the matter of vegetarian etiquette remind me that in a civilized world food and religion don't mix. Conviviality matters more than adhering to principles, whatever they are. But, as I began by saying, probably the reason for the huge growth in pseudo- or quasi-vegetarianism in Britain in the last twenty to thirty years is that it hardly signifies a belief entailing moral commitments, and doesn't have to try too hard to be sociable. Nor is it gastronomic sacrifice, and thank God for that, for practical vegetarianism probably owes its spectacular growth in Britain to the superior supply of varied fresh vegetables we all now enjoy, and the coincidental decline in the general quality of meat.

There are health arguments against too much, or even any, red meat, which may or may not be valid. Avoiding meat may make us live longer and feel better. None of these factors make vegetarians essentially more moral than anyone else, nor gastronomically more discriminating. After all, many of them buy pre-packaged and processed foods, which is the usual fare of the mass of carnivores and herbivores alike.

Yet perhaps vegetarianism is not just any old choice. Some years ago, when Russia first opened up to the West, I was struck by the pathos of middle-aged women envying their Western counterparts their slim figures. "We would be vegetarian too, if only there were enough vegetables." One of the innumerable ghastlinesses of the Communist world was that it shoveled meat at its citizens because that was the cheapest fodder, served in large quantities that kept them filled up for hours, so they didn't yearn for cafes and snackbars in their woefully inhospitable towns. There is a case for saying that all meat eating was a hangover from a 19th-century view of affluence, gastronomically speaking, and also that it was a continuing reaction to the deprivation of the war. But it struck me then that vegetarianism in the West is actually a beacon of the luxury the free world managed to create for itself, three-quarters of the way through the 20th century. We don't really worship Krishna, but rather the freedom to feel good. In fact we worship choice, our present condition, which is not exactly heroic, merely a confirmation that we live in times of extreme affluence.

MAGIC BULLETS AND PHILOSOPHERS' STONES

Marco Riva

Spinach is rich in iron. Pasta is fattening. Mozzarella is a low-fat cheese. Frozen bread is carcinogenic. An apple a day keeps the doctor away. He who drinks beer will live to be a hundred. Swiss chocolate is the best. Vitamin C cures colds. . . .

What confusion is caused by myth and prejudice! Misleading is the term we use to define all the tendentious or oversimplified assertions that attribute to food a property, quality, or defect that has not or cannot be verified scientifically and rationally. In a way, these are metropolitan fables (urban myths): some are rooted in our history and folklore, others are deliberately induced by the market and spread through our tendency to exaggerate. Once upon a time, they were passed down by word of mouth; more recently, they have been the object of unscrupulous campaigns; no doubt in the future they will reach us through the Internet.

Curiously enough, the increase in misleading assertions about food and nutrition has been proportional to the development of a scientific, positivist approach to the subject. And yet for centuries rational thought has participated in spreading information that would have been hard to verify. In Mediterranean countries, sick people were urged to eat "white food" (dressed only with oil or butter rather than with meaty sauces) because white was wrongly held to be the neutral color par excellence, so that white food was bound to be easily digestible. In ancient times pork meat was often impure from a hygienic point of view, and the resulting prejudice led to entire populations banishing it from their diet. Another correct prejudice concerned the vital, tonic, and curative power of eggs, especially in times when animal proteins were a luxury and people had no worries about excess fat and cholesterol. The triumph of modern scientific thought is associated with the development of a new kind of prejudice, strictly linked with the complex language involved. Nutrition is a very fertile industry: most of its achievements are recent and in constant evolution, many of its ingredients are impalpable. A whole market has developed around food, one in which information—and its deformation—count more than pleasure.

Simplifications

The most absurd simplification consists in ascribing out-and-out advantages or drawbacks to the consumption of a product and the introduction or limitation of a single nutrient. Food is either glorified or damned: vegetables are in and butter is out, cholesterol is bad, vitamin E improves sexual performance, coffee is a (healthy or unhealthy) stimulant, and so on. People are much more inclined to embrace such detrimental simplifications than to accept the more complex idea that good nutrition is the result of a delicate (and, in a way, mysterious) balance between multiple nutrients.

The result of all this is that eating is increasingly becoming a medical process. The more scientific research proves that some ingredients have a positive or negative impact on health, the more people develop ridiculous simplifications that are then spread as gospel truth. Asserting that food with high cholesterol content increases the risk of heart attack is much simpler and more immediate than explaining that only a part of the cholesterol contained in food is used by our organism to produce endogenous cholesterol; and the latter circulates in our veins in two different forms (one good, the other bad) depending upon the excessive presence of calories and, especially, saturated fatty acids; that the endogenous synthesis capacity of cholesterol (partly genetically predetermined) is much more important than its quantity when calculating the risk of developing cardiovascular disease. It's much easier to describe eggs and butter as killers than it is to articulate a complex explanation of this sort.

The problem is that this extremely simplified way of reasoning induces lots of people to sit at the table with a long (positive or negative) list of things that can or cannot be eaten. These people have such a probing and anxious attitude toward food that the pleasure element is entirely removed from eating.

Sometimes prejudice can actually lead to dangerous obsessions. Since it was suggested that vitamin A has a protective effect against some forms of cancer, many cases of liver disorder and jaundice due to the excessive consumption of carrots have been reported. A hospital once asked me my personal opinion about the case history of someone who got intoxicated after eating all the fruits of the persimmon tree he had in his garden in just a couple of days. He was really convinced that the fruit would do him good. Guidelines for a good diet in industrialized countries have recently started to warn against excessive vitamin consumption because many people (wrongly convinced that their diet is poor in vitamins and that vitamins would do them good) have begun to take them in the form of drugs. Not to mention the fact that industrial products are frequently integrated and enriched with vitamins.

Scientific information is largely to blame for the development and consolidation of nutritional prejudice. Fearing that their complex dietetic explanations would be incomprehensible, nutritionists have often used hyperbolic images to convince people they were telling the truth. Most researchers live in a laboratory, refer to food in terms of weight, and in specific fields consider nutrition to be the result of a dose-effect ratio. My personal opinion is that most of them use their heads instead of their senses when eating, and some of them actually hate food. This explains why they either overestimate or underestimate the grassroots impact of their scientific finds. The fall of ideologies promotes minimalist myths, be they about garlic, lecithin, or cabbage (it has actually been proven that broccoli is also effective against cancer).

Metropolitan Fables

Quantifying nutrients and comparing nutritional contents is another field in which absurd prejudice seems to prosper. The prejudice: mozzarella is a low-fat cheese. The fact: mozzarella is usually classified as a fat cheese since it is produced with whole milk. Behind the scenes: mozzarella is very wet and therefore the fat it contains is very diluted. Let us put things straight: when you eat a whole mozzarella (about 120 grams), you absorb 20

grams of fat; a slice of Gorgonzola (about 40 grams, and I defy you to eat more!) contains no more than 12 grams of fat.

The prejudice: I drink coffee without sugar because I do not want to put on weight. The fact: then I gobble down a croissant. Behind the scenes: I do without 5 grams of sugar in the coffee and absorb at least 20 grams by eating a croissant.

The prejudice: I'd rather have honey than sugar because honey is richer in vitamins. The fact: honey contains 0.04 milligrams of vitamin B_2 (riboflavin) and sugar contains none. But we need to absorb about 1 milligram of this nutrient per day. Even if we ate 100 grams of honey, we would meet only 4 percent of our daily requirement in riboflavin. And if we ate much more honey, we would put on a lot of weight!

Misinformation is often due to the intrinsically complex character of nutritional problems. A balanced diet depends on the quantity of nutrients contained in food and on their requirements, which are aspects we are not immediately aware of. This prejudice is the reason why the business of light or low-fat products is so successful.

But the problem gets more serious and rife with anxiety when the threat of degenerative diseases such as cancer hovers over our nutritional habits. There's a lot of information in circulation that is lacking in the necessary quantitative parameters to support it.

It has recently been discovered that resveratrole, a component of the phenolic fraction of grapes and (red) wine, is able to prevent a certain type of cancer (at least, in guinea pigs). This information has become widespread without its indispensable corollary: positive results can be obtained only by absorbing doses corresponding to the intake of about 15 liters of wine per day. Yes, you can fight cancer, but only by becoming an alcoholic!

Here is another example. Selenium can prevent cancer (this the conclusion of research summarized in an article by Larry C. Clark et al. 1996. "Selenium and Cancer Prevention." *Journal of the American Medical Association* 276: 1957–1963). So go for it, gulp down unlimited quantities of selenium-based pills and drugs (the selenium market is already rocketing in the United States). Steven J. Milloy criticizes all the hyped research in a very serious Web site (The Junk Science: www.junkscience.com). He says: "Yes, selenium CAN prevent cancer. Unfortunately, you would need to have a lethal dose of selenium. So that instead of dying of cancer, you would die of a specific intoxication!" That's not all. Many studies similar to the one mentioned refer to the beneficial effects of the substances under examination (in that case: the intake of selenium brings about a decrease in prostate, intestine, and lung cancer, but has no impact on leukemia or esophagus, skin, bladder, and breast cancer), but they do not take into consideration the side effects. The tendency of researchers to oversimplify is

perfectly in line with the public's need to be reassured (and make do with simple solutions). But this attitude is a source of danger and damage.

The (temporary) moral of the fable is: Beware of those who advise you to eat healthy food, such as bran or acorns. Remember that philosophers' stones are not edible.

Beware of those who tell you—with a conspiratorial tone—that a certain product is rich in a certain substance. The hamburgers you eat in fast-food outlets are not (yet) made with mouse meat, despite what an excited consumer told me last week when she phoned me at the university!

And this brings us to the last of our prejudices, a kind we can describe as metropolitan fables. Such popular beliefs are usually generated by the fear of reality. They circulate in crumpled leaflets, through specific systems such as chain letters, or simply door-to-door. But when you read a leaflet in a hospital or you find it in a supermarket, your prejudice acquires an aura of justification. I learned that frozen bread is carcinogenic by reading one of these leaflets, distributed in a traditional bakery. With pseudoscientific language, the author referred to research carried out in an undefined university. This white lie is probably the expression of the legitimate aspiration of traditional bakers to hinder the spread of industrial bread-making methods. Clearly the end does not justify the means.

Chapter EIGHT

Poultry

BICYCLE OR AIRPLANE CHICKENS

Ettore Tibaldi

Hens (and their macho male partners, the cockerels) are multicultural animals. Unlike many other creatures, hens have never—or very rarely—been the object of disgust, bans, or prohibitions. This explains why they have become so widespread all over the world and are in integral part of the food habits of many populations. Since gaining their place at table in the global cuisine, hens have taken a leading role in many different adventures. It is as though they were endowed with a magical formula that makes them welcome as tasty food wherever they happen to be. You can easily find people in our world who do not want to (or cannot) eat pork, horse, sheep, goat, beef, or camel meat. But everybody can eat poultry and eggs, except of course the vegans who make no distinction between these and other animals. Much of their worldwide success is no doubt due to their anatomy, physiology, and behavior. However, the history of their domestication also explains a great deal about how they came to be so widespread.

Chickens have been global international animals since their own particular dawn of time, meaning about five thousand years ago. Everything started in the Indus Valley, probably with *Gallus bankiva*, the golden chicken of the jungle. But one thing is certain: the species currently farmed *(Gallus gallus)* is the product of a crossbreed of several local species from Indochina and the Sunda Isles that subsequently became widespread in Persia, Egypt (during the 5th dynasty), and Greece at the time of the Persian wars. The Celts probably took these precious birds from the Persians, and developed poultry breeding to such an extent that chroniclers from ancient Rome decided to call the region where this population had settled Gaul (from Latin *Gallus,* that is, chicken). Cockerels, hens, and young chickens soon integrated with local cultures. Moreover, they traveled the world in the ships of conquerors and explorers, and came to colonize lands far and wide. Imbued with meanings and values of their own, they acquired new ones as they were introduced into new territories. The stone that is sometimes found in the stomach of cockerels brings luck and the art of foreseeing the future. A dragon, the terrible basilisk, was born from a rounded egg laid by a cockerel. The crowing of cockerels can put evil night spirits to flight and break up witches' Sabbaths. Many gifts are to be had by sacrificing a black hen to the devil, including a hen that lays golden eggs. In voodoo rites chickens can be killed and brought back to life. No wonder the creatures are so extraordinarily popular.

Breeding Farms

Breeding habits have made chickens and hens very dependent on the social environment in which they live. Their behavior adapts easily to the surrounding family situation. They can just about endure being reared in factory farms, they obligingly accept the leftovers from people's meals, and they are able to find their own food by scratching around in grasslands and orchards and gleaning in fields after harvesting. Paolo Sorcinelli, who has been studying the evolution in eating habits from *polenta* (cornmeal mush) to crackers, has come to the conclusion that the nutrition of the poor oscillates between making do, dreaming, and privation. This being so, West Africa provides an interesting case study. In these countries culture is closely linked to farming and breeding and cockerels, hens, and chickens are both victims to tradition and agents of change.

In the southern Sahara there are plenty of villages where poultry is considered an extremely important source of wealth. What is known as "courtyard animal capital," though modest, can be ceded, traded, offered as a gift,

133

or sold on several occasions. Such property is more easily sold than cattle, sheep, or even goats, which are worth much more. The only requirement is protection from human or animal predators and the provision of a modest food supplement for the chicks. And since the chicks mainly eat termites, they do not compete with the human population for food. The small termites' nests, which can often be found in cultivated fields, are broken with hoes and hurled, still swarming with "white ants," among the ravenous chicks, which gobble up the excellent proteins thus provided. Cash is strictly limited in rural areas, so that cockerels, chickens, and hens are generally sold to address some particular necessity. Demand is growing in both local and urban markets.

As a consequence, medium-sized breeding farms are mushrooming. A chemist from Barnako, Seydou Sow, devotes half of his time to his 15,000 chickens: "They are not hens laying golden eggs, but they are a profitable business." Darko Farm, founded in Ghana in 1962, currently has a capital investment of 250,000 chickens. Many years ago the owner, Kawabena Darko, known locally as the "chicken billionaire," set up a "chicken-connection" which now enables him to export his poultry to neighboring countries. Sedima, a farm based in Malika, Senegal, produces and sells 120,000 chicks per week. Recently it has also started supplying eggs for hatching and chicken feed. In the words of the owner, Babakar Ngom: "This is just the beginning."

Africa wakes up early in the morning and every day those who have something to sell leave in the dark, before dawn breaks. Meat trots to the market: short-horned calves, hunched zebus, as well as sheep and goats spurred on by impatient shepherds. The "cold chain"—which in the global economy makes it possible to ship Argentinean meat, Canadian lobsters, and Thai orchids everywhere in the world—does not exist in these countries. Here you find dusty lanes, sandy tracks, scorching hot asphalt roads, incredibly overloaded *taxi-brousses,* and a stifling hot climate that persists throughout the day and only gets milder at night. So animals walk to their own slaughter at nighttime. But for poultry the situation is completely different. It is impossible to get a group of chickens, let along a flock of speedy guinea fowl, to behave with disciplined masochism. You have to tie their feet and carry them head down in an upturned world. And if that makes them dizzy, well so much the better: it will be easier to bleed them once they have been sacrificed.

Bicycles are an ideal vehicle for transporting a number of chickens. Feet to feet and upside down, they can be attached to the handlebars, to the crossbar, or beneath the saddle. Amid this beady-eyed ball of feathers the impassive cyclist rides to the Big Market of Ouagadougou, in the city center, not far from the main mosque. Some of these chickens will be killed and plucked before appearing in the spotless windows of the neighboring Marina Market. This is a classy Lebanese shop offering frozen poultry imported from Europe alongside the local variety. You can tell the difference between the two by the labels: bicycle chickens for the locally raised sort, and airplane chickens for those flown in from afar.

Bibliography

Aime, Marco, *Le radici nella sabbia: Viaggio in Mali e Burkina Faso*. Turin: EDT, 1999.

"Poulet connection," *Eco d'Afrique: le magazine afro-optimiste de Norbert Navarro*, www.rfi.fr and www.cfi.fr.

Sorcinelli, Paolo, *Gli italiani e il cibo, dalla polenta al cracker*. Milan: Bruno Mondadori, 1999.

Tarozzi, Alberto, *Sviluppo e impatto sociale, valutazione di un progetto CEFA in Tanzania*, with texts by Guido Giarelli, Laura Cioni, and Paola Pirani. Bologna: EMI 1992.

Tibaldi, Ettore, *Uomini e bestie, il mondo salvato dagli animali*. Milan: Feltrinelli, 1998.

EIGHT:2

THE WRETCHED AND THE NOBLE

Michel Smith

With annual sales of 570 million chickens, cocks, hens, pullets, and capons, there can be no doubt that France deserves a place of honor on the rostrum of world poultry production. Whether it's a good year or a bad one, the French eat a per capita average of 23 kilos of chicken each year. The birds they eat range from the awful to the very best, which in some cases means exceptional.

From Dunkerque to Perpignan the Mad Cow scare triggered a boom in the already fabulous poultry market, which provides employment for as many as 12,000 breeders. However, in the wake of the dioxin scandal (and we are assured this was confined to Belgium), French consumers are tending to buy fewer chickens. The good news, according to some producers, is that the French are increasingly moving toward *fermier* (farm), organic, or at least "certified" birds. In other words, for their own peace of mind consumers are currently prepared to pay more for "safer," better-fed, older birds. Yet this trend is still far from becoming consolidated behavior; indeed, some see it as a mere fashion. For the moment, the phenomenon is swathed by the reassuring aura that surrounds traditional produce from specific regions or villages.

Be that as it may, the "organic" or "farm" chicken, which is subject to the strictest breeding standards, is unquestionably much more sought after by the informed consumer, even though quality entails a price two or three times higher than normal, especially in the case of the Bresse chicken, certified thirty years ago as a product of controlled origin. "When I buy a chicken," says one gourmet, "it's for a special occasion. What I want is to be able to tell my guests where the bird comes from, who bred it, and what it was raised on. Plus, of course, it has to have an exceptional flavor!"

These are objectively wise demands, especially considering that only 3 percent of chickens and the like consumed in France can claim to be organic, farmhouse, or, better still, "AOC Bresse." Even if we add so-called "labeled" chickens—birds with a trademark guaranteeing that they have been bred in the open air in a well-defined geographical area (Saint-Sever, Janzé, Challans, Loué, and so on) according to relatively severe and relatively respected standards—the percentage of "respectable" poultry still fails to exceed 20 percent of the total market. The production of poultry whose quality is certified on the packaging by the very official-looking *label rouge* granted by the Ministry of Agriculture and generally associated with a regional trademark (about one hundred of which exist to date) continues to grow, partly for export purposes. This is a wise precaution, since it is common knowledge that three-quarters of French production is managed by the large-scale retail network—meaning the powerful lobby of the supermarkets—which blackmail producers, paying them such low prices that one can't help wondering how they have been able to ensure their birds better feed, more space, and a longer life, three evident prerequisites for quality. Yet to be fair, at the moment one of the merits of large-scale retail chains is that they attach the greatest possible attention to provenance; in some cases, they even stick a portrait of the breeder and his full "pedigree" on the packaging! Alas, all this fails to stem the sharp increase in the number of processed products such as chicken sausage, croquettes, and kebabs on sale in the delicatessen departments of supermarkets. These products are totally lacking in any indication of the parts of the bird used. "A good way of stimulating new consumer habits by continuing to fob us off with shit," complain consumers sensitive to the problem. In this they echo the convictions of Jean-Pierre Coffe, the outspoken media critic, and of José Bové, the farmers' leader who has spoken out about the trend toward "bad eating."

That, basically, is the situation at the moment. It is worth pointing out that a regular "class A" chicken, one of the cheapest on the market, is bred together with twenty-six others in a space of just one square meter for a period of 40 days and weighs just over two kilos. An industrial breeder may produce up to 800,000 such chickens every year. By contract, his cereal suppliers ensure him perfectly balanced feed. Some industrialists opt for "certified" production, and are controlled by independent organizations such as Veritas. This is the case of the Duc brand, whose chickens live for 57 days in climatized pens on beds of shredded hay. This is a huge step forward if we consider what was happening only twenty years ago. Chickens are mostly fed on wheat, but also on soya beans and corn supplemented with phosphor and calcium. To this day, the use of antibiotics and genetically modified feed is cloaked in mystery.

The figures change completely if we move on to "red label" chickens. They live not in large concentrations but in conditions of semi-freedom. A *label rouge* chicken lives for at least 81 days, and possibly even 110, in which case its life extends beyond the fattening stage. This bird spends its days hunting for insects and

137

worms in a hectare of grass (with about two square meters per bird) and its nights with no more than ten others (per square meter) in small aerated pens—almost a sort of Club Med! "What counts most of all is the length of the rearing period and freedom of movement on natural land," explains one breeder. Another expert in the industry, who is attempting to relaunch the *géline*, an old breed increasingly in demand by the large-scale catering trade, has decided to breed a maximum of 2,000 chickens per year; subdivided into groups of 250 over a total area of five hectares, each group with its own comfortable hut for shelter. The price of these "farmyard" or "free-range" chickens can reach 50 francs per kilo at poulterers in the posher parts of Paris or Lyon. If the bird has been free to roam in woodland, it may cost even more. This is the case of the ancient "bare neck" chicken, which runs in flocks in the forests of Landes, and was the first to be granted the *label rouge* in 1965. The Saint-Sever chicken, duly certified and widely distributed in butchers' shops, has a completely different flavor—and price—from the "standard" chicken mentioned above. Prices thus vary from 10–15 francs per kilo to 30–40 francs. Whether it's a farmyard or a free-range bird, this chicken is clearly a luxury suitable only for special occasions.

Recipes

Unless they breed their chickens themselves, good chefs use the birds for boiling, "stuffed with a sprig of tarragon, with garlic cloves to perfume the skin and a few gray shallots". They are also used for spit-roasting, where they cook in their own fat with a stuffing of rosemary, thyme, and bay leaves; to heighten the flavor, old vine branches are burnt on the barbecue. In Gascony, around Bordeaux, or in Languedoc, toward Carcassonne, one variation is to baste the skin with slightly rancid fat, previously melted in a funnel fixed to a handle and then scorched over the flame. This invaluable implement is known as a *capucin* or *flambadou*. The slightly smoked flavor of chicken roasted in this way is truly unique!

Innumerable other traditional dishes exist: chicken with peas; chicken casserole with bacon cubes and button onions; chicken *à la normandaise*, cooked over a low flame with a good liter of vintage cider; chicken with cabbage; the list is endless. In the Périgord region, chicken is grilled *en crapaudine*, cutting the skin round the fat of the legs and opening the breast so that the whole bird can be spread flat and pressed between two grills; both sides are then rubbed with sea salt and pepper and grilled in the fireplace, flavored with bay leaves and rosemary. In the farms of Burgundy, old cocks are still kept for *coq au vin* (in Alsace they use Riesling), while old hens end up cooked gently with rice, cream, and large onions with cloves, or with cream and morels. In Tours, you can rediscover the exquisite flavor of the *géline noire de Touraine* breed, which the chef Jean Bardet boils in stock with the finest vegetables from his own garden. In Paris, another chef, Alain Dutournier, prefers the chicken of Landes, which he blanches in stock before roasting it golden brown in the oven (a trick recommended by gourmets, who abhor "dry" chicken flesh). And then there is Alain Passard, who cooks chicken gently in straw as his grandmother used to do. Like mine, she probably also kept the heads and claws to make delicious soups.

Alexandre Dumas's *Grand Dictionnaire de Cuisine*, a flavorsome *summa* of recipes, culinary tips, and anecdotes published in five volumes just before the writer's death in 1873, sets off in fine style with the word *abatis* (giblets). The author of *The Count of Monte Cristo* and *The Three Musketeers* opens his chapter on "Poultry and Game" with the words, "Giblets are the crests and kidneys of the cock and the wings of the pullet . . ." At the time, it was popular to use the crests and kidneys to garnish *grands ragoûts* and straightforward *vol-au-vents*. Dumas pointed out that with such ingredients it was also possible to prepare a single dish, cooking the giblets in stock with beef marrow and mixing them with mushrooms, sliced artichoke hearts, and slices of celery. In the same period, the *poularde*, or young hen—its flesh refined by being treated with milk—was also highly popular. Anyone was

capable of plucking it and singing it over the flame! To prepare it for trussing, its claws were carefully cut and it was drawn, paying attention not to burst the bitter gall bladder; the wings were then folded over, the legs boned, and the delicate breasts larded, Finally, the bird was trussed and stuffed with truffle and *foie gras*.

The capons of Bresse

If we go back in time to the splendors of the court of the Sun King in Versailles, to an era when meals were staged like veritable theatrical productions, we shall find that pullets played a leading role. The most renowned were those from the region around Le Mans, north of the Loire and south of Normandy, which were raised exclusively for the royal table with the same care and attention reserved today for the chickens of Bresse, a region northeast of Lyon. Some of these Bresse chickens are still castrated to carry on an ancient tradition of capon breeding. These eunuchs are the very finest French poultry specialty.

Anyone who has never eaten a perfectly cooked capon doesn't know what true chicken flesh tastes like. "The male bird was castrated when it was young, between its eighth and fourteenth week of life: in this way it fattened better and took on an almost feminine rotundity," explains Jean-Claude Miéral, one of Bresse's most illustrious *coquetiers*. Donning his wide-rimmed black hat, Miéral does the rounds of farms and markets in search of the finest specimens to deliver to France's greatest restaurants and to the odd private customer. He doesn't mince his words. "Here the best breeders only produce 200–300 birds each, for a total of 7,000 capons a year. In other regions, they produce about 200,000, with a number of breeders ten times lower than in Bresse". The man who is speaking is the son of one who in 1967 was among the first promoters of "controlled denomination."

In a delimited area of 3,200 square kilometers, fifty or so producers keep the capon tradition alive.

A true capon has to be at least seven months old and has to be fed, like a Bresse chicken, on natural feed and, if possible, with even greater care and attention. Its selling price can reach 200 francs per kilo. "First of all," points out Jean-Claude Miéral, "the capon loves loehern, which in these parts they call *terre à pisé.*" Loehern is a decalcified silt, which, along with snails and small insects, the birds feed on when they are allowed to roam free. Weakened by their operation, capons are treated to a great deal of attention and protected from the elements. Their feeding and hygiene are also supervised. Before they are slaughtered in December, the birds spend at least five weeks in the *épinette,* a sort of cage where they are fed on a special fattening diet of milk and cereals (black wheat, yellow wheat, and corn) as part of a *finissage.* The gentle ritual of their sacrifice is designed not to damage their delicate flesh. The capons are then carefully plucked to the base of their heads, then their bodies are covered to protect their delicate skin and further wrapped in canvas to allow the fat to impregnate the flesh. The purpose of this is to further soften the flavor. If the bird has been fattened properly, its spine will be invisible. The skin must be white, almost mother-of-pearl in color and the feet should be blue. The ideal weight of a capon from Bresse varies from four to four and a half kilos. At about 200 francs per kilo, it is obviously much more of a luxury than your common or garden-variety Christmas turkey. *Noblesse oblige!*

EIGHT:3

TANDOORI

Radha Kapoor-Sharma

India has different meanings for different people. From saffron-robed, white-bearded, trident-carrying sages to long-haired, full-breasted, elegantly clad women in saris, from the silent, meditating yogi in lotus pose to the noisy clamor of crowds that throng the streets, from the sweet scent of jasmine that pervades the moonlit nights to the stench of open gutters, India is a sight, a sound, a smell. Close your eyes and you can conjure up instant visions of India, both exotic and modern; you can sway to her music, get high on her perfume. But that is not all, for, almost unbidden comes the taste of a delicately spiced, aromatic dish, *tandoori* chicken, and India is transformed into a flavor.

Indian cuisine has done the round of the world and is now deeply entrenched in most world capitals and urban centers. Of all the offerings to the palate that India is capable of making—and they are numerous—it is undoubtedly the North Indian *tandoori* chicken that rules the menu virtually undisputed. This dish of a deep red color has taken on the hues of the Indian identity in the Western imagination and more than any other has become synonymous with Indian food.

Chickens, hens, and roosters have of course long been a part of the essentially rural society that India was and still largely is. Driving along national highways that slice villages into two, one is forced to slow down to let squawking fowl scuttle to safety. To spend a night in the country means resisting the urge to wring a few necks as the competition between roosters to crow the loudest heats up with the sun still nowhere in sight. My own memories of chickens go back to childhood holiday afternoons spent in their company. Undaunted by the smell of droppings, I discovered that the hen coop was a great place to read and play without being disturbed by adult directives and reprimands. Intimacy breeds trust, and I often caressed the chickens, burying my face in their soft down. My feathered friends and I were however soon parted when my mother discovered white chicken lice clinging to my eyelashes: the eyelashes were snipped off and a big lock placed on the hen coop. That put an end to my association with chickens as pets and playmates. Over the years, these memories receded until chickens became only an item on the menu.

Cooks' choices

In the hierarchy of Indian menus, chicken occupied pride of place amongst nonvegetarian delicacies, for it was by far the most expensive meat to serve. To honor a guest necessarily meant placing chicken on the table.

141

Though today, in the age of mass-produced industrial chickens, chicken is cheaper than mutton, it still retains the aura of a special dish. By Indian reckoning, it still works out to be more costly, as the amount of chicken a guest is likely to consume far outweighs his consumption of mutton, and if the dish served is a dry one—like *tandoori* chicken, which contains no sauce—then the quantity eaten is likely to be even greater. Cooking a chicken dish involves a series of choices right from the very purchase of the bird itself: spring chicken (very succulent, ideal for the *tandoori* form), broiler (fleshy and tender), or a regular open-air-bred chicken (scrawny and tough, but tasty) brought into the cities alive with hundreds more, all crammed squawking into the back of pickup trucks, to be slaughtered and plucked on the spot. The last solution—one that is not for the fainthearted or squeamish—is slowly losing ground before the onslaught of produce from poultry farms that have mushroomed around towns and cities. Once the kind of chicken to be bought has been settled, there are still myriad other questions to be decided. To skin the chicken or not, with the majority of people removing the skin as it is generally considered to be unclean, and this is just as well perhaps, considering the high blood cholesterol levels of Indians; to cook it whole, joint it, or serve bite-sized boneless pieces; to serve it dry, in a thin gravy, or a thick sauce; to use onion, tomato, yogurt, cream, or coconut as the base for the gravy or sauce; to throw in whole spices, ground ones, or a mixture of both; to make the final color yellow, light brown, dark brown, whitish, or a deep red; to cook it alone, with a vegetable like spinach or with rice (*biryani* or *pulao*); to let it simmer on a stove or roast in a traditional clay oven, in a modern substitute, or a vessel tightly sealed with dough (*dum phukt*); to garnish it with coriander, green chilies, onions, fried raisins, or almonds; and so forth.

In a country where cooking is a skill passed on from mother to daughter and not one learned through recipe books, the style of cooking in a family is a hybrid of community and caste dictates, economic status, family tastes (read: master of the house), as well as a matter of personal invention. There are of course the regional influences as well, which are linked to the availability of ingredients, such as the liberal use of coconut in the southeastern state of Kerala where coconut groves abound. There are chicken dishes typical Bengal, Andhra Pradesh, Kerala, and so on.

Hands on

Tandoori chicken is a Punjabi specialty that derives its name from the traditional clay oven, the *tandoor*, in which it is cooked. Traditionally made from young chickens weighing not more than 500–600 grams) that have been marinated for many hours in yogurt to which cooking oil, salt, pounded garlic, ginger juice, and a heady mixture of crushed spices such as turmeric, cumin, *garam masala*, and coarsely grounded red chilies (which give the rich red color) have been added, it is roasted whole on skewers in rudimentary charcoal-fed clay ovens. It is served garnished with onion rings and wedges of green lime.

This is a festive dish, a convivial one. A dish that is served at wedding receptions, dinner parties, and social gatherings. It is certainly not a food to be consumed in solitary splendor, as the whole process of heating up the *tandoor* is terribly tedious. If ever there were a dish that could be considered symbolic of the traditional Punjabi male, it would be *tandoori* chicken, right from the cooking itself, which is normally done by male cooks in the open air (they plunge their hands into the hot *tandoor* unmindful of the searing heat) to the manner of its being eaten. Though a main dish, it is often served with a green mint chutney at the long male drinking sessions that precede dinner, as it makes an excellent accompaniment to whisky or country-made liquor. More often than not served whole or half, the chicken is torn into smaller bits with the hands. Eaten with the fingers, it is devoured hot in large bites interspersed with onions (known for their aphrodisiac properties). Whether it is eaten sitting on rope-strung cots *(charpais)* in village courtyards or standing around, glass in hand, in posh urban drawing rooms, the scene is one of bonhomie and cheer.

Curiously at some level there appears to be an association of masculinity if not downright virility with *tandoori* chicken. If the villain of Hindi films—normally a fierce hunk of a man with a pronounced fondness for subjugating the fairer sex by brute force—is shown eating, the dish is invariably *tandoor* chicken. With its strong tendency toward the use of not-so-subtle metaphors, Hindi cinema thereby signals the man's weakness for all flesh. Could the deep red color of the chicken—so similar to the red powder a woman adds to her hair parting after marriage—perhaps evoke a woman who is already spoken for, as is the case of the Hindi film heroine whose heart belongs to the hero?

Its attractive color, in contrast to the dull brown of most meat curries, the versatility that allows it to be sampled either as a main dish or a starter, its rich yet mild flavor and exotic look, all make *tandoori* chicken an immensely popular dish in restaurants in the West. Moreover, leftover *tandoori* chicken is very easily disguised into another popular dish, butter chicken, which owes

143

its rich red color to tomatoes. The question, however, still remains as to why this Punjabi delicacy rather than another from India's vast repertoire has become the dish synonymous with India. The answer lies very simply in the fact that the first waves of Indian immigrants to the United Kingdom consisted mostly of Punjabi males, either bachelors or married men who had left their spouses behind in India. To cater to their home food needs a series of simple eating places sprang up. Over the years these became more elaborate, with the ever swelling numbers of South Asian immigrants as well as the increasing popularity of Indian food among the local inhabitants. Since initially the large majority of restaurants were run by Punjabi men, they tended very naturally to give pride of place on their menus to *tandoori* chicken. It has quite literally ruled the roost of Indian cuisine undisputed ever since, even though today Punjabis are perhaps outnumbered by Bangladeshis, Pakistanis, and Sri Lankans in the restaurant business.

EIGHT:4

SPOILT CHICKENS

Manfred Kriener

Frank Richter and Anton Pohlmann—two German poultry farmers. The former owns 4,700 hens, the latter millions of them. The former set up a model ecological farm in Brandenburg, Germany, the latter has served prison sentences and raised endless scandals. These are stories of happy hens and tortured hens, of free-range and industrial farming, and of a perfect food: the egg.

Who wouldn't feel unnerved when faced by 4,700 pairs of eyes? This is no exaggeration. A sea of brown necks, combs, beaks—an ocean of hens. Head to head, they sit on the ground and perches, their feathers ruffled, looking for some warmth. We are in the cold land of Uckermark, 20 kilometers from the Polish border, and spring is hardly at the door. Outside, a few snowflakes dance here and there, blown by the chilly April wind. Inside, the birds improvise a concert of their own. It is eleven o'clock in the morning. Most of them have already laid; dozing off and cackling, they are now recounting their daily good deed. Their eggs have already been carried away by the conveyor belt, and are being weighed by automatic devices, channeled off into the appropriate weight category by prehensile rubber arms, and boxed by nimble fingers.

Once the eggs are laid, the henhouse opens up. A covered passage leads onto 5 hectares of paddock, where a protective embankment provides shade and shelter from birds of prey. The first hens come rushing toward us, curious, hopping between our legs and pecking our shoes. Chickens like everything that glitters, which they examine with their beaks. As a matter of fact, Frank Richter's birds are still capable of a proper peck. Their beaks are not cut, as happens on other poultry farms, where the chicks' beaks are burnt to prevent cannibalism. With a swift move, the thirty-two-year-old Mr. Richter grabs a hen, opens up its beak to show us the spotted pink inside: finely chiseled nervous tissue. The beak is the main instrument of hens, a sensitive organ of touch and ingestion.

Beaks are not the only things worth seeing here. The whole complex in the tiny village of Grimme in Brandenburg, two hours from Berlin, is a sort of model farm: modern, but tailor-made for specific needs, rational but ecologically oriented. Respectfully referred to as "the Popes of Poultry," the ethologists of Kassel University recommend visiting and copying the Grimme in Brandenburg complex. In this era of mad cows, genetic engineering, price collapses, and a jungle of subsidies, the best poultry-raising method is here for visitors to see.

Yet those who expect to find an idyllic environment will feel disappointed. Only in illustrated books or small, self-sufficient farms do you still come across little colonies of hens placidly pecking around a heap of manure presided over by a multicolored cock. Though plump countrywomen with rosy cheeks may still exist, such models of egg production are now definitely outdated. If you want to make a living at poultry farming, you must raise at least three to four thousand birds in a highly functional and largely automated farm. In other words, conveyor belts for birdseed, eggs, and efficient ventilation systems. All in the name of quantity.

Then, you need "turbo" hens, as Frank Richter calls his brown team. What he means is that his birds are real athletes, whose bodies are geared to a single purpose: laying eggs. Not even this ambitious poultry farmer can afford to keep different breeds of hens, even if they would be stronger, more vital and natural. "An egg could easily end up costing one mark," he says. Why? Because the other breeds—

Sussex and New Hampshire, Leghorn and the Italian varieties, Rhodeländer and Barnevelder—cannot guarantee half the egg production of hybrid breeds specially bred for top-level performance. "Warren-Isa-Brown" is a cross between four different breeds; here, each bird reaches an annual yield of 240 eggs.

Such production levels are the fruits of various decades of poultry farming and are achieved at a high cost. Males are selected as chicks, gassed, and turned into feed; females are aggressive and frequently subject to ailments. Richter's hens often peck at one another, especially in wintertime when they cannot go out, and from time to time a few deaths occur, birds that fall prey to stronger colleagues. In any case, they do not run the risk of getting old. After fifteen months, Richter's egg layers are removed from their henhouse, sold to the butcher, and replaced with younger birds. The old ones—whose destiny is to end up in broth—are often worth but a few pfennig: according to official statistics, the price of a bird ranges from 0.40 to 0.65 marks. Housing hens for two years would mean shouldering the burden of the awkward molting period, during which they do not lay for six to eight weeks, an experience that the newly born ecological farm is not ready to face just yet.

When you are idealists like Frank Richter and his wife, Christian Binsfeld, you tend to neglect the market rules and defects that farming itself generates, letting the birds lead as nat-

ural an existence as possible. They can move about, scratch around in the manure, and bathe in dust to get rid of excess fat that builds up between their feathers; they can run around, look for worms and insects, and peck at green stuff and seeds. The litter running across the henhouse is tree-shaped, with various surfaces to climb. Daylight, sunshine, and seasons enter into the henhouse, and the birds lay their eggs in communal, slightly shaded nests. The next group to come will also include a few cocks, which play an important role as peacemakers and leaders within the social pyramid of the henhouse. There is only organic feed, no soybeans, no permanent prophylaxis, no drug pumping, no artificial yolk coloring, no enzyme and hormone-based therapies.

Hapless hens

Are Richter's hens happy? Those who wish to find an answer to this question should get acquainted with how the other half lives. Actually they're not half, but an absolute majority. Ninety-five percent of German laying hens live cloistered in cages, 4 percent are raised on litter floors, and no more than 0.9 percent in the open air. Raising poultry in cages means cramming up to 300,000 birds into a single battery. According to European Union directives, each bird should be given a surface area of 450 square centimeters, that is, as much room as a shoe box. No daylight, no seasons, no weather, no sun, no worms, no manure, no room to move or stretch, eighteen hours of artificial light in aseptic conditions and without any stimulus whatsoever, the claws deformed by the inevitable contact with the floor wire, ulcers, sore cloacae, hysterical head movements, swollen combs, weak connective tissues, lacerated feathering, whole sections of the body completely featherless, and, to top it all, cannibalism.

In Switzerland, this model of poultry farming was banned in 1991, branded as cruelty. After the initial protests of poultry farmers, conversion was successfully achieved, even without state and other subsidies. The main chain stores—Coop and Migro—undertook not to import cheap eggs from battery farms in foreign countries. Now, five years later, this new system works perfectly, and consumers are quite willing to pay a bit more for good eggs. "It was a necessary and fair step," says Niklaus Neuenschwader, head of the federal office for agriculture in Bern. In Sweden, a similar ban is currently being devised, whereas in the rest of Europe, poultry raising in wire cages is still a sad reality.

This year, the utter cruelty of cage raising will be unveiled before the Court of Oldenburg. During recent weeks, the interest of the German population has been focused on the spectacular trial of Anton Pohlmann, for many years one of Germany's leading egg producers and object of a surge of campaigns organized by the animal rights' movement. With ten million egg layers, Pohlmann used to be a leader in the poultry industry

EGG LAYING · The ancestors of our mass-producing hens—the red jungle fowl found in Southeast Asia—used to lay from six to twelve eggs per year. By 1870, poultry farmers had managed to bring production up to 80 eggs, reaching 120 in 1950. Nowadays, hens are expected to produce twice as much, or more; birds housed in cages now reach a yearly production of 300 eggs, whereas free-range ones reach 270. A possible limitation to this ever-increasing yield is not foreseeable. When are we going to see the first two-eggs-per-day bird? "The current egg production of a hen," wrote the scientific journalist Dieter Zimmer from Hamburg, "corresponds to that of a woman with a menstrual cycle of fifteen hours."

worldwide. In February 1996, he sold his farms for 330 million marks, after being deprived of his hen-farming license. That same month he was arrested in connection with the egg scandals. In April he was released on bail, upon payment of five million marks. In the meantime, he has set up large-scale factory farms in the United States with more than six million fowl.

Pohlmann is an old acquaintance of the German authorities. In the past he has cooped up his hens in less-than-regulation space, sold eggs contaminated by salmonella, and, according to the accusations, run unauthorized factory farms and counterfeited the egg-laying date. Two years ago he mali-ciously choked to death 60,000 ill hens by switching off the air conditioning system—it seemed the cheapest way to kill them. In the indictment that has just been brought against him he is once again accused of a series of crimes against humans and animals:

• In order to eliminate mites, Pohlmann allegedly instructed some of his workers to spray a highly noxious nicotine solution into the hen-houses without providing them with the necessary protective clothing or warning them about the considerable risks; furthermore, he removed the producer's warning labels from the containers. While spraying this sub-

THE CHICKEN · The domestic chicken is the descendant of *Gallus bankiva* (*Gallus gallus*), which is found in the forests of Southeast Asia. It is brown, with yellow neck feathers. The ancestors of domestic chickens used to live in the underbrush in small groups of five to twelve birds; they ate small animals, seeds, and buds, and slept in the trees. Fowl started to be domesticated approximately five thousand years ago in India. Initially the birds were raised for their meat and later as egg producers. In the wild, chickens lead a stable and gregarious life. Cock crowing announces the start of day; at dawn, the birds carefully clean their feathers, then start searching for food and eventually lay their eggs and cackle to celebrate this act. At noon, they take a rest basking in the sun, and in the afternoon, they take a dust bath and begin once again their quest for food. Mating also often takes place in the afternoon. Toward evening the cock leads his hens back to their perches. In a day, these birds may cover a distance of between 1 and 1.5 kilometers, and they can live approximately seven years.

stance around, one of the workers fainted, ending up in a dangerous apneic condition with corrosion wounds all over the body;

• Nicotine traces were found on chickens' feathers and eggs, thus breaching the legislation on food-stuffs. An indefinite number of hens choked to death in the nicotine fog;

• Five and a half tons of Virkon-S, a disinfectant utilized to eliminate salmonella in the gastrointestinal tract, were found in Pohlmann's farms. The tests performed proved that Pohlmann had mixed this substance with hen feed, though strictly forbidden by the law.

The whole cage-raising industry is on trial with Pohlmann. During the last two decades, large-scale producers have progressively stripped hens and eggs of their natural character and plunged one of our most precious foods into a disgusting abyss. Thus, the delicious little breakfast egg has gradually turned into a receptacle of the most hideous of sins. A few years ago, the German market was flooded with eggs from Holland that were polluted with hen embryos, blood, and feces. The deteriorated substance was sold as "liquid egg" to pasta factories and pastry-makers at a low price, and ended up in zabaglione, mayonnaise, and dressed pork products as well as in homogenized products of babies. As a consequence, the Federal Republic of Germany was hit by the most striking food scandal ever: the whole nation was retching.

At the beginning of the 1990s, the salmonella plague reached its peak. Health authorities recorded a sudden rise in salmonellosis cases, which were often lethal. It was ascertained that the main causes lay precisely in contaminated eggs. In 1962, 2,254 cases of salmonella infection were observed; in 1972, they had already reached 13,842, in 1982, 40,977; to top 114,110 in 1999. Salmonellosis casualties are now two hundred every year. "Here comes the hen's revenge," wrote *Der Spiegel*, whereas the satirical magazine *Titanic* presented an "innovative euthanasia set"—a carton of eggs.

In Northern Rhineland West-phalia, veterinarians have made alarming discoveries: one-third of the eggs analyzed contained high residual quantities of Monensin, an antibiotic drug, 18.2 percent were polluted by the antiparasitic Nicarbazin, and 6.9 percent contained traces of Meti-clorpindol, another substance utilized in the struggle against parasites.

In the early 1990s, the gourmet magazine *Der Feinschmecker* per-formed a test on the quality of German eggs. Twenty-one random samples were collected in the three major German cities, Hamburg, Berlin, and Munich. The outcome: in twenty cases, eggs were either flawed or too old, or their weight was not correct—that is, fraud was the name of the game.

Moreover, finding out that many "free-range hens' eggs" were ordinary factory farm eggs was particularly disturbing. In Germany, France, Holland,

and Belgium, the official number of free-range hens does not exceed eight million, yet thirty million "free-range eggs" are sold every day. Which means that hens should be laying four eggs a day. The press has been talking about the existence of an egg mafia for quite a while. Moreover, many "free-range hen" farms simply practice litter-floor raising; openings are often used only by the staff for supervision purposes, since egg laying falls on open grounds.

And what about Frank Richter and his small-scale model farm? The cock in the basket, a small sign of reconciliation? In the jungle of frauds, ill-treatment, and cruelty, the hens of Uckermark are a tiny oasis, a ray of hope. A few willing farmers can prove that it is possible to act in a different way. A real U-turn could only be reached by prohibiting at a Europe-wide level poultry raising in cages; in many countries, the legal framework regarding animal protection provides insufficient juridical tools. The fact remains: Cloistering hens in cages is barbaric.

IN THE STREETS, AT HOME

Nelly Krowolski

In Vietnam, there are chickens everywhere. You can see them in the villages scratching around in the streets, gardens, and fields, often far from their henhouses.

You often see them in the roads, their legs hobbled. They peep out of the baskets of country women on the way to the market. In the city, they can be found in all the markets, as well as on street corners: even urban housewives insist on buying their chickens live. Nowadays cage-raised chickens are also available, but the meat is not highly regarded and hardly features at all in the markets. (Breeding chickens in batteries of cages was experimented with in the south of the country, before 1975. Known as "Yankee chickens," these creatures met with utter disdain). In Vietnam chicken meat is firm, sometimes even tough, since these are free-range birds that have largely been forced to find their own food.

A village where no roosters crow, no dogs bark, and no pigs grunt is a place that has fallen to such a level of misery that it is doomed to disappear. Not all households can afford a buffalo or a cow, of course, but they generally raise a few chickens and a pig. Together with the dog that guards the house, the chicken and the pig represent the three pillars of village prosperity. Tenth among the twelve animals of the sun and moon calendar, the chicken, followed by the dog and the pig in the last two places, concludes the cycle of the years.* Popular images portray it in different ways. A plump, prosperous hen surrounded by her chicks, whom she teaches how to feed. A rooster with beautiful feathers accompanied by a hen and her chicks. A powerful rooster with a caption in Chinese characters: *thiên ha thai binh,* "Peace in the Empire." The year bearing its name is not associated with any notable event. Maybe this is because the rooster stands for peace and therefore, in line with the saying according to which "Happy people have no history," so happy years have no history, either. There is a folk song that reveals chicken is also part of a second trilogy, considered as a generator of wealth:

I raise fish in the large tank
I raise ducks in the large pond
I raise chickens in the large garden.

The more roosters crow, the more prosperous the village is. There is certainly no ignoring a feathered friend who wakes the family up at three different times: at the first cockcrow, *gà gay dâu,* at nearly four o'clock in the morning; at the second, *gà gay giua,* at almost five; and at the third, *gà gay tan,* at five thirty or six. But if a hen crows instead of making her usual cackle-cackle, watch out: it is definitely a *gà mai gay go,* a bad omen.

The return of chickens to the coop at night is another crucial moment. As soon as the sun goes down, the chickens leave off scratching around for food and return in noisy haste to their coop

---

* Domestic, wild, or legendary, animals feature in the calendar in the following order: mouse, buffalo, tiger, cat (or rabbit), dragon, snake, horse, goat (or ram), monkey, chicken, dog, and pig.

above the pigsty. There is always a great turmoil on the farm before everything calms down in the henhouse. . . . In Vietnam, as in other parts of the world, chickens have little in common with night owls.

Chickens provide the most popular meat after pork. Nonetheless, chicken is eaten very rarely at the daily tables of country folk. During these frugal meals, eggs are consumed more frequently and children go searching for them as soon as the hen, with its cackle-cackle, announces she is laying. They must be taken before predators such as snakes and rats discover them. Chickens appear on the table as a fitting sacrifice for feast days. If you enter a temple or a pagoda in the north of the country on a feast day, you will see trays piled with offerings to the tutelary gods, left there on the altars by the faithful: in the center is the chicken, its head held aloft.*

The ritual rooster

In the past, for the annual ceremony in honor of the tutelary god of the village, a rooster called the *gò thân* (god's rooster) would be specially raised so that it could be sacrificed for the village banquet. The person in charge of feeding the bird carried great responsibilities. The rooster was kept in a cage and carefully fed each day to fatten it as much as possible for the day of the sacrifice. Considering the frequent outbreaks of epizootic disease, the farmer was in constant fear of his rooster falling sick or even dying. Such an event would be an extremely bad omen for him, his family, and the whole village.

Even the way the rooster was cooked was special. There was no question of simply throwing it into the pot to boil because that would have spoiled the way it looked. The night before the meal, the dressed bird was continuously doused on all sides with hot water. It thus cooked slowly and to perfection, its head held proudly aloft. At this point it could be cut into as many pieces as the number of participants gathered for the banquet. That

---

* This can take place only in the north of the country, where all functions can be held in a pagoda. In the central and southern regions, the cult of Buddha and that of the tutelary gods are completely separated. The strictly vegetarian Buddhist clergy would not tolerate the offering of meat inside the pagoda.

involved considerable art. Every portion had to include the three inseparable elements that make boiled chicken so delicious: a piece of skin, a piece of meat, and a piece of bone. The famous writer Ngô Tât Tô describes in lyrical terms the accomplishment of a town crier who managed to cut one of these sacrificed chickens into no less than eighty parts, so thinly sliced that they looked like butterfly wings. Each slice was then placed on the portion of sticky rice served to each participant. Rice and *xôi* (boiled chicken) are still the quintessential or most common ritual food, though boiled and occasionally glazed pork is the king of banquets.

Prepared as a ritual food, chicken is a way of questioning fate, by observing the "phalanges" of the legs of the birds cooked for the ceremony. Usually reserved for the master of the house, the deliciously crispy feet are offered on such occasions to the master of the cult, who will draw all possible lessons from them before eating them. Yet the role of the feet is not limited to clairvoyance. Eating them can actually induce strange consequences: according to popular wisdom, they should not be consumed by young students of literature in particular, since this might provoke trembling of the hand, which would compromise handwriting, making it look as scratchy as chickens' footprints on the threshing floor.

Chicken is not simply an offering, it accompanies every festive or important occasion and is a testimony to abundance. It always has a place at wedding tables and at meals prepared to commemorate the anniversary of the death of a relative. It features at New Year's meals, especially in the north of the country, alongside pork. It is right and proper to honor the guest with it; more so than with duck, which are not raised as universally and are often used when chicken is lacking.

Choosing the right chicken is no easy matter. According to popular wisdom, frogs (also called "field chickens") are best in their third month and chickens in their tenth. Since the fowl is bought while still alive, it is advisable to choose those with black feathers and white feet, avoiding at all costs white chickens with gray legs. Nowadays, the most popular variety is those with white feathers and black feet, called *gà ac* and considered "invigorating."

Recipes and aphorisms

Everything is good in a chicken, though there are plenty of sayings in favor of one part or another. According to some people, "first place goes to the skin and second place to the head," while others believe that "The best piece is the parson's nose, followed by the wing tips." Everything is eaten, though: the blood, religiously collected after the bird's slaughter, is simply cooked in water or used to prepare a savory dressing. The intestines are carefully cleaned and make the rice soup richer. The heart, the gizzard, and the liver are boiled, but not for too

153

long, to keep them firm. Then they are thinly sliced and dipped into a mixture of salt and pepper. They are a delicacy reserved for children. If you open a now fashionable cookery book, you soon see that there are many ways of preparing chicken: grilled; stewed and scented with lemon grass; with ginger and accompanied by bamboo shoots; steamed and stuffed with lotus seeds . . .

The traditional and most popular preparation still remains boiled chicken, though cooking methods differ slightly according to the various regions. In the north, as we said in describing the preparation of the chicken for the village banquet, the cooked bird is cut into small pieces (each including skin, meat, and bone), simply flavored with young, thinly sliced lemon leaves and lightly dipped into a mixture of salt and pepper or sometimes into a salted blood dressing. This is in keeping with the will of the bird, whose trembling voice is said to call for tender lemon leaves, while the pig roots for onions and the dog whines for some *galanga*. In the central and southern regions, the flesh of boiled chicken is removed from the bones by hand, then chopped into small pieces, *gà xé phay*, which are dressed with *nuoc mam* (fish sauce), lemon, pepper, and the particularly aromatic persicaria. This cold salad comes with rice or *chao*, the rice soup prepared with chicken broth.

Chicken is so present in everyday life that it has become a basis for popular wisdom. There are more sayings, songs, and aphorisms devoted to this fowl than we could possibly mention here, and many of them are used to describe certain events in life or particular facets of people's characters: "A rooster raising his chicks" is a widower with children. "Mother hen and children ducks" is a woman who raises somebody else's children, or a situation of conflict. "Mister, says the chicken; madam, says the duck" means to strike blows in all directions. "Brave as a rooster on a heap of manure" is said of man not given to bravery. "Unable to tie a chicken" is an epithet for a weak or clumsy person. Those who "take a quail for a chicken" are wont to take one thing for another, are gullible, or have confused ideas. And if when the cat's away, the mice will play, in Vietnam "When the master's away, the chickens will scratch around in the kitchen."

A symbol of peace and prosperity, chickens are indispensable for feasts and rituals. But until these occasions arise they keep up their cocky pecking around the gardens and rice fields searching for something to eat. By doing so, they strengthen their legs and make their meat firm. Which is just as the Vietnamese like it.

Chapter NINE

ſour Power

THE LEBANESE CALENDAR

Aïda Kanafani-Zahar

For the Lebanese, the start of every season is marked by the appearance on tables of still unripe vegetables and fruit, simply seasoned with a pinch of salt and served as appetizers: green plums and almonds in spring, unripe grapes and pomegranates at the start of summer, and when the winter comes, whole lemons. This liking for sour flavors is evident at Lebanese tables every day.

Daily life

Lemon juice is a basic ingredient in the preparation of *yakhani*, ragouts of vegetables, meat, pulses, and *confit* of mutton, and *mahâshi*, stuffed vegetables (vine leaves, cabbage, chard, zucchini, eggplant, and peppers) and meat (tripe, for example). It also provides the base for the magnificent *arnabiyyi*, a sesame-cream-based dish that requires a certain amount of acidity, hence lots of juice of citrus fruits (bitter oranges, mandarins, and lemons) to attain the right balance of flavor.

According to an old Lebanese proverb, the olive is the *cheikh* (or sheik) of the table. Olives are invariably served with one or two halved lemons in the same dish. These lemons serve to flavor ragouts and sautéed vegetables, as well as vegetable, pulse, meat, and chicken soups.

Another sour taste common to everyday tables is the one produced by fermentation: in other words, yogurt and its by-products. During the fermentation process, lactose (the sugar contained in milk) turns in to lactic acid, which causes milk to acidify and also happens to be an effective preservative. The conditions of fermentation partly determine the degree of acidity and intensity of flavor. The staples of the food civilization of the Lebanon are not only wheat and olives but also yogurt, which is eaten natural at both lunch and dinner. It is often flavored with crushed garlic or powdered, dried mint and used to thicken the ragouts that accompany rice or *borghol* (steamed cracked wheat). Yogurt is also used for cooking. To prevent it coagulating with the heat, a binding agent such as cornstarch or egg white (which contains lecithin) is added. The most typical dishes are *laban ommo*, yogurt cooked with lots of onion and meatballs (once it is cool, immediately before serving, the mixture is sprinkled with pine kernels); *shish barak*, meatballs (made of *kibbi*, a mixture of minced meat and *borghol*) cooked in yogurt; stuffed zucchini and eggplant cooked in yogurt; and *fatti* (pieces of toasted bread and chickpeas in yogurt flavored with garlic and dried mint). By-products of yogurt include *labni* (produced by draining the yogurt whey), *shanklish* (buttermilk produced by churning the yogurt, fermenting it, drying it, and flavoring it with herbs) and *anbaris* (pasteurized milk fermented in an urn). These preparations are often preserved in oil or brine, which further accentuate their acid flavor. A key ingredient in peasant cooking is *kishk*, a mixture of fermented *borghol* and yogurt that is normally eaten in winter.

To accompany meats

As if to exorcise the compulsory abstinence from meat in the period of Lent, Christians organize meat dinners during Carnival Week. On such occasions, they drink *arak*, a traditional anise-flavored alcoholic drink. The climax of the week is the so-called "drunks' Thursday," when people get drunk at a great party, knowing that they won't be able to drink alcohol during Lent. In reality this abstinence is a choice, since although the precepts of the Church advise against alcohol, its consumption is not regarded as a major sin. Nonetheless, as peasants point out, the consumption of alcohol would be pointless at meals without meat. Only meat goes well with strong drink, tempering its alcoholic content and attenuating its "brutal" character. *Tabbuli*, a salad of *borghol*, onions, chopped tomatoes, mint, and parsley dressed with olive oil and lemon juice, and *fattush*, a salad of lettuce, cucumber, tomato, and toasted bread flavored with *sumach* powder, are both served as accompaniments to meat dishes whose intense flavor they help mitigate. *Sumach* is produced by crushing the berries of the Mediterranean shrub of the same name; its sour taste heightens the flavor of a number of starters, salads, and sautéed dishes. Moslems who celebrate events such as the Feast of the Sacrifice (the re-enactment of the replacement of Ishmael with a sheep) with meat dishes or take part in Christian banquets always abstain from drinking alcohol. Salads play a fundamental role in meals in this kind. The stuffed intestine of the animal is flavored with a sauce of vinegar, garlic, and dried mint. In the absence of alcohol, the acid tones down the "gamy" flavor of the meat, neutralizing the fat, and making it acceptable to eat.

Symbols of asceticism

Sour and acid flavors are a constant feature of everyday eating and are always present on the meatless Lenten table. In addition to lemon juice, in most Lent dishes considerable use is made of vinegar and *sumach*, which is widely used during the period to add or accentuate acidity in dishes.

While Carnival is the period of feasting in which the most meat is eaten, Lent implies a return to vegetarian asceticism with the use of cereals, pulses, and wild plants. Lentils also play a symbolic role, in that they stand for the tears of Christ. The traditional dish on Ash Monday is thus *mujaddara*, lentils and rice, or a salad of lentils dressed with vinegar. Lent cooking is rounded off by the daily use of the wild plants such as althea, *eryngo*, *Portulaca oleracea*, dandelion, cows-and-calves, and hawthorn, which are all in full bloom at that time of the year. Wild plants are used as a complement to garden vegetables such as spinach, beet, and cabbage, all boiled in water and dressed with lemon juice or *sumach* and olive oil. Alternatively, they may be sautéed in a frying pan with onion and garlic. Olive oil, the undisputed sovereign of the Lebanese kitchen, is loaded with biblical symbolism.

Another delicacy prepared at Lent is vegetable *kibbi*, or *kibbi triste—borghol* balls stuffed with sorrel, the sourest wild herb of all, and *sumach*—which is eaten for lunch on Good Friday. The classic *kibbi* is a mixture of meat and *borghol*, which is either crushed or worked with the hands, rolled into balls, stuffed with more meat, and flavored with spices. During the period of fasting, the meat is replaced by pumpkin pulp mixed with *borghol* and a little flour flavored with cumin. The filling is prepared with potatoes, sorrel, and lentils or chickpeas. After being boiled in water, the balls are flavored with *sumach*. At the climax of Lent on Good Friday, some people drink a glass of coffee with vinegar to commemorate Christ's sufferings.

NINE:2

BALSAMIC VINEGAR

Giorgio Triani

The genesis of traditional or "typical" products—by which I mean "real" traditional products—is always cloaked in mystery. Maybe that's what makes them traditional! The products at the top of any scale of typicality are unrepeatable because the factors and processes that have combined to make them possible are not entirely clear. The balsamic vinegar of Modena (like its neighbor, the *culatello* of Zibello) is one such product.

For a start, the environmental, climatic, and cultural characteristics of the limited area in which it is produced are not all that different from those of the broader surrounding area. The fact is that through-out the Emilian plain, from Piacenza to Bologna and along the lower Po Valley, the natural and human environment is more or less the same. Yet *culatelli* and balsamic vinegar are only made in the provinces of Parma and Modena (and to a lesser extent in Reggio). True, "more or less" may mark the imperceptible distance that makes the difference between a good vinegar and an extraordinary condiment. Yet it is also true that no historical, scientifically valid reason exists to explain why, how, and when balsamic vinegar—the fruit of a very complex technique and manufactur-ing process—began to be produced. As a result, comparative analysis simply cannot tell us why such a refined, spe-cial "culture of vinegar" grew up and developed in Modena and in no other province of Emilia.

The authoritative work on the sub-ject is *L'aceto balsamico tradizionale di Modena*, edited by Gianni Salvaterra for the producers' consortium and pub-lished by Calderini. This study explains that "the story of how bal-samic vinegar came into being is too old to be told with absolute certainty. Some reckon that its birth was a chance event: a certain amount of boiled wine must (the *saba* used in Modenese cooking) must have been forgotten in a jar somewhere, then found later in an advanced state of acetification." But surely similar phe-nomena must have taken place on countless occasions in other areas of

Italy without giving rise to a special way of producing vinegar. So it certainly wasn't only a question of chance. For example, the *Vita Mathildis* written by the Benedictine monk Donizone recounts that Matilde's father Bonifacio was producing a fine vinegar in the castle of Canossa in 1046. Yet the term "bal-samic" was only associated with vine-gar for the first time in 1747, when it featured in the *Register of grape har-vests and wine sales on behalf of the Private Ducal Cellar* of the Duke of Modena.

A gastronomic glory

The exceptional character of the balsamic vinegar of Modena is also underscored by the obvious historical observation that vinegar was used in the earliest civilizations. The Egyp-tians, Chinese, Greeks, and Romans knew how to produce it and use it accordingly as a condiment, a drink, and medication. In the Middle Ages, the alchemist physician Basilius Valentinus wrote that "in medicine and alchemy, it is impossible to do any-thing useful without the help of vine-gar." Later, during the cholera epi-demics of the late-19th century, vine-gar was officially recommended for washing fruit and vegetables. Vinegar can be used not only as a disinfectant but also as a preservative. Indeed, until recent years it played a predominant role in the tradition of marinating food. Today the tendency is to consider it an almost residual ingredient in the

159

fine art of *haute cuisine*, though in the classic "oil and vinegar" formulation of everyday salads and greens, its presence is perceptible as a contrast to the food thus dressed.

Until a few decades ago, the renown and use of Modena balsamic vinegar was exclusively confined to the area in which it is produced. Pellegrino Artusi failed to mention it in his classic *La scienza in cucina e l'arte di mangiar bene*, while Luigi Carnacina, the chef who left his mark on cooking in the 1950s and 1960s, was unaware of its existence. It was not until the 1980s that the balsamic vinegar of Modena rose to gastronomic glory, and this was entirely thanks to *La cucina regionale italiana*, a collection of recipes by that great innovator of national cuisine, Gualtiero Marchesi. Once Marchesi had set the trend, the product lost no time in achieving international recognition and making its appearance on the tables and menus of international *haute cuisine*. This speedy elevation of status actually coincided with the passage from essentially domestic production largely for home consumption to market-oriented production. It is a change that is very recent. Not until 1965 did a ministerial decree establish precise "Characteristics of composition and methods of preparing the balsamic vinegar of Modena." The Ministry of Agriculture and Forestry

finally granted the DOC designation in 1983, while the producers' consortium came into being in 1979.

Though official recognition of a traditional or typical product may respond to a particular demand, the actual development of the market for such products obviously depends on a number of social and cultural factors that can influence scale of production and the distribution of the product, both nationally and internationally. What counts most is clearly the values and perceptions of individuals and groups as they go about the business of eating both in their own homes and elsewhere. Diet and hunger, the two extremes of gastronomy, appear to converge in the case of balsamic vinegar. Indeed, this actually explains balsamic vinegar's rise to "cult product" status, a must on any table. Without overly stretching the point, it could be said that the success of Swatch watches is a textbook case of the same phenomenon. Swatches possess the same capacity to evoke and satisfy a very widespread social feeling, which goes under the name of "mass elitism." This is a deceptive but effective way to meet the general public's need for "designer" products. For the fact is that "true" balsamic vinegar remains a product accessible only to the happy few, those with cultural and gastronomic as well as financial capital. Let me explain. Balsamic vinegar can be found both cheaply on supermarket shelves and in costly specialized food shops and delicatessens in phials that are as tiny as they are expensive. There is obviously an abyss between the two products, the first being a normal wine vinegar with added caramelized sugar, the second the result of twelve years' aging, twenty-five in the case of a refined extra-old variety. For the moment, however, the image of the product counts more than the product itself.

Global and local

The reasons for this are many and various. The first is that the name "balsamic vinegar" sounds good, while the product itself has a very characteristic color and flavor, plus that touch of eccentricity that never goes amiss. As a "balsam" it conjures up images redolent with nature and its gifts, the healthy attributes that are bound to be "good for you." With its pronounced but delicate flavor, balsamic vinegar heightens the taste of meats, sauces, and especially the vegetables and salads that are no longer necessarily a side dish in these days of fashionable diets. In fact, the increased consumption of vegetables, with the advent of the most wild and wonderful dressed and mixed salads, is the main cause for the growing balsamic vinegar craze.

There is no doubt that it is a remarkably versatile product, able to satisfy both the palates of people on low-calorie diets and connoisseurs attracted by the significant variations in taste it can create. Balsamic vinegar should be used neither too abundantly nor too parsimoniously. As the producers' guides and manuals prescribe, "balsamic vinegar is versatile, but also tricky. If you don't know how to use it properly, you risk ruining everything. Oddly enough, it is impossible to establish how much to use and when. In short, balsamic vinegar is a solo player; so it's best to savor it first on the tip of a tablespoon and gradually assimilate its rotundity or its tart acidity (. . .). For special uses, deciding on the right amount is up to the sensitivity of the user."

Balsamic vinegar is literally the acid test of gastronomic skill, though its internationalization is more a matter of savor than savvy. It owes much of its success in English-speaking countries (especially the United States), the rest of Europe (especially Germany), and Japan to the appeal of refined, Italian-made niche products in general. It manages to be "glocal," at once global and local, exotic and national, typical of its place of origin and adaptable to the tastes of consumers the world over. Crossing the classic geographical and gastronomic borders, it has become a part of the most various national and traditional cuisines. In oriental cuisine, for example, it is a perfect replacement for soy sauce, while in the U.S. it is ideal as a barbecue sauce. Likewise, it goes well with northern European dishes and supplements wine vinegar in meat and fish marinades.

In conclusion, what better image than that of balsamic vinegar ice cream to sum up the success of this strongly typified product in the modern cuisine? A bittersweet image blending history and modernity, mixing classicism and extravagance, and bringing together high and low, far and near. An image that stands for the strength and independence implicit in the belief that anyone anywhere can "invent themselves a tradition" on the basis of the conviction that balsamic vinegar of Modena is the mother of all vinegars.

NINE : 3

PICKLES

Elizabeth Clift

Pickles must surely qualify as a poor relation in the history of food. They suffer from such a lack of documentation that it is difficult to place them in a historical context. Though they have always been a way of preserving vegetables and fruit (and thus valuable vitamins) and storing gluts of valuable crops through winter periods, unlike other forms of preservation they do not seem to have enjoyed any great periods of particular fashion and popularity. In fact pickles seem never to have benefited from imaginative treatment in general, except perhaps in America where the word "pickle" refers specifically to a pickled cucumber, of which there are now some fifty or more variations, depending on type of processing, flavoring, and cut. Indeed, in America the "pickle" has found its way into some incredible concoctions, pickleloaf luncheon meat, for example! A staggering five million pounds of pickles are consumed daily in the United States, and the Pickle Packers International, Inc., even goes so far as to define the perfect "pickle" as having no less than seven warts per square inch.

It is generally agreed that the Egyptians and Sumerians discovered fermentation about 2000 B.C.E. and with it the ability to preserve fruit and vegetables, particularly the cucumber, a plant introduced to the Tigris valley from the Indian subcontinent. Some fifteen hundred years later, Roman civilization had mastered the art of preserving by salting, and the combined techniques led to what we know today as pickling: first steeping a vegetable in brine or dry salt and then preserving it in acetic acid.

Pickles are rarely mentioned in early historical manuscripts, though cucumbers feature here and there in the Old Testament. "We remember the fish which we did eat in Egypt freely; the cucumbers, and the melons, and the leeks, and the onions, and the garlick," wail the people of Israel when faced with a diet of manna. Among the ancients, Aristotle, Cleopatra, and Tiberius are all thought to have appreciated the qualities of the

"spiced and preserved cucumbers" mentioned in Pliny's writings. Julius Caesar included them in his legionnaires' rations, and the quartermasters for the early merchant seamen were later to follow suit, since such provisions were a guard against scurvy during the long sea voyages. Pickles turned up again in French army rations during the Napoleonic wars, and I was curious to discover that they also featured in the American troop rations of World War Two. But given the nation's "pickle" consumption, perhaps that's no wonder.

It was during the 13th century that pickles gained a place in the diet of the English aristocracy. Indeed, they became a dish in their own right at feasts at the court of King John. For pickles were more than a way of preserving food, although this was obviously important. They also gave piquancy to a diet that must often have been very bland. By the time Gervase Markham came to write *The English Housewife* in 1615, the range of pickles had increased to encompass samphire, asparagus, onions, as well as cucumbers and a "world of others too tedious to mention." Most were consumed as "sallats," and Markham goes on to describe a very elaborate one suitable for a great feast fit for princes. It contained almonds, raisins, capers, olives, currants, red sage, and spinach, all mixed together with sugar and then placed in a dish with vinegar, oil, and more sugar. Thin slices of orange and lemon were laid over this, followed by a layer of well-pickled cucumbers, a layer of shredded cabbage lettuce, and a subsequent layer of oranges and lemons. This leaves out another prized ingredient for sallats, the pickled flowers that Markham advised the prudent housewife to preserve in distilled vinegar to keep their color.

It is worth considering the main preserving ingredients involved in this process, given that salt was an expensive commodity with great hierarchical traditions and grape vinegar was a luxury certainly not available to the ordinary households of northern Europe, where strong traditions of pickling were evolving. The salt used by all these busy housewives laying down their winter stores was not the expensively refined table salt, which was in any case too fine. In England at least, the home-produced salt was augmented by Bay salt, a coarse, dark salt full of impurities, derived from the Bay of Bourgeneuf and later from all down the French Atlantic coast. Its coarseness was especially suited to preserving of all kinds, although one presumes that the clarity of some of the pickles may have been compromised a little. As for vinegar, for those without access to grape verjuice, it would have been made either from strong ale fermented in the sun or from crabapples left to rot and then pulped by hand using wooden hammers and strained

into barrels, to be kept together with a dozen handfuls of damask rose leaves for every hogshead of verjuice.

But what exactly is a pickle? I believe the British must be held responsible for any confusion in terminology between pickles, chutneys, and relishes. The dreaded Branston pickle, the scourge of many a poor ploughman, is not a pickle at all but a chutney, and chutneys are a much later introduction into the European diet. A pickle is usually a vegetable first steeped in brine or dry salt and then preserved in liquid with a minimum acetic acid ration of 5 percent. Refinements over the last centuries have been few and far between. Commercialism has crept in, but with little imagination, and the outcome has been a mouth-puckeringly sharp acid pickle.

The heartland of good pickles is still in the home though, with that band of dedicated storage cupboardists who are often the backbone of the Women's Institute. A well-stocked storage cupboard is something both to envy and to marvel at. I take great pleasure in viewing someone else's neatly stacked jars, labeled and dated in neat little writing; even more fascinating is viewing a storage cupboard in a different culture to see the staple pickles of another country and of course to steal a few ideas to take home. There can be no one more smug than the prudent housewife on a cold, damp, winter evening reflecting on the contents of her storage cupboard and deciding what crunch and flavor to eat with that evening's supper, particularly in the presence of unexpected guests.

I myself run a traditional country inn with my sister in the depths of rural Worcestershire, and our pickled storage cupboard is an essential part of our menus throughout the year. Radishes, rocket pods, and nasturtium seeds garnish cooked lamb dishes; carrot and celeriac sallat accompany dishes of cured pork; the strong little tree onions are served with bread and cheeses, sweet pickled damsons with rich vanilla ice cream. Pickled cherries go perfectly with cold spiced meats and smoked duck breast, autumn field mushrooms are a treat with smoked eels, and green walnuts and horseradish are a must for cold beef. Moreover, pickled octopus and sepia fish (which almost fall over the fence into the chutney category, but I refuse to see them there) form part of a mixed hors d'oeuvres, while baby beetroots (both red and yellow) and red cabbage find their way onto the inevitable ploughman's plate.

Then of course is the list of the pickles yet to be tried, given the availability of ingredients and time. This year I may travel with the big pan to be in the right place at the right time to try the central European plum and pepper pickles, the American bread and butter pickle that was taken from Europe by the early settlers, watermelon rind, garlic—the possibilities are endless. Yet for most Europeans nowadays, pickles imply little more than gherkins, onions, and cucumber. If I have my way, the list will soon be expanding and pickles will again enjoy fortunes long lost.

CHUTNEYS

Radha Kapoor-Sharma

The camera moves slowly around the rustic kitchen, stopping an instant on the gleaming brass pots and pans before settling on the frame of a slim, young woman in a simple cotton sari, her hair in an untidy knot at the back of her head. She delves deeply into a large jar containing what appears to be mango pickle, leans back on her haunches and sucks noisily on a piece. An expression of pure contentment crosses her face. The subtle message of the scene is not lost on the Indian viewer: the young woman is evidently expecting a child.

This cinematic euphemism for pregnancy derives from the Indian woman's relish of all things sour, particularly pickles. Pregnancy of course only heightens this desire. Strangely, though men and women in India seem equally fond of salt and sweet dishes, the sour is largely the preserve of the women. A taste for pickles and chutneys crystallizes early when young children are often fed from their mother's plate, but it is the girl child who, by virtue of hanging around the kitchen a great deal in traditional households, is unconsciously much more influenced. Or perhaps initiation into the realm of the sour takes place when village children raid trees in the neighborhood in search of tamarind or green mangoes.

The prized fruit is dipped into salt (sometimes salt mixed with red chili powder) and is immediately devoured with great zest. For city children today, the only readily available, comparable substitute is a wedge of lime covered with salt.

For urban and rural households alike, no meal is really complete without a judicious mix of the salty, the sweet, and the sour. The sour takes several forms ranging from cooling drinks made with either lime juice or green mango pulp to a thin tomato-based sauce *(rasam)* that accompanies certain South Indian dishes and is either drunk from small bowls or is poured over steamed rice; from lentil dishes that are cooked with tamarind juice to vinegar-blended meat preparations; from pickles that are made to last a full year to chutneys that can last a few days at most. Variety is definitely the life of Indian cuisine, and it is the vast palette of pickles and chutneys made to tickle the palate that add spice to a meal.

Homemade

Pickles and chutneys form a vital part of an Indian meal, and all self-respecting housewives ensure that their table boasts, if not an array then at least one or two pickles or chutneys. Meant to be eaten in small quantities, both pickles and chutneys are accompaniments to the main meal and serve to perk up the fare offered. Sluggish summer appetites are revived with the addition of these relishes. They are believed to aid digestion as well. In fact, in south India the best way to end a meal is inevitably curd and rice with pickle. And, astonishing though it may seem, in the south a combination of *rasam*, pickle, and rice is advocated in cases of nausea and retching.

Pickles and chutneys have been made in India for centuries and the recipes passed down zealously from generation to generation. English, French, and other languages have borrowed the word "chutney," and *achar*, the Indian word for pickle, has been incorporated into Portuguese and been adopted by English through the Portuguese. *Achar* carries the same meaning as pickle in English. To the popular mind, pickle seems to be an innovation of the British that has spread its roots all over the world. This culinary "imperialization" of a basic part of an Indian meal has certainly furthered the cause of pickles and the pickle industry.

In India, though bottles and tins of pickles are sold in stores all over the country, each family prides itself on the homemade ones it can offer family members and guests. Pickles are usually made from seasonal fruits or vegetables (though meat and fish pickles also exist) and so pickling time must be carefully set aside during the season of a particular fruit or vegetable when it is abundant and therefore cheap. The summer months are the mango pickling months. Large jars, crocks, and bottles are brought out in preparation. They are washed and dried very carefully, for one undetected droplet of water could cause the full year's supply of mango pickle to mildew. The fruit is washed and dried thoroughly before being cut into small pieces or strips according to the requirements of the recipe. Children happily join in the work, as it is vacation time. The mango is then pickled with a host of spices and one or more preserving agent. Pickles are preserved with salt, oil (generally mustard oil), vinegar, or lemon juice. Some are cooked while others are left to mature in the sun. The wait for sun-dried pickles to become ready for eating can seem painfully long for the young and even the not so young.

Some condiments must be consumed within a few days, whereas others can last years. The popular favorites are mango, lime, chili, garlic, mixed pickle, and, in north India, a sweet and sour pickle made of winter vegetables such as turnip, cauliflower, and carrots. Pickles are adapted to family tastes. They vary from hot and sour to sweet and sour to tangy and spicy.

Two differences

Similarly, chutneys cover the full gamut of tastes but also include sweet and mild flavors. They are made from standard or seasonal fruits and vegetables, herbs, and dried fruit or nuts. Chutneys differ from pickles on two counts essentially. The first is the consistency. Chutney is of a reasonably smooth consistency, with the fruit or herb having been either ground to a paste or cooked to a mashed pulp. The grinding is usually done on a special flat stone called a *sil* with a small round stone called a *batta*, though electric grinders are now beginning to be used. A mortar and pestle can also be used to pound the spices and other ingredients to a pulp-like texture. The requisite consistency is obtained by the judicious addition of water, vinegar, lime, or tamarind juice. The second difference is that chutneys are made to be eaten fresh or within a few days at most. They generally contain no preservatives. Like pickles they add a new dimension to the meal, add color to the table, and revive dull appetites.

What is more, they are particularly rich in vitamins. Coconut chutney is virtually an omnipresent feature of south Indian meals, whereas in the north, in Muslim and Hindu households alike, a hot favorite is mint chutney. This cooling relish goes well with both vegetarian and nonvegetarian dishes and can be put together in a jiffy. Mint chutney sandwiches are a very popular snack with children of today, who love to take them to school for their mid-morning break, and they are equally popular with working mothers who are perpetually short of time. In India, chutneys are a daily affair, therefore quick to make. They have nothing in common with their bottled counterparts in the West that are the end result of a fairly long cooking process, and that are sweeter, more elaborate, and contain preservatives.

Still, for Indians living abroad the bottled varieties of pickles and chutneys remain a very welcome way of enlivening bland meals. However, since nothing can really compare with the homemade ones from back home, the earnest request of Indians abroad when asked what they'd like from India is inevitably some homemade pickle. This is a request that it is better to turn down heartlessly, unless you particularly like the look and smell of pickle oil in your suitcase!

Mint Chutney

INGREDIENTS:

1 medium-sized onion

A few cloves of garlic

1 sprig of mint leaves

2–3 sprigs of coriander leaves

1–2 green chilies

Juice of 1 lime (or lemon)

Salt to taste

1 small green mango (optional)

METHOD:

Grind the onion, garlic, mint, and coriander leaves coarsely in an electric mixer with one green chili. Add some salt and the juice of half a lime, and grind to a finer texture. Add more lime juice, salt, and another green chili if necessary after tasting. Mix a little water if you prefer a thinner consistency. Serve chilled.

All ingredients can be varied to suit personal tastes. Remember that the quantity of coriander should be double or more the quantity of mint, as the inverse would result in a very bitter taste.

Chapter TEN

Frankenfoods: Biotechnology

TEN:1

TRANSGENESIS

Arnaud Apoteker

 The recent series of scandals in the food production industry (Mad Cow disease, chicken containing dioxin, the use of waste sludge from sewage treatment plants in animal feed, etc.) has shattered the consciences of European consumers. Suddenly they have been rudely awakened to the growing process of "artificialization" of food products, to the complexity and total lack of transparency in the production methods underlying the food they eat every day. Cows no longer munch grass, industrial residues are now introduced into the food chain, and the vegetables and animals we eat are no long exactly living organisms cultivated or bred by farmers in different locales but rather disparate elements in an assemblage of

glucides, protides, and lipids associated in increasingly mysterious preparations. Consumers are thus becoming aware of the increasing divide between food and nature. Not surprisingly, the sudden introduction into food of genetically modified organisms (GMOs), manipulated in laboratories by the engineering of genes from different species into vegetables or animals, is cause for considerable discomfort among the citizens of Europe.

GMOs are, after, all just the latest mirage of an industrialized agriculture that has caused glaring damage: soil, water, and even atmospheric pollution, a dramatic decrease in the biodiversity of agro-ecosystems and the areas surrounding them, toxic residues in crops and thus in food, the standardization of taste, a dissolution of the bond between product and area of origin, and a disappearance of food diversity. It is grotesque to note that the same agro-chemical companies that have given rise to GMOs, promoting them as an alternative to chemical pollution, are also responsible for that pollution—though they denied the fact for decades and firmly opposed any attempt at regulation.

Evolution in reverse

The perfecting of cultivated species through the creation of chimerical and artificial species has nothing in common with the varietal improvements carried out by farmers ever since agriculture began. Farmers have always strived to create new varieties by cross-breeding characteristics of the same or similar species. Yet they have always remained within the natural constraints of sexual reproduction and the natural compass of agricultural ecosystems. With transgenetics, it is possible to free species from the last barriers that exist between them. But such barriers are the result of billions of years of evolution in reverse.

This radically new technology is based on scientific discoveries that are still in their infancy. As a technology, it therefore presents totally new risks whose long-term consequences no one is currently in a position to evaluate. Be that as it may, in the United States transgenic crops have been spread over millions of hectares of land in the past few years and are indirectly present in various forms in tens of thousands of food products through the feed given to livestock. In the majority of cases, the presence of GMOs is not acknowledged to consumers. After chemical and radioactive pollution, which we inherited from the industrial era and which coming generations will have to address, will transgenetics lead us to genetic pollution too?

Like other forms of pollution, genetic pollution consists of the dissemination of a particular substance in the environment—in this case, artificial genetic elaborations. All cultivated plants still have wild ancestors, often improperly referred to as "weeds." With these "weeds," agricultural crops exchange their genetic material, primarily through pollination. In this way, sooner or later the genes introduced into cultivated plants are found in wild plants of the same species. Unlike chemical or radioactive pollution, genetic pollution—that is to say, contamination of the genetic inheritance of living organisms—is irreversible and self-multiplying. A gene that "escapes" from a cultivated plant cannot be captured and enclosed in a laboratory, but is certain to multiply by reproducing contaminated organisms. The consequences of this diffusion in the environment are unpredictable. The tools for evaluating the present situation are seriously deficient, and the models necessary for predicting the dispersion of genetic contamination are highly complex, almost as much so as weather forecast models. Alas, only paltry resources are made available for studies and research on the risks deriving from transgenic pollution.

Though this new technology may appear extremely complicated, the logic pursued in the development of transgenic plants or animals is the same that led to intensive agriculture. Intensive crops need to be protected from the environment, since the emphasis on high-yield varieties and large-scale monocultures has made them more vulnerable to all kinds of attack. Quantitative yield has become practically the sole objective, to the detriment of quality food. In organic agriculture, there is energy between the plants cultivated and the ecosystems in which crops are developed. Instead of seeking such "collaboration," industrial agriculture is waging war on the environment, which is seen as a hindrance to development. In short, standards are being downgraded.

The fight against insects

More specifically, using transgenetics to make plants resistant to insect attack is a glaring example of the reductionist vision of industrial agriculture with its crude, myopic view of reality. Agriculture systems ought to be considered much more holistically as sets of complex interactions.

At world level, sizable loses have been recorded due to the attacks of plundering insects. Almost a third of harvests worldwide are eaten by insects, and the indirect effects of such attacks exacerbate the total loss. The damage suffered by plants as a result of the destructive passage of insects opens a breach for viruses and other pathologies typical of vegetables, which can become so weak as to be unsuitable for consumption. To protect crops from insects, the first move was to use insecticides, powerful mortal poisons originating from research into gases used on the battlefield in the course of World War Two. The growing use of chemical insecticides provoked the rapid development of insects resistant to these insecticides. The need to invent new poisons pushed intensive agriculture into a vicious circle of consumption of chemical products whose sole beneficiaries are the insecticide producers themselves.

Transgenetics has developed at a moment in which public opinion is extremely critical toward the tainting of the biosphere by persistent poisons produced by the agrochemical industry, and likewise when the public is concerned about the residues of toxic products in food. The idea embraced by agribusiness is to make the plants themselves produce their own insecticides. No one is prepared to admit that the majority of losses caused by the attacks of parasites is a direct result of the industrialization of agriculture which, year after year, covers immense surfaces of land with monocultures, thus fostering viral epidemics and the development of colonies of insects. It has been calculated that percentages of insect-related harvest losses have never notably decreased since insecticides were invented.

Plants cultivated today have been implanted with the genes of a soil bacterium, *Bacillus thuringiensis* (Bt), used in organic agriculture for decades on account of its high insecticidal

properties and its positive impact on the environment. The chemical and seed multinationals are proud of their new creations, since they pre-empt the need for insecticides. Such plants are even referred to as "organic crops." Meanwhile the consumer is caught between the prospect of chemical insecticides or manipulated vegetable organisms. No mention is made of alternative methods of production such as organic agriculture or the use of biological methods, including the use of the natural parasites of destructive insects. The chemical approach and the biotechnological methods share the same paradigm. The idea is to arm crops against insects, which are seen as a scourge that can be eliminated by using a chemical product or a bacterium gene inserted into a plant.

Consumer guinea pigs

It is wrong to believe that insecticides are not used on crops of insect-resistant transgenic plants. When insecticide plants are sown over millions of hectares, the quantity of insecticide they develop is huge, since every single cell in every single plant produces insecticidal substances twenty-four hours a day, thus spreading them over the whole cultivated area. The quantity of insecticide thus becomes much higher than that produced with external spraying at given intervals. This system stimulates the appearance of super-insects that develop a resistance to the toxin, so that the transgenic plants become totally defenseless. As a result, agrochemical companies are forced to create new genetic modifications or new insecticides. This is an example of the inexorable cause-effect mechanism that builds up between chemistry and biotechnology.

It is also worth pointing out that treated plants have to undergo genetic manipulation to be able to produce an effective insecticide by themselves, and that they are subsequently consumed by livestock or human beings. What will the effects of these self-produced insecticides be on the health of animals and humans? Here we are no longer speaking about insecticide residues from the spraying of fields, but of substances intrinsic to the plant itself. In this case, the fact that the Bt toxin deteriorates very quickly and has been used for over 40 years in agriculture (organic agriculture included) is in no way reassuring, since the toxin produced by transgenic plants is substantially different from that of the bacterium.

In Novartis transgenic corn, the first GMO authorized for cultivation in Europe, the gene of the *Bacillus thuringiensis* bacterium engineered into the plant is shorter than the gene that exists in nature. Its way of acting and its toxicity on nontargeted insects might thus be different too. It has been observed in the laboratory that the toxicity affects insects that are not deemed harmful and are situated higher in the food chain. Yet no long-term study of toxicity on human beings, was made before these products were marketed. Consumers themselves will be the guinea pigs for the agrochemical industry in a "real-life" experiment.

All major crops are manipulated to achieve higher resistance to an allegedly hostile environment. About 90 percent of them are genetically modified to acquire so-called agrochemical properties, meaning higher resistance to insects and viral diseases and better tolerance of herbicides. Plants, increasingly seen as "molecule factories," are being turned into production processes for the components developed by agribusiness and are expected to behave effectively in any climate, soil, and environmental condition. By responding to the demand of industry and the supermarkets for standardization, and only managing to offer advantages for the most productive varieties, transgenic agriculture effectively undermines local specificity and the diversification of agricultural production methods. Hence a standardization of flavors, despite the growing diversification of the range of food available. All over the world we are seeing a proliferation of exotic restaurants and even ethnic fast foods. It is now possible to eat the same snacks—pizzas, *tacos*, *nems*, and *kebabs* in Paris, New York, Mexico City, or Sao Paolo. They give us the impression we are living in a cosmopolitan environment. In reality, the appearance of diversity conveyed by industrial food preparations is an illusion, since modern people are consuming fewer and fewer vegetable varieties. Wherever industrial agriculture has asserted itself, the number of varieties cultivated has dropped rapidly.

The introduction of GMOs, the manipulation of the genetic inheritance of living organisms, poses a conundrum: Will the food of tomorrow maintain a bond with the soil, the land, and the farmer who "plows the field and scatters," or will it simply be the product of the genetics lab, irrespective of where it is produced? Will it be a gift of nature, warts and all, or will it be an insipid, rigorously codified industrial product?

TEN : 2

GENETIC FREEDOM

Vandana Shiva

Cultures that regard nature as life have always considered the divine presence in nature and seen any expression of nature as an expression of its divinity. A mechanistic culture, on the other hand, divorces god from creation, thus making the deity a sort of super-engineer, a watchmaker. Cultures looking at nature as a living organism respect its diversity and variety, they recognize that everything grows by itself, out of itself, and all creatures develop by themselves, whereas in a mechanistic culture, all forms of nature appear more and more as made things. The privileged members of such a culture detach themselves from nature by identifying with the divine principle that has seemingly been disconnected from the whole. In contrast to cultures relating to nature as a partner, today's mechanistic culture with its genetics and biotechnologies is forming a sort of right of intellectual property over animals and plants that thus appear increasingly as products of the human mind. Countries, peoples, and rivers have been colonized: what has remained is the inner space of beings, especially that of women. This inner space is now becoming an object of colonization.

Only where cultural diversity has been able to persist does biodiversity continue to exist; it can be found in the few niches that have not yet been completely modeled after the Western pattern and its mechanistic metaphor.

The destruction of biodiversity follows the logic of projectability and feasibility; it necessarily pushes for the simplification and uniformity of complex, self-regulating living systems. The transformation of complex ecological systems such as the rain forests into monocultures is the most immediate expression of this logic. A living forest with living trees is extremely important for the people in the rain forest; the trees collect the groundwater, stabilize groundwater level, and supply green fodder for the cattle—that is, they provide the essential living conditions for the forests' inhabitants. This is the reason why cutting trees to obtain lumber or firewood has traditionally been but a limited element of life in and with the forest.

There has been an increasing trend in India and Latin America to replant forests with eucalyptus trees, which originate from Australia, because they grow extremely fast and are therefore especially "useful" in terms of timber production, this being the only criterion that modern forestry will consider. But their leaves cannot be used as fodder, and the trees do nothing for groundwater storage. The gigantic monocultures, while increasing the profits of the lumber industries, locally cause poverty and render the land barren.

The same principle of cultivating an ever-decreasing number of species, and solely those suitable for global trade, has gained ground in corn growing as well. A great number of cereals have disappeared worldwide, the only exceptions being wheat, rice, and corn whose cultivation, however, has been reduced to a few types. Monocultures do not only entail poverty, they are also particularly susceptible to pests and diseases: if plants are afflicted by a disease, it will immediately spread to the entire monoculture, whilst the extent of spreading diseases is far less in diversified agriculture.

The logic of monoculture

Livestock farming in India may serve as an example to illustrate the far-reaching consequences of the destruction of diversity for all areas of human life. Traditionally, India had a great number of cattle breeds that, just as the trees in the rain forest, catered for a variety of needs. As a rule, the males were used as draft animals and the females as milking cows. About 80 percent of all the energy and more than half of the fertilizer needed in Indian villages were provided by them. Then Western agro-engineers started to influence this organically grown system. They introduced the logic of an agriculture based on electrification and mechanization instead of animal force. In their perspective, cattle served the sole purpose of milk or meat production, wherefore the diverse cattle breeds—above all the zebus that are especially suitable as draft animals—were replaced by Charolais or Holsteins. European crossbreeds took over, chiefly cattle incapable of moving and therefore unfit for use as draft animals. The ecological and economic consequences reached far. At first the farmers became dependent on motor tractors and the like, which poor farmers could not afford and had to borrow or rent from richer neighbors. In addition, they usually had to wait until the rainy season—when the owner would need the machines himself— was over. This caused the farmers double distress. Another effect was that now they needed to use artificial fertilizers, which led to an increasing pollution of the groundwater and soils. Moreover, many jobs that were once part of village life—like pressing oil and raising water—and for which the cattle had previously been used, could not be pursued any longer; they were industrialized and necessarily centralized. New dependencies developed; for the first time, oil and even water had to be bought. At the same time, the creative life of the village community was reduced with each task evacuated from the village. While statistically an increase in productivity can be construed for specific items (for example, the milk yield in India), these figures do not show the deprivation the villages suffered when such monocultures were carried through. These losses find no symbolic expression in the centers, for instance, at the Chicago grain market. They are, however, directly felt in the villages of the poor.

This is by no means a closed chapter of long bygone colonial times. On the contrary, the European Union has designed a program to standardize the Indian livestock, according to which more European cattle breeds are to be introduced in India. As the green fodder available in India is not suitable for these breeds, the fodder will have to be imported from Europe as well. Again, the situation of the poor farmers will deteriorate: they happen to be in the maelstrom of a debt crisis that obliges them to use more and more artificial fertilizer in order to obtain the desired increase, the "surplus."

In contrast to the logic of monocultures, a perspective that focuses on biodiversity will state a surplus only if a living system flourishes with all its interrelated components. Many initiatives have presently been launched in India in an attempt to return to traditional agriculture. The people inhabiting the southern slopes of the Himalayas have partly come back to the traditional mixed cultivation of twelve local cereals in the same field. These twelve cereals have gone through centuries of mutual adjustments, resulting in a positive coexistence in which none deprives any other of nutrients nor diminishes their growth and productivity. These mixed crops certainly yield more than India's corn or wheat monocultures, but they are deemed "unproductive" because their produce is not fit for global export, it is all the more adequate for the traditionally balanced and diversified alimentation of the farmer families themselves.

Patented genes

The issue, however, is not simply whether we recognize that diversity is the actual basis of productivity, but whether we understand that diversity has an intrinsic value and should therefore be saved. Only then will it be unthinkable to regard biodiversity as raw material for the uniform fabrications of the genetics industry. The conflict between the two concepts—diversity as an intrinsic value and diversity as a material resource—touches on issues of power, control, and property. Many people in all cultures share the opinion that life is not something one can own, and that any exploitation of living beings has to be governed by respect. The notions of modern science and biotechnology are irreconcilably

opposed to such respect: according to them, living beings can be claimed as intellectual property and become objects of patent law.

There is a fundamental distinction between two kinds of patents. One class of patents does not claim an invention but rather a discovery to be the "property" of an industrial corporation, for instance. These patents chiefly deal with the exploitation of knowledge common in the "Third World" but unknown in the industrialized countries. There is, for example, an utterly effective traditional pesticide that the inhabitants of the rain forest brew from the leaves of the Indian neem tree. A team of American researchers nevertheless had the results of their observations of this traditional technique patented; they can now claim the right to the use of neem tree leaves—the grotesque consequence being that those who have used this technique for many generations may now face prosecution for offending the patent law.

The other class of patents really deals with "new" genetic products. However, patenting does not only protect the inventors' property rights, but extends to all offspring of the manipulated organism. These patents are based on a crude, reductionistic notion: as the mechanistic concept says that organisms have been "made up" by genes, anybody recombining these genes in a new way consequently has to be regarded as the actual "creator" of the entire organism, although a new combination of genes is by no means equivalent to the creation of a living organism. It is a contradiction that biotechnologists on the one hand insist that their "products" are novel, basing their owner status on this claim, while on the other hand they attempt to play down the risks by pointing out that a manipulated pig is still "nothing but a normal pig."

The language of biotechnology clearly reflects the push for control that is gaining ground through this kind of intensified monoculture. It speaks of "biotechnological resources" instead of creatures, thereby making life seem an object and indeed a product of the human mind. It thus becomes more and more difficult to recognize the intrinsic value of biodiversity and the right of every living being to its own existence.

Note: This text is based on lectures given by the author on the occasion of the "Karl Jaspers Lectures on Issues of our Time" at the Oldenburg University.

TEN : 3

THE SECOND REVOLUTION

Manfred Kriener

The "gun" system is new and successful. How does it work? Tiny golden particles are covered with a vegetal DNA solution. Just as a well-made sauce adheres to meatballs, so the solution with the genetic substance sticks to the gold fragments. Then the noble metal, together with its attached DNA sauce, is laid upon a glass sheet placed in the middle of a pressurized chamber. Corn broth media are present on the floor of this chamber. An engineer pumps gas into one half of the room, while another pump opposite sucks up the air. Suddenly there is an explosion, the glass cannot hold the pressure and shatters. The gold particles spread in

179

all directions at an explosive speed. Like shrapnel, they fall onto the corn medium, making tiny holes in the plants and penetrating their cells. After the bombing, the DNA sauce around the gold core remains attached to the plant, just as a meatball leaves residues in the mouth as it is being swallowed.

"Particle-Gun" is the name of this system used to transfer foreign genes onto plants. As if they were shot by a shotgun, corn, rice, and wheat cells are studded with genetic matter. The rifle range is a genetic engineering laboratory where, 113 years after the death of Gregor Mendel, the Augustinian monk who founded plant genetics, grain species with new qualities are created—the new frontier of plant cultivation on the verge of the new millennium.

The promising results obtained from the Particle-Gun have allowed genetic engineers to widen their range of action decisively. Before this, the carriers used to introduce the foreign genetic substance into the plant were generally viruses and bacteria. Until not long ago, the researchers' favorite toy was the *Agrobacterium tumefaciens*, a parasite well known for being smart at getting into plants. It attaches itself to the plant roots and hoodwinks its host by introducing a plasmid—the carrier of a small part of genetic information, a sort of behavioral instruction—well hidden in the host cells. The plant takes the plasmid for its own genetic substance, reads it, and carries out the orders, which are coded on foreign genes. This way, it produces nutri-

ents for the bacterium, offering its parasite a princely welcome.

Genetic engineers have shamelessly made use of this trick: they "wipe away" the old genes in the plasmid of the bacterium and add new ones. In the same way, the manipulated load is now secretly introduced into the plant cells by the microbes. This way, the cheater is cheated and the microbe becomes a useful idiot.

Manipulations

By means of this and other transfer systems, genetic surgeons have managed to manipulate nearly all known species of useful plants (see the list on page 185). Extreme limitations have thus been surpassed. Seed companies and farms are no longer constrained to one single species, but are now able to take useful genes from one plant and transfer them to another. The gene supermarket is open, offering a green light to the inventiveness of farmers.

Genetic matter from animals or microbes can also be transferred into plants. An example is a "corn with inner pesticide," made in a U.S. laboratory. To protect corn from the voracious corn pyralid caterpillar, genes of *Bacillus thuringiensis* have been introduced into the plant, so the manipulated plant produces poisonous bacterial substances that fight the caterpillar.

Faced with such spectacular genetic creations, we sometimes tend to forget that genetic engineering is very young. In 1983, a foreign gene was transferred for the first time onto a tobacco plant.

Now, fourteen years later, countless experiments have been carried out. The introduction of genetic engineering in agriculture has "taken off like a rocket," to use the words of Andreas Büchting of Kleinwanzlebener Saatzucht AG, based in Einbeck, in the north of Germany.

Other scientists go even further: the group of biochemists Gassen, Bangsow, Hektor, and König, from the Technische Hochschule in Darmstadt, refer to the future prospects of genetic engineering as a "second revolution." After the triumphal development of preservation techniques and frozen foods, in the next decade genetic engineering will bring about further turmoil in the food industry. Gassen and company believe that, after the year 2000, all drugs will be produced with the help of genetic engineering, as well as all "seeds of the plants that we use to produce food." Over the next three years, a growth in sales to two billion dollars is projected for the transgenic plant industry. In Brussels, the European Commission estimates that "in the future genetic engineering will be used for nearly half of all foodstuffs."

Perhaps many of these estimates are deliberately exaggerated, to convince the most skeptical consumers that their resistance is useless. The pace of the actual progress of genetic engineering in agriculture and foodstuff production can be expressed in a different set of figures. In 1996, over 3,500 cases of genetically manipulated plants used for open field cultivation were recorded. They mainly involved tomatoes, pota-

toes, rape, soybean, sunflowers, and tobacco, since it is very easy to transfer genes into monocotyledonous plants. The best profit opportunities are probably to be found in soybean as animal fodder and a lubricant for the food production industry. Already it is included in no less than 20,000 foodstuffs.

In Canada and the United States, two of the leading transgenic countries worldwide, huge surfaces are now exclusively cultivated with manipulated plants. In the U.S. alone, twenty-five transgenic plants have been approved for marketing.

Poisons and savors

Transgenic plant species have been planted and marketed not only in the large industrialized countries, but also in developing countries such as Zimbabwe, Eastern European countries such as Bulgaria, Hungary, and Russia, South Africa, and especially China. China is now the world leader in the production of virus-resistant plants. With over sixty new cultivated plants, including tobacco, pepper, rice, tomatoes, and potatoes, China has even surpassed Germany.

In Germany, by August 1996, there were exactly fifty-two new cultivated plants. Yet in half these cases the enemies of genetic engineering managed to destroy experimental cultivations by means of "field-mouse actions." In Austria, the acceptance of genetic engineering experiments on plants is even lower than in Germany: by means of a referendum held this year, a large majority voted against any genetic manipulation of food. Currently, most genetic engineering experiments are still mainly focused on how to make plants more resistant to parasites or diseases, or on how to program them so that they become insensitive to specific manufactured pesticides, in order to make the use of such poisons easier and more intense. Needless to say, the manufacturer is a monopolist.

There is also a growing number of experiments whose objective is to improve taste, appearance, and preservation. The "Flavr-Savr" has become famous, a tomato that does not spoil, produced by the U.S. biotechnical company Calgene, the first genetically engineered food to be approved worldwide. Researchers managed to block the gene responsible for tomato fruit rot. The Flavr-Savr tomato concentrate can now be found in British supermarkets as well. Following the same principle, scientists are trying to engineer the maturation process of many other fruits. Should they succeed, a new age would open for the world trade of fruits and vegetables, since paths and transportation times could be redefined.

Rape oil has recently been introduced into Calgene's list. Produced from the laurel plant thanks to gene transfers, it seems to taste like coconut oil. Some Swiss biologists are working on a "natural" quality of decaffeinated coffee. Genetic engineers at the University of California–Berkeley have created lettuce plants that lay a sweetener on their leaves.

Utopian promises

The future undoubtedly has a number of surprises in store. Researcher Andreas Büchting has tried to imagine how current trends will develop and what consequences might derive from the very rapid change of useful plants that have developed over thousands of years. His projections for genetic engineering in agriculture may seem somewhat utopian, but here they are:

• Plants cultivated in temperate climates, including our grain species, will be adapted to tropical climates. New hybrid qualities will grow in Africa as well.

• The nutritional value of staples such as rice, wheat, or potatoes will be improved by the addition of vitamins and amino acids.

• Plants equipped with special binding genes will "gather" nitrogen directly from the air, where there is plenty. The atmosphere will become a universally available fertilizer.

• Crop losses due to high ultraviolet rays or ozone pollution will be avoided. Corn and rape made resistant by the new genes will be able to tolerate even particularly intense environmental stress.

• Medicinal plants such as chamomile, valerian, and mint will become real bioreactors for drug production. By means of genetic manipulation, it will be possible to strengthen their action.

• Potatoes and sugar beets will be manipulated to produce large quantities of antibiotics, coagulants, and antibodies.

Accidents

What may now seem like science fiction is already the object of experiment in genetic engineering laboratories. Chinese researchers are working to improve the nitrogen-fixing capacity of barley, rice, wheat, and watermelon. Many other experiments aim at improving resistance to pollutants like ozone or heavy metals, drought, or heat. In many countries research projects are being carried out to improve the vitamin and amino-acid content of plants. Some British researchers have developed a "healthy tomato" that boasts a higher content of beta-carotene and antioxidants and thus seems to have a preventive effect with regard to heart disease.

However, one of the most consequential accidents in the history of genetic engineering took place during an experiment for improving nutritional value, involving the transfer of genetic matter from Brazil nuts to the soybean plant. The food surgeons of the seed group Pioneer Hi-Bred were trying to optimize the soybean plant, which lacks two amino acids, methionine and cysteine. It was believed that this shortcoming could be remedied by transferring the genes of the Brazil nut. Unexpectedly, during the manipulation the allergic potential of the plant was also transferred. Experiments with the manipulated soybean on people allergic to the nut produced the same symptoms in both cases. Had they eaten the manipulated soybean, "even lethal symptoms" might have appeared, wrote the *New England Journal of Medicine*.

This experiment underlined the point that gene transfer may also have negative consequences, which has refueled the debate on the safety of such experiments.

Mutant vines

"The Germans are the biggest cowards in the world," complains Wolfram Siebeck, the most famous German gourmet. He has certainly not embraced genetic engineering, but he is not happy that the debate is almost exclusively about safety and not taste, heterogeneity, and authenticity of foodstuffs. As to the future, Siebeck fears that genetic manipulation will end up by

183

leveling the taste of food. "For each food, there will be three versions: one with a peach taste, one with raspberry taste, and one with a banana taste."

The Provence-based food expert hopes that a counter-movement will be started up to promote and protect authentic foods free of genetic manipulation. He envisages a reaction similar to the movement created by the advocates of organic foods. However, he acknowledges that genetic engineering will become more and more popular, "since there is an immense power concentration in the big groups of the food industry." Siebeck does not see what is happening as a second revolution, but the continuation of current evils in different guise. Today, most vegetables on sale are large and long-lasting, "more suited to repairing bicycles, and therefore inedible."

This is certainly not true for wine, whose quality has improved over recent years. Yet genetic engineering does not balk at Bacchus either. Last year two Australian scientists, Tricia Franks and Mark Thomas, triumphantly presented the first kind of genetically manipulated grapes. This was only a test experiment: the Australian researchers simply wanted to show that the technique used to infect plants with external genes with the help of the *Agrobacterium tumefaciens* microbe also works with the vine. And they were right. Since then, even the most biblical of all plants can be genetically manipulated.

Now that the technique has been finalized, foreign genetic material can be introduced into the plant with a specific target. Franks and Thomas say they are pursuing three main objectives: new high-tech vines that will produce fruit of a better quality and that will be more resistant to disease and decay in the long run.

Genetic engineering on vines has also got under way in France, and the first manipulated species have been planted. The goal is to make the famous Burgundy Chardonnay vine more resistant to viral infections. With the introduction of a particular gene, the new Chardonnay clone can withstand viral attacks thanks to antibodies in the plant itself.

Super-yeasts

Despite such experiments, Ernst Rühl, responsible for vine growing at the Institute of Research on Wine in Geisenheim, does not believe that genetic engineering can produce extraordinary results in this field. Similar practices are not easily accepted in drinks such as wine, whose identity so much depends on its genuine, natural aura. Moreover, consumers are far more careful about wine than they are about any other food. Rühl rather expects genetic engineering to reach wine through bottling techniques. Genetically manipulated yeasts are already available, and just waiting for an opportunity to be used.

South Africa is at the forefront in this field. South African genetic engineers have made special types of yeast available whose action goes well beyond the mere transformation of

GENETICALLY ENGINEERED CROPS ALREADY OPEN-FIELD PLANTED IN EUROPE AND THE UNITED STATES

alfalfa	gladiolus	potato
apple-tree	grape	pumpkin
barley	lettuce	rape
belladonna	maize	rice
birch	marigold	soybean
broccoli	mountain cranberry	strawberry
carnation	Norway spruce	sugar beet
carrot	onion	sugar cane
cauliflower	papaya	sunflower
chicory	pea	sweet potato
chrysanthemum	peanut	tobacco
cotton	pepper	tomato
cucumber	petunia	walnut
eggplant	plum	watermelon
eucalyptus	poplar	wheat

sugar into alcohol. Some of these manipulated yeasts can curb wine acidity during the fermentation phase, turning the more aggressive malic acid into lactic acid, or can take an increased quantity of pectin from the berry cell walls, thus giving the wine a more intense red color. Some specific organoleptic or sensual features of the wine are affected as well. New varieties of yeast developed in genetic engineering laboratories intensify the formation of glycerin, thus making wine acquire a fuller flavor. As for industrially produced wines, genetic engineering provides a wide range of

opportunities for manipulation thanks to yeasts alone. Even though these are not yet in use, nobody thinks that vine growing will remain an island unblemished by genetic engineering.

No doubt, many vine growers would be in favor of genetic engineering if the outcome were vines that are resistant to fungi attacks and thus require a less extensive use of fungicides. This is precisely where the very limits of the transgenesis method become more apparent. The immunity struggle of vines against the impending attack of fungi is a complex game, where various plant genes interact. Rühl is convinced that "transferring the reactive potential of fungi from traditionally grown wild species is easier than doing the same with genetic engineering."

We can thus find solace in the conviction that not all that genetic engineers threaten or forecast will turn into reality in the next few years. The history of medicine shows that reality is more complex than researchers usually expect, and the same is true for genetic engineering. It will take another decade for two U.S. companies to fully decode the genetic material of maize, with an annual cost of ten million dollars. Indeed, many growth and metabolic processes in plants are not attributable to a single gene, so that removing or replacing it would not suffice. Very often, these processes result from the interaction of various genes.

Finally there is another open question: to what extent will the public at large be ready to accept genetically manipulated food? Virtually all the literature available on the future of genetic engineering indicates that eight out of ten consumers are not too happy about the prospect. Fear and mistrust will thus have a major role to play in defining the time frame of this "second revolution."

TEN:4

THE VINE AND THE ENGINEER

Ivana Gribaudo

Genetic engineering in grape growing: some readers will be startled just reading the words. For many Italian consumers, grape growing, and thus wine, conjure up hedonistic images and sensations rather than technical reflections. Yet there are very specific reasons why the vine-growing world could benefit considerably from the new techniques.

Understandably, the subject is hotly controversial. Some address the question from an ethical standpoint, arguing that to introduce genes into a plant is "to alter the course of life," which is tantamount to replacing the Creator and therefore morally censurable. It is hard to reply to questions of principle. All we can do is point out once more

that what we are doing today is, in a sense, simply a further step in the process of domestication of wild vegetable species. Humans have always selected, improved, and crossed plants, creating hybrids that previously did not exist, if only because the parents grew in different continents. What we can and must do is offer the public information so that they can judge for themselves, without denying or underestimating the risks inherent in these biotechnologies. Many of the articles written on the subject contain more errors than they do correct information. Some authors can't resist yelling like soccer fans at their "opponents." Clearly this does not contribute to proper assessment and civilized discussion.

Engineered chardonnay?

But let's return to the vine. The vine species normally cultivated is *Vitis vinifera*, and genetic improvement involves features that differ from those of cereals or other crops, including perennials. In European vine and wine growing, the variety cultivated is a factor of great importance and stability, both because the consumer is loathe to accept new flavors and because it is not simple, legally speaking, to introduce the cultivation of new grape varieties (either for table wines, or indeed for *d'Origine Controlée* wines). It is a different matter for "new" vine-growing countries. (the U.S. and Australia, first and fore-most), in which the market and the environment determine which grape varieties are cultivated. Unfortunately, the European vine suffers from a number of serious diseases, particularly fungal and viral ones. The former can be cured, but at the price of a relatively widespread use of phytochemicals. But the only weapon we have against viruses is the use of healthy young plants and operations to counteract the carriers of viruses (insects and nematodes). Other species of the *Vitis* genus of American or Asian origin reveal characteristics of resistance to many pathogens. Traditional methods of genetic improvement make it possible to hybridize *Vitis vinifera* with virtually all wild vine species, but the resulting hybrids will bear no great resemblance to our original grape varieties. They will in fact possess the characteristics of both parents and, possibly, negative genetic characteristics that were not present in them. In the course of many years, however, no vine geneticist has ever managed to create a barbera or a chardonnay, say, resistant to mildew or peronospora. It has been claimed that in the vine it is possible to transfer these characteristics of resistance using classic methods of genetic improvement, but this is not true. After decades of hard work, only in recent years have more rustic grape varieties obtained from repeated hybridization been presented in Germany, but they are new varieties, different from those cultivated to date. With genetic engineering it would be possible to draw a resistance gene from another species of the *Vitis* genus itself, or from miscellaneous genera, and transfer it to *Vitis vinifera* without transmitting other undesired characteristics to the descendants (for example, the "foxy" taste associated with *Vitis labrusca*). One difficulty derives from the fact that we are still unable to transfer resistance based on the expression of many genes, and several resistance characteristics in wild vines are polygenic.

So what has been achieved to date by using genetic engineering techniques in the wine sector? One thing is certain: as far as the interests of the multinationals are concerned, the vine is not even remotely comparable to corn or soybeans. This stands to reason, not only on account of the difference in turnover, but because the vine is a perennial as opposed to an annual species, which means that experimentation is inevitably much slower. This explains why it is generally not large biotechnology companies that work on the genetic engineering of the vine, but public research institutes. The laboratories of one large champagne company spent a long time working on these problems in collaboration with public bodies, but recently they have drastically reduced their commitment in the sector. Such choices are also determined by the fact that, for the moment, nothing has been decided on how genetically modified vines are to be named; that is to say, whether they can conserve the name of the original grape variety. This decision will clearly

have a strong influence on the commercial success of transgenic vines and consequently the economic return of those who produce them.

Twenty-eight experiments

According to the most recent updates, twenty-eight field tests with transgenic vines are currently underway worldwide, obviously at an experimental level and on a small scale. Many laboratories are developing research on this and other related matters: from the perfecting of protocols for regeneration (the production of plants from single cells) to gene transfer and the identification and cloning of genes that might be transferred for agronomic or pathological purposes. These laboratories are located in various parts of the world, especially in the U.S., France, Germany, Austria, Australia, Israel, Switzerland, and Italy, but also in Ukraine and Bulgaria. Of course, not all of them have managed in pots or in the field to produce plants that are definitely transgenic, and research often concentrates on one or another of the states outlined above.

Another point worth stressing is that a lot of work has been done on vine and stock and less on wine and table varieties. There are technical reasons for this, as it is particularly difficult to perfect transformation and regeneration protocols for *Vitis vinifera*. However, this in itself is somewhat reassuring since it implies that the vines would be modified only at the root. So what are the characteristics transferred into the wine? In the vast majority of cases, it is resistance to agent viruses or viruses associated with viral diseases. There are three basic reasons for this: because such pathologies may be a serious problem for the wine (as we have said, no effective chemical cure exists against viral diseases); because it is relatively easy to build a resistance gene from the virus genes themselves; and because these monogenic characteristics are simple to transfer. Some research groups are contriving to produce vines resistant to fungal diseases (the great cryptogamic diseases of the vine, such as peronospora, mildew, and botrytis force vine growers to perform numerous treatments every vegetative season) or bacterial diseases. Very few laboratories actually handle genes that modify the biochemistry of the fruit or create codes for other characteristics.

These characteristics, theoretically acquired with the introduction of new genes, need to be verified. The first data can be acquired in a confined environment, but it is only with implantation in the field and exposure to normal cultivation conditions that reliable responses can be obtained on the effective expression of the gene introduced and its interference, if any, with other genes. In practice, there must be a proven advantage for that given aspect that does not change the behavior of the plant with regard to all its other characteristics. Of course, experimentation must also cover any other risks that might be involved. In any case, at the moment and for some time yet, vines will be modified with the introduction of very few genes, and it is absurd to describe them as being resistant to all diseases or as non-rotting. It is also worth stressing that, in general, the alternative is not between grapes from transgenic vines and grapes produced using "natural" methods, but between grapes from more resistant vines (hence less needy of chemical treatment) and those produced from plants subjected to all the necessary fungicides or insecticides.

Advantages and risks

Such are some of the potential advantages of genetic engineering. As to possible risks, the story is a long one, too long to tell here in a few lines. As many people are aware, the matter is beset with all sorts of grave social, ecological, and environmental dangers as well as risks for the health of the consumer. Obviously much still has to be clarified with regard to the impact of transgenic crops on the environment, though a great deal depends on the type of genes transferred. Indeed, even some of the champions of engineering acknowledge that there is still a lot of work to be done. Some authoritative voices argue that the future lies not in the transfer to vegetables of genes from systemically very different organisms (like the famous gene of resistance to cold that has been transferred from a fish into strawberries, raising understandable ethical anxiety and serving as an easy target for those opposed to such techniques) but, for example, in the study and use of promoter and regulator genes for similar species. Greater knowledge of these aspects might make it possible for substances synthesized from new genes to be produced only in some parts of the plant, if need be excluding the edible parts and/or only in response to external stimuli—for example, as a reaction to attacks by the pathogen to which resistance is sought.

My personal opinion is that it is counterproductive to call for total blocks on research and experimentation as well as on the importation and cultivation of transgenic plants. It is unquestionably necessary to make serious and scientific assessments of the possible medium- and long-term risks. The problem is: what is the time limit, and which and how many tests can ensure that no risks exist? Considering that we live in a world in which it is practically impossible to block the circulation of goods, to hope that a country such as Italy can become and remain a happy bucolic island uncontaminated by genetically modified foodstuffs is purely utopian. Another reasonable argument is to demand proper labeling and broad information that enables the consumer to choose in total, unbiased freedom.

Anyone who sees a danger in transgenic vines can rest relatively assured that their cultivation and commercial vinification is still a long way from materializing. Those interested in the possibility of having transgenic vine varieties resistant to viral or other diseases and therefore less needy of chemical treatment should wait for the results of experiments in the field (which will last an estimated ten to twenty years) and hope that any moratoria on transgenic foods will, for the moment, concern commercial and not experimental crops, cultivated on a small scale in non-vine-growing areas, and subject to careful control. In any case, more widespread information and better communication among the parties (especially researchers, politicians, and consumers) can only be a good thing, leading to the sort of serenity of discussion and appraisal that is conspicuously lacking at present.

TEN:5

A MIRACLE?

Vandana Shiva

Genetically engineered crops and foods were to have been the miracle solution to world hunger and the ecological crisis created by industrial agriculture. However, genetically modified organisms (GMOs) in agriculture create new hunger and new ecological risks.

The myth of saving the planet

As the Green Revolution miracle fades out as an ecological disaster, the biotechnology revolution is being heralded as ecological miracle for agriculture. It is being offered as a chemical-free, hazard-free solution to the ecological problems created by chemically intensive farming. The past forty years of chemicalization of agriculture has led to severe environmental threats to plant, animal, and human life. In the popular mind, "chemical" has come to be associated with "ecologically hazardous." The ecologically safe alternatives have been commonly labeled as "biological." Biotechnology has benefited from its falling under the biological" category, which has connotations of being ecologically safe. The bio-tech industry has described its agricultural innovations as "Ecology Plus."

It is, however, more fruitful to contrast the ecological with the engineering paradigm, and to locate biotechnology in the latter. The engineering paradigm offers technological fixes to complex problems, and by ignoring their complexity, generates new ecological problems that are later defined away as "unanticipated side effects" and "negative externalities." Within the engineering ethos it is impossible to anticipate and predict the ecological breakdown that an engineering intervention can cause. Engineering solutions are blind to their own impacts. Bio-tech, as biological engineering, cannot provide the framework for assessment of its ecological impact on agriculture.

Genetic engineering is creating the risks of a new form of pollution or "contamination" called genetic pollution or bio-pollution. In certain cases, bio pollution can have major health and environmental impacts and create biohazards. Introduction of new species into ecosystems had led to the phenomenon of bioinvasion, which is one form of biohazard. Introduction of exotic genes into crops can have unpre-

dictable ecological impacts. Some organisms can be pushed to extinction by crops that release toxins. Other organisms can become invasive species, dominating ecosystems and displacing native biodiversity. Unlike toxic hazards, biohazards multiply and cannot be recalled.

There are multiple ways in which GMOs will increase the ecological vulnerability of agriculture. Firstly, GM crops will increase rather than decrease chemical use. Chemical corporations pushing genetic engineering have used various strategies to make the public believe that bio-tech in agriculture implies the end of chemical hazards and that biotechnology "protects the planet."* However, there are four reasons why biotechnology will lead to an increase in chemical use in agriculture.

1. The predominant agricultural application of genetic engineering is herbicide resistance. This will increase rather than reduce herbicide use.

2. The use of chemicals will spread to new regions of the world that were formerly free of intensive chemical use in agriculture.

3. Applications such as Bt resistance, which are supposed to get rid of pesticides, can actually lead to increased

---

*For instance, consider the speech delivered by Hendrik Verfaillie, president of Monsanto, at the Forum on Nature and Human Society, National Academy of Sciences, Washington D.C., 30 October 1997.

pesticide use through buildup of Bt resistance and the destruction of ecological alternatives for pest control.

4. The engineering of a toxin into the plant itself can have the impact of increasing toxins in the plant and the ecosystem.

RoundUp Ready Soya (RRS) is the most widespread genetically engineered crop introduced so far. The strategy for RRS is basically to sell more of the herbicide RoundUp. Monsanto's RoundUp accounts for 95 percent of all glyphosate sales (glyphosate is the world's best-selling total herbicide). The worldwide sales of glyphosate products are currently worth approximately US$ 1,200 million annually and represented about 60 percent of global non-selective herbicide sales in 1994.

RoundUp sales are nearly US$1 billion. The patent for RoundUp expired in 2000. RoundUp Ready crops are a strategy for Monsanto to protect its sales of the chemical RoundUp through its life sciences division, which is separated from the chemical division as a public relations ruse, but which is still involved in pushing chemicals.

The second strategy used by Monsanto is to spread RoundUp in countries where it was not used before. Monsanto has greatly increased its manufacturing capacity of glyphosate, investing US$200 million in production and formulating technology in Australia, Brazil, Belgium, India, and China as well. The use of RoundUp in

biodiversity-rich regions and where biodiversity is the resource of the poor will destroy species as well as the livelihoods of the poorest.

The advertisements of the genetic engineering corporations, which call themselves the Life Sciences Corporations, are all directed at making the public believe that genetically engineered crops are ecologically safe and reduce the use of chemicals. In an advertising campaign in Europe in 1998, Monsanto claimed that Monsanto's genetically engineered crops reduce pesticide use and provide a safe and sustainable method of weed control. As one of the ads stated, "More biotechnology plants mean less industrial ones." However, while Monsanto was selling its RoundUp Ready crops, it was also setting up new RoundUp factories in India, China, and Brazil. More biotechnology plants mean more industrial ones, since herbicide-resistant crops are designed to be tolerant to the propriety herbicides of the company, which makes money selling both seeds and chemicals. Monsanto makes farmers buying its RoundUp Resistant crops sign a contract that they will not buy chemicals from any other company and will not save seed. Monsanto has thus retained its monopoly through genetic engineering at a time when its patent for RoundUp was expiring.

Herbicide-resistant crops are designed to increase herbicide use, especially in those regions of the world where farms are small, labor is abundant, polycultures control weeds, and women use the weeds for food and fodder. Weeds are part of biodiversity in small farms, and a useful resource. The spread of herbicide-tolerant seeds would destroy biodiversity, destroy sources of food and fodder, destroy women's livelihoods, and introduce toxic chemicals.

Farming systems in the Third World depend on 100–200 plant species. The introduction of herbicide-resistant varieties will push the rich diversity of small farms to extinction. Monsanto's RoundUp ads in remote villages of India declare: "Are your hands tied up by weeds? RoundUp will set you free." As the sole purpose of RoundUp Ready crops is to increase the use of RoundUp herbicide, so Monsanto's claim that their use will reduce herbicide use is sheer deception. RoundUp is Monsanto's largest selling product, accounting for 17 percent of total annual sales of US$9 billion.

Biopollution

Genetically engineered transgenic crops can contribute to genetic pollution or biological pollution in many ways.

1. In herbicide-resistant varieties, transgenes can spread to wild and weedy relatives, creating superweeds.

2. Contamination or pollution of biodiversity can destroy the unique characteristics of diverse species.

3. Transgenic crops engineered to produce pesticides can lead to evolution of resistance in major insect pests.

4. Toxins from the genetically engineered crop can kill beneficial species.

In addition to creating superweeds and superpests, GMOs can also spread disease. Breeding plants resistant to viral infections by inserting virus genes in the plant genome can create new superviruses which have new hosts and new properties.[1]

Genetic pollution or bio-pollution can also occur through horizontal gene transfer. Horizontal or lateral gene transfer is defined as the nonsexual transfer of genetic information between organisms. Horizontal gene transfer is therefore different from the ordinary form of gene transfer, which takes place vertically from parent to offspring. One instance of such transfer is the genetic parasite belonging to yeast that has suddenly jumped into many unrelated species of higher plants.

Our knowledge at the genetic level is too immature to assess the probability or consequences of such horizontal gene transfer and the resultant genetic pollution. Little has been done to understand the ecology of genes, though much effort has gone into the engineering of genes without any knowledge of the impact of genetically engineered organisms on other organisms and the environment. The lack of knowledge concerning ecological impact has been taken as proof of safety when in fact it is evidence of ignorance of biohazards.

The myth of feeding the hungry

GMOs will increase hunger because they will introduce a chemical- and capital-intensive monoculture agriculture, displacing small farms and small farmers who use biodiversity to feed themselves and their families. Small biodiverse farms are more productive than industrial monocultures.

Yields usually refer to production per unit area of a single crop. Planting only one crop in the entire field as a monoculture will of course increase its yield. Planting multiple crops in a mixture will produce lower yields of individual crops, but a higher total output of food. In the biodiversity perspective, biodiversity-based productivity is higher than monoculture productivity.[2] The Mayan peasants in Chiapas are characterized as unproductive because they produce only 2 tons of corn per acre. However, the overall food output is 20 tons per acre.

In the terraced fields of the high Himalayas, women peasants grow *Jhangora* (barnyard millet), *Marsha* (amaranth), *Tue* (pigeon pea), *Urad* (black gram), *Gahat* (horse gram), soybean (Glycine max), *Bhat* (Glycine soya), *Rayans* (rice bean), *Swanta* (cow pea), and *Koda* (finger millet) in mixtures and rotations. The total output is nearly 6,000 kilograms per acre, which is nearly six times more than industrially farmed rice monocultures.

The work of the Research Foundation for Science, Technology and Ecology has shown that farm incomes can increase threefold by giving up chemicals and using internal inputs produced by on-farm biodiversity, including straw, animal manure, and other by-products.[3]

Research done by FAO, the United Nation's Food and Agriculture Organization, has shown that small, biodiverse farms can produce thousands of times more food than large, industrial monocultures. Indigenous farmers of the Andes grow more than 3,000 varieties of potatoes, and in Papua New Guinea as many as 5,000 varieties of sweet potatoes are under cultivation, with more than 20 varieties grown in a single garden.[4] In Java, small farmers cultivate 607 species in their home gardens, with an overall species diversity comparable to a deciduous tropical forest. In sub-Saharan Africa, women cultivate as many as 120 different plants in the spaces left alongside the cash crops. A single home garden in Thailand has more than 230 species, and African home gardens have more than 60 species of trees. Rural families in the Congo eat leaves from more than 50 different species of trees. A study in eastern Nigeria found that home gardens occupying only 2 percent of a household's farmland accounted for half of the farm's total output. Similarly, home gardens in Indonesia are estimated to provide more than 20 percent of domestic food supplies.[5]

The assumption of an inverse relationship between biodiversity and

195

productivity has guided all technological change in agriculture, destroying biodiversity. Yet it does not hold when one takes diversity of crops and their diverse outputs into account. The increased yields from genetically engineered crops is the most important argument used by the genetic engineering industry. However, genetic engineering has actually led to a decline in yields. Bill Christianson, a soybean farmer in the U.S. who participated in a 1998 conference on "Biodevastation" held in St Louis, Missouri, home of the headquarters of Monsanto, says that in Missouri, genetically engineered soya had a bushel per acre decrease in yield.[6] According to Ed Oplinger, Professor of Agronomy at the University of Wisconsin, who has been carrying out yield trials on soybean for twenty-five years, genetically engineered soybeans had 4 percent lower yields than conventional varieties on the basis of data he collected in twelve states that grow 80 percent of U.S. soybeans.[7] In a study by Marc Lappe and Britt Bailey, in 30 out of 38 varieties, the conventional soybeans outperformed the transgenic ones, with an overall drop in yield of 3.34 bushels per acre, or a 10 percent reduction compared to conventional varieties.[8] Dr. Charles Benbrook has reported a 6.7 percent decline in yields in soybeans engineered to be resistant to RoundUp on the basis of 8,200 university-based soybean varietal trials in 1998. In his view, "If not reversed by future breeding enhancements, this downward shift in soybean yield poten-

tial could emerge as the most significant decline in a major crop ever associated with a single genetic modification."[9] The yield of Bt cotton was found to be dramatically reduced in the first Bt trials undertaken in India.

Speed and biohazards

Speed has been at the root of ecological crisis in agriculture. Speed is the justification for shifting from organic manures to synthetic fertilizers. Speed is the justification for shifting from harvesting the biodiversity of "weeds" to destroying them with herbicides such as RoundUp. Speed is the justification for using genetic engineering on crop breeding. Speed is the justification for rushing GMOs to the marketplace without tests and evaluations. GMOs were rushed into the marketplace with a *declaration* of safety, not tests for safety, without assessment of productivity or risks.

The safety debate has been repeatedly suppressed by bad science parading as "sound science." One of the unscientific strategies used to extinguish the safety discussion is to tautologically define a novel organism or novel food created through genetic engineering as "substantially equivalent" to conventional organisms and foods. However, a genetically engineered crop or food is different because it has genes from unrelated organisms—it cannot, therefore, be treated as equivalent to a non-genetically engineered crop or food. In fact, the biotechnology industry itself gives up the claim of "substantial equivalence" when it claims patents on GMOs on grounds of novelty.

When the claims for safety and for intellectual property rights in the genetic engineering industry are put together, what emerges is an unscientific, undemocratic demand for total control, whereby absolute rights are claimed and all responsibility is denied and disclaimed. This ontological schizophrenia is based on and leads to incoherence, which is characteristic of bad science.

The global citizens' call for a five-year freeze on release of GMOs into our agriculture and food systems is a necessary pause that should induce responsibility, sanity, and safety in the insane rush to sell GMOs at any cost, including irreversible risks to biodiversity and human health. Slowing down the GMO madness is an essential part of the Slow Food Movement because the transgenetics culture will destroy the ecological and economic foundations on which Slow Food cultures have been based. In this pause we can build and strengthen food cultures based on small farms, biodiversity, and ecological time in place of giant corporations, monocultures, and Wall Street time.

Notes

1. A. E. Greene and R. F. Allison, "Viruses and Transgenic Crops." *Science* 263 (1994), pp. 1423–1424.

2.a) V. Shiva, *Biodiversity-Based Productivity*. New Delhi: Research Foundation for Science, Technology, and Ecology, 1996.

b) P. Rosset and M. Altieri, *The Productivity of Small Scale Agriculture*, IFA White Paper, 1999.

3. D. Deb, *Case study: Bengal*, and V. Bhatt, *Case Study: Himalaya*, RFSTE, 1999.

4. V. H. Heywood, *Global Biodiversity Assessment*, UNEP, Cambridge University Press, 1995, p. 724.

5. FAO, *Women Feed the World*, World Food Day, 16 October 1998.

6. Statement of Bill Christianson at First Grassroots Gathering on Biodevastation, St. Louis, Mo., 18 July 1998.

7. D. Holzman, *Agricultural Biotechnology: Report Leads to Debate on Benefits of Transgenic Corn and Soya bean crops*, "Genetic Engineering News," Vol. 19 No. 8, 15 April 1999.

8. M. Lappe and B. Bailey, *Against the Grain*, Earthscan. London 1999, pp. 82–83.

9. C. Benbrook, *Evidence of the Magnitude and Consequences of the RoundUp Ready Soybean Yield Drag from University-Based Varietal Trials in 1998*, Ag Biotech Info Net Technical Paper Number 1, 13 July 1999.

Chapter ELEVEN

Cheese and Cheese Makers

ELEVEN:1

TYPICAL?

Piero Sardo

The history of Gorgonzola is an ideal "case in point." It is not known exactly when this famous blue cheese was invented, but it derives from *stracchino*, one of the most widespread cheeses in northern Italy. *stracchino*, incidentally, is so named because it is made of milk from cows tired out *(stracco)* by their return from summer pastures.

What probably happened was that a dairyman forgot some curds dripping in a sack overnight: the next morning, to avoid his employer's reprimands, he decided to crumble the curd that had hardened in the meantime and to add it to the fresh curd. The result was surprising: after a short time the cheese became naturally streaked with green mold, which gave it a more agreeable piquancy. A different version tells how an innkeeper in the town of Gorgonzola was left with a quantity of unsold *stracchino* that grew mold all over. Instead of throwing it away, he decided to offer it to his customers as a specialty. The success was such that from then onward the innkeeper ordered artfully moldy *stracchino* from the dairies. The so-called "double curd" or "old-style" Gorgonzola was born.

The mold proliferated naturally in the spaces that inevitably formed after combining the mixtures, and its development was favored by the environment in which the cheese matured. Gorgonzola was left to age in *casere*, the naturally damp and ventilated caves in Valsassina. Transporting the rounds of cheese to the mountains, arranging them on planks, then turning and cleaning them with exasperating regularity was a thankless task. However, the cheese made following this procedure was excellent, indeed so good that it was exported throughout the world. Demand grew to such an extent that it was no longer possible for all the cheese to be aged in *casere*. In 1860, Mattia Locatelli, the owner of a large cheese factory, decided to build a big maturing plant in Ballabio, where modern techniques were used to mature and refine the cheese. That day marked the end of "old-style" Gorgonzola, which was made by mixing two different curds. It also marked the birth of soft, dripping, industrial Gorgonzola, which today dominates the market.

But why is the history of Gorgonzola emblematic? Because it illustrates a case in which industry plays its role to the full: inventing, rationalizing, mechanizing, and transferring a process to a large scale without misrepresenting the allegedly traditional product. Indeed, with soft, single-curd Gorgonzola impregnated with mold, industry invented a new cheese. Over time, industry dictated the rules, methods, and timing for its production. The outcome is thus a typical cheese, in the true sense of the word.

Local and traditional

What considerations underlie this statement? The word typical derives from the Latin *typum*, which in turn can be traced to the Greek *typtein* (to beat), and means: statue, model, manner, character. Furthermore, the use of the word typical in everyday language is relatively recent: in the Rigutini-Fanfani dictionary of 1893, the term *tipicità* ("typicality") is not included. Today the term is so overused that it is hard to work out where it should apply. We propose that "typical" should be used to refer to certain food products that meet codified regulations.

The term typical can be applied to Gorgonzola, Parma ham, DOC, and DOCG wines. This does not necessarily imply that typical goes hand in hand with "industrial," but it certainly does not exclude modern production methods. To remain within the compass of cheese, Parmigiano Reggiano provides an example of large-scale production (approximately three million rounds of Parmesan per year), which is rigidly codified at every stage, from the raising of the cows to the maturing of the rounds of cheese. Production is colossal in financial terms, yet it remains an artisanal process. Parmesan is made in small dairies scattered throughout the area with which they have a strong interactive relationship. Parmesan is not a standardized product, yet it is a typical product.

On the other hand, "local produce" is an appropriate epithet for all produce outside the specific regions of origin, particularly in Alpine and Apennine huts and in small sheepfolds, which in the main use milk from indigenous and rare breeds. Most of the cheese they produce is also "traditional." Within the overall picture of Italian cheese production, this galaxy of historic local cheeses barely makes up 1 percent of the total. This is a trifle from the point of view of quantity, but constitutes an exceptional cultural patrimony.

These cheeses are made with rudimentary techniques from unpasteurized milk in places that do not meet current health and safety regulations. The equipment used is often handmade and crafted from materials considered to be unhygienic. Though such cheeses often reveal defects of production or maturing, they embody time-honored skills and a unique link with the land. Moreover, when they are free of defects they can achieve exceptional organoleptic qualities. Being a local product is a necessary but not a sufficient condition for being deemed an excellent complex cheese. Industrial cheese can be pleasing, seductive, light, and of a constant, guaranteed quality, but it will never be a complex cheese. On the one hand, we have a food that can often be very good, and on the other we have a cultural treasure.

ELEVEN:2

TUMALO TOMME IN OREGON

Sarah Heekin Redfield

It's been over a decade since lawyer-*cum*-cheese maker Pierre Kolisch bought his orchard-studded farm in the high desert territory of central Oregon in the western United States, a place far from the enchantment of the Alps and best known for its cowboy lore and desolate big-sky sunsets—quite an unlikely place in which to become both a producer and purveyor of gourmet goat cheeses including *chevre*, *buche*, and most recently an alpine *tomme*.

"*Tomme?*" I asked my husband. He came walking into our kitchen carrying a 4-pound wheel of cheese wrapped in brown parchment paper. "*Tomme*," he said knowingly as he shook flakes of hay off his shoulders and onto the floor. My husband is a farmer and wastes no time. "Let's try it, now," he said as he set the wheel on the worn wooden counter and opened the paper wrapping, exposing a blotchy, orange-colored, washed rind with the aroma of wet grass. I quickly opened the utensil drawer and pulled out our sharpest knife.

As befits a farmer, my husband came by way of this cheese through barter. He supplies Kolisch with lucerne (alfalfa) for his ninety-plus goat herd, and the wheel of *tomme* was partial payment. I, on the other hand, came by way of my ignorance about cheese varieties from growing up in southern Indiana where a sharp cheddar made up north in Wisconsin was considered exotic. "Taste this," my husband said, cutting me a small wedge from the wheel and placing it onto a plate. I sliced bread from a loaf, coupled the two and took a bite.

Then I took another and another and another, finally deciding that this *tomme*, this rarity that I had never tasted before, was one of the best cheeses I'd ever eaten. Its semi-soft texture, pitted with very small holes, had a subtle but rich, earthy flavor that

conjured up the notion of early rural traditions, the product of a family recipe shared through the generations like an heirloom. Knowing that this wheel of *tomme* was fresh and delivered directly from the cheese maker, not in a supermarket bag nor in plastic wrap with a label, made the experience of eating it all the more special— it was a step back in time.

Tomme was first introduced into French cheese culture during the 14th century, when the monks of L'Abbaye de Saint Abondance, situated in the Alps on the Swiss border, were charged with the responsibility of supplying the Pope in Avignon with savoyard cheeses. The Tomme d'Abondance, which is still available today, was named after the breed of cow that produced the milk for the cheese. The other varieties of *tomme* found throughout the Alpine region, including the Basque country, are named after their respective villages, towns, and provinces: Tomme des Chouans, Tomme de Savoie, Tomme d'Arles, Tomme Brûlée, and Tomme Lullin, to name a few. Characteristics also differ from *tomme* to *tomme*: rinds are washed, floured, or seared; shapes can be round or cylindrical; some *tommes* are made with cow's milk, skimmed milk, or ewe's milk, all unpasteurized—though few are produced from goat's milk. Thus Kolisch's Tumalo Tomme, also named after the region where the cheese is made, is not only unique to its surroundings but also to the international cheese market.

201

Raw milk

It is mid-morning and the sun is shining at Juniper Grove Farm, Kolisch's five-acre parcel that houses several goat sheds, grazing pastures, a cheese production facility, garden, orchard, and home. This is where Kolisch began his dream. A longtime enthusiast of all things rural, Kolisch finally left the fast-paced life of corporate law in southern California to begin "a life that allowed me to live in a natural and harmonious setting." After an apprenticeship lasting several years in Normandy with teacher and mentor François Durand, Kolisch came back to Oregon and started his herd with four goats. And in the small, rustic kitchen of his house—experimenting with recipes and techniques he'd learned in France—Kolisch adapted and perfected methods so as to make gourmet goat cheese, desert-style.

"This region of Oregon has absolutely no history of cheese," says Kolisch amid a chorus of bleating coming from the goat sheds. "This region has traditionally been used for cattle ranching and limited farming, and still is today, though the variables here are excellent for making good cheese. I'm still the only non-industrial cheese maker for hundreds of miles around." The variables Kolisch speaks of are the dry climate, high elevation, air quality, lack of insects, and most importantly, purity of water—which he and his family drink from the tap. "Eighty-eight percent of milk is water," Kolisch adds, "so having quali-ty water for your goats, cows, or sheep is one way to contribute to the goodness of the cheese."

Another way, one that is well rooted in the cheese-making philosophy, is to adhere to the tradition of making *tomme* from raw milk. Because production of Tumalo Tomme is still small enough, Kolisch explains, even here in the United States the government standards can't interfere with his decision to use unpasteurized goat's milk.

"But if I increase my output, I'll have a problem," he admits. As it is, he is obliged by law to use pasteurized milk for the making of his *chevre* and *buche*.

"Probably the most important reason behind my choosing to make *tomme* my priority for production and sales is the fact that it calls for the use of raw milk. That's how it has to be made, it's the way I think all cheese should be made; 'modernizing' the process detracts from cheese making as an art form and it changes the taste radically. Even specialty cheeses like mine can become generic in taste."

Kolisch's version of the ideal cheese-making scenario is as follows: A farmer with his an wooden bucket milks the cows, sheep, or goats until the bucket is full, then places it where the milk can turn and become the type of cheese the farmer desires. Natural bacteria from the farmer's hands, from the air, from the age of the bucket, all take part in the curdling and fermentation of the milk. It is this organic process that gives the cheese its savor, its identity, its soul. "Every farm has a different set of variables," says Kolisch, "and those differences give each cheese from each farm and town and region its very own unique taste. Each cheese tells its own story." As Italo Calvino declared, "behind every cheese there is different green pasture blessed by a different sky."

At present here in the United States, the American Cheese Society is taking action to help enable specialty cheese makers such as Kolisch to use unpasteurized milk for cheese making. And not just for the aesthetics and taste. Cost of production is also an issue.

The American cheese culture for years has been limited to the state of Wisconsin and to industrial dairies. It's only been in the last forty years that small regional farmsteads specializing in gourmet cheeses have come into existence. "We need to be here," Kolisch insists. "Not only does the American consumer want local gourmet cheeses, but our culinary culture can't evolve if we're not here." The problem, Kolisch adds, is that with the required use of pasteurized milk, yes, there is the loss of flavor in the cheese but there are also overwhelming costs for production. "The economics of the laws mandated to small cheese makers and small dairies makes it hard for us to survive." Cheese sales for Kolisch have been steady over the past few years. His distributor, Eurobest—based in Portland, some 160 miles northwest of Tumalo—places his cheeses in supermarkets as well as specialty shops and delis. But the affinage (period of maturization) for the *chevre* and the *buche* are so short that Kolisch is more interested in focusing solely on the *tomme,* a cheese that can easily be shipped worldwide and has a longer affinage, ideally three months for *tomme* produced from summer milk and four months plus for *tomme* produced in the fall.

Kolisch says he also likes the variety of uses for *tomme*: aside from the joy of eating it with good bread, it makes an excellent fondue, cheese sauce, and stuffing, and once hardened is a great alternative to Parmesan. In its flexibility it also goes well with both red and white wines, and most fruits as well. Kolisch's Tumalo Tomme is truly a cheese for all seasons.

The sun is now higher in the sky and Kolisch dons his white boots and apron. It's time to cut, then hand-ladle the whey from the curd and set the forms. Kolisch looks at the milk tubs thoughtfully. "I think about my son being a cheese maker," he says as he begins to cut the large curd with a tool that resembles a saw blade, "so he continues the traditions that I've started and borrowed from: preserving the old ways. Maybe it's just me, but sometimes I think there's more progress in taking a giant step back rather than forward."

On the table in Kolisch's spartan office there is a cheese board with a wedge of the *tomme*.

I smile to myself, inhaling the lingering smells from the storeroom as I reach down to slice a piece. How often do we get to taste history?

"TOMA": TO BE OR NOT TO BE

Vincenzo Gerbi

Ever since it was awarded the National Denomination of Origin in 1993 and Community-wide Denomination of Protected Origin in 1996, Piedmontese Toma cheese has acquired the masculine article "il" like other stars of this region's dairy universe—"il" Grana, "il" Gorgonzola, "il" Bra, and so forth. To its people, however, this product will always remain "la Töma," though they feel proud that the distinctive quality of this most ancient product of their alpine valleys has finally been recognized.

Together with other agencies and producers' associations, we were able to contribute to a recent survey of Toma conducted by Piedmont's regional authorities. The outstanding feature turned out to be the great variety of producers: from the *margaro*, who makes Tomas with rudimentary equipment only in summer when grazing his herds, to the plain-based dairy producing cheese all year round in technologically advanced facilities.

In terms of volume, the production of Toma is outstanding, although the amount sold directly by producers cannot be assessed with certainty. It ranks third in Piedmont, coming just after the more famous Gorgonzola and Grana, and thus outdoing such noble products as Bra and Raschera. Indeed, Toma is enormously popular throughout almost all the mountainous and hilly areas of Piedmont's alpine chain. The province of Turin, including the Susa, Lanzo, and Chisone valleys, takes pride of place, followed by Biella, Cuneo, Vercelli, and Novara. Based on the data supplied by the Consorzio di Tutela (Protection Syndicate), 30 dairies alone account for over 60 percent of the entire production, the remainder being supplied by 321 processing facilities. Traditionally, Toma is a single-cream cheese—that is, made from partially skimmed milk. It is made by letting the milk drawn off at night come to the surface then mixing it with the one drained in the morning. When the uncooked milk is left surfacing, its acidity increases due to its spontaneous microflora. Today, milk is still skimmed by most producers, although the tendency is to abandon this practice gradually in view of the

decreasing interest in butter. As a consequence, Toma is becoming fatter, creamier, and less resilient.

The traditional production of cheese from uncooked milk presents some health hazards associated with the possible presence of a scarce, abundant, or anti-cheese microbial colony in the raw material. Today's dairy practices are based on the use of pasteurized milk, subsequently inoculated with efficient and safe micorobial cultures. Pasteurized milk is safer, in that the process kills possible pathogenic microorganisms. Indeed, all bottom-of-the-valley and plain-based dairies process pasteurized and whole milk to obtain the so-called *toma grassa* (fat Toma), which is now the product most frequently supplied to dairy shops and supermarkets.

Generally speaking, the consumption of cheese made from uncooked milk does not pose any health hazards to consumers when eaten at least 30 days after production. This applies to Toma as well, which is usually sold after 45 to 60 days of maturation. The drawbacks of uncooked milk are mainly technological: the presence of an unsuitable micoroflora can produce negative effects on the maturation of cheese, form low acidification and insufficient bleeding to excessive formation of holes and anomalous smell and flavor, just to mention a few. Obversely, thanks to the assets of natural microbes resulting from environmental conditions, uncooked milk can give cheese a unique flavor and taste rarely obtainable in products made from pasteurized milk. In other words, uncooked milk provides greater opportunities to produce original cheese, maybe with some defects, but with a strongly characterized taste and flavor.

Bacteria and bureaucrats

The enforcement of D.P.R. (Presidential Decree) 54 of January 14, 1997, implementing European Community directives 92/46 and 92/47—which impose stricter controls on milk and dairy products with the aim of safeguarding consumers' health—could jeopardize the survival of the *margaro* and consequently undermine the use of summer pastures.

On the one hand, we agree unconditionally on the limits set by directives for the content of bacteria and somatic cells in milk. There is no doubt that producers should do their utmost to improve the hygienic conditions of their farms and business premises. Yet it is also true that small producers would go out of business if they followed all the bureaucratic standards and facility specifications to the letter.

Fortunately, the above-mentioned directives do not apply to businesses selling directly to consumers, and special conditions are envisaged for small plants with an output of less than 5,000 kilograms of milk per day.

The survey reveals that 50 percent of all dairies sell Tomas in-house or at outdoor markets, even though in most cases, a part of their production is supplied to wholesalers, retailers, or supermarkets. There are only a few businesses whose facilities have been certified by the relevant health authorities and who thus market their entire output directly. Such certification is clearly an insurmountable obstacle for summer pastures, some of which cannot meet such vital requirements as the availability of fresh water for the processing of milk. Many producers may thus be forced to close down their dairies and restrict their activity to the sale of milk, because they cannot afford the cost of complying with the law.

Would this be a great loss or simply a natural step in the direction of increased product rationalization and standardization that would ultimately benefit the consumer? At this point we should perhaps add that, according to our survey, the vast majority of the hundreds of cheese samples examined conformed to the limits of pathogenic microbes set by D.P.R. 54 for cheese, which rather suggests that after 30 days even cheese made from uncooked milk in deficient hygienic conditions pose no serious hazards to consumers' health.

As far as chemical composition is concerned, single-cream Tomas (with a fat content between 20 and 40 percent assessed on the dry substance) are now a minority (appoximately 25 percent), since this cheese type generally contains 40 to 48 percent fats. The remaining Tomas are very heterogeneous, both in terms of maturation and salt content.

Categories

The Tomas supplied today by large, medium-sized, or small dairies can be divided into three categories, based on their sensory qualities.

• The first includes Tomas made by large, usually plain-based dairies form pasteurized milk. They are generally softer and creamier, have a pleasant, rather sweet taste, show no organoleptic defects, but also no unique traits. They are often similar to other types of cheese, Italian-style soft cheese.

• The second includes Tomas made in medium-sized, alpine valley-based dairies, mainly from partially skimmed, uncooked milk. Their organoleptic features vary largely in terms of acidity, softness, proteolysis, and taste. Sometimes their defects are very marked (bitter taste, smell of ammonia), other times their quality is excellent. This is the most promising category as far as enhancing the image of Toma is concerned.

• The third includes Tomas made with rudimentary equipment by small or very small businesses or dairies such as those set up in the mountains

in summer pastures. Their quality varies even more than the previous category's, as it is sometimes excellent but often extremely poor, due to unacceptable defects caused by serious mistakes in milk processing and cheese production. Yet, owing to the great demand for these types of Toma from consumers who like traditional alpine products, they continue to sell quite well. However, this is no justification for the intolerable backwardness of some of their producers' facilities.

Greater standardization of production would be good. Standardizing does not necessarily mean massifying small-scale production up to industrial levels, but making use of the sort of technology that can guarantee a "zero defect" output while preserving diversity that derives from local traditions and the raw material used.

To safeguard and enhance the traditional Toma, it is necessary to preserve summer pastures and stimulate the *margari* to upgrade their technology. This also requires an extensive professional retraining program, as well as targeted business reorganization schemes. If this is not done, not only will the Toma lose its ancient taste, but the whole alpine environment will change irreversibly, and not for the better.

ELEVEN:4

FARM WITH A VIEW

Sarah Freeman

If you travel around the cheese farms of Britain and Ireland, you cannot fail to notice how many of them are in exceptionally lovely locations. You might expect them to be in attractive parts of the country, since the hillier, wetter, western side of the islands is more suitable for dairy farming than the east; this, however, is not enough to explain the number with splendid views or situated in isolated spots that you could hardly imagine still exist in modern Britain. Sleight Farm, where Mary Holbrook makes some of the most outstanding cheeses in the United Kingdom, is on the summit of a hill near Bath with a view over the Bristol Channel to South Wales; Charlie Westhead of Neal's Yard Creamery works on top of Dorstone Hill in Herefordshire, from which you can see as far as the Malvern Hills; Isle of Mull Cheddar, to name another, is produced on that island against a skyline of the mountains of the west coast of Scotland. Similarly, Leon Downey, whose hard cheeses consistently win top awards, also deserves an award for the prettiest farm in Wales. Penybont, a hard goats' cheese made by Alan and Karen Reynolds; John and Patrice Savage-Onstwedder's Teifi, the Supreme Champion at last year's British Cheese Awards; Carraig,

St. Tola, and Coolea from Ireland; the Nut Knowle Farm goats' cheeses; and many others all come from places that seem completely cut off from civilization. Do cheese and an aesthetic appreciation of the countryside go together?

The answer is that nearly half the farmhouse cheese makers in Britain now do not come from farming or cheese-making backgrounds but have "downshifted," rejected the consumerist values of urban society, and opted for a rural way of life. The most publicized example of downshifting is the case of Alan and Karen Reynolds, who were among the subjects of a four-part television documentary, *The Good Life*. Both of them grew up in the London area: Alan worked at an employment agency and Karen for Shell in the Shell building on the South Bank. To start with, Alan enjoyed his job, but Karen found hers increasingly boring. Then she was laid off, and while she was unemployed had their two daughters, Alice and Katie. Soon, Alan too began to feel dissatisfied: "I was working long hours and never saw the children except at weekends. The job seemed totally pointless. I felt that I was going nowhere. We spend a lot of time discussing possible alternatives. Neither of us is afraid of hard work, so we felt sure that we could make a success of some kind of small business." They chose cheese-making because "we wanted something to do with animals, and Karen likes cooking, which isn't the same as cheese but is still a food product."

They now live on a small farm in one of the loneliest areas of central Wales. At the time they moved, the farm was depressingly shabby and run-down, though potentially very charming. The first year was hard. The goats developed worms and played any number of tricks, including going into the milking parlor twice for the sake of an extra ration of the food that they are given during milking. As the Reynolds soon found, the milk changes with the seasons and the cheese making process has to be modified accordingly. However, they survived, and are now supremely happy, not only on their own account but the children's. "The life here is fantastic for children. We don't worry about crime. The whole environment is friendly. People will help you just because you're a neighbor." As for missing anything from their past life: "We never have the time. We don't even have a TV."

Mary and Leon

The only instruction Alan and Karen had before moving was a course in goat-keeping and a fraught weekend learning how to make the cheese with their predecessor. Mary Holbrook and Leon Downey were in an easier situation in that both had farming connections, although neither had had any formal training in cheese making. Mary worked for many years as a museum curator: she eventually resigned because she was "fed up with bureaucracy." Of course, as she says, there is now more bureaucracy to contend with in farming than there was then in curating; however, "it postponed it for a few years." As it happened, her husband's family were farmers and they went to live on the family farm, which was not Sleight, on top of the hill, but in the nearby village, Timsbury. In due course, her husband took over the farm; they bought Sleight, with its view, later. Mary had no particular thought of making cheese, but bought a couple of goats, which led to her making feta simply because she had to do

specialist cheesemakers' association

One Saturday morning in February 1989, the British Minister of Agriculture announced his intention of banning the sale of cheeses made from unpasteurized milk. On that very morning, the Specialist Cheesemakers' Association was founded. Their immediate objective was to clarify the matter and to explain the consequences of this decision to the Minister. It was clear from the outset that they had wide support from producers and the public. The Milk Marketing Board soon provided help with funding, secretarial staff, and administrative support.

Thanks to the work completed over the years, the Association is today in a position to communicate with the government, media, and the public, but above all it is influential in ensuring that output of quality cheese is on the increase and that the growing public is duly informed of such developments.

According to chairman Randolph Hodgson, the Association's strength lies in communication. "There is no sense on going flat out to produce the best cheeses in the world if no one knows of their existence." For years it was thought that there was no market for excellent handmade cheeses that were only available locally. As a result, many farmhouse cheeses were unknown to enthusiasts simply because they were not in the usual shops and markets.

The aims of the Specialist Cheesemakers' Association are to promote the knowledge and appreciation of specialist cheeses, provide a forum in which members can exchange ideas and points of view, present a united front to the authorities and the media, and encourage the small-scale production of excellent cheeses made according to traditional methods and even using unpasteurized milk. The Association's members include British and Irish producers, wholesale merchants, shopkeepers, restaurants, journalists, and cheese enthusiasts. Members keep in touch through the newsletter, occasional conferences, and meetings, which Hodgson believes have proved to be extremely useful. "An example of what the Association can do . . . A producer who had only just set up in business came to the Harrogate conference with his cheeses. In a matter of a few hours he succeeded in contacting a farmhouse Cheddar selector, production experts, four buyers, and a large number of producers. I would have given anything for a day like that at the beginning of my career."

Under the patronage of Prince Charles, Juliet Harbutt has compiled the *Guide to the Finest Cheeses of Britain and Ireland* for the

Association. Besides listing all the types of cheese, which are cata-
logued according to the milk used, the guide provides information
about cutting, packing, and storing, as well as the addresses of
about one hundred of the best British and Irish cheese shops. The
guide can be ordered from the Association.

—Simona Luparia

Specialist Cheesemakers' Association
PO Box 448
Newcastle under Lyme
Staffordshire ST5 OBF England
Tel. ++44/1782/580580
Fax ++44/1782/580680

something with the milk (a common situation: Lyn and Jenny Jenner, who make the Nut Knowle Farm cheeses, are among those who started for the same reason). Later, Mary added sheep to the goats because authentic feta is a sheep's cheese. She now makes a total of seven cheeses, including Tilleys, a hard goat's cheese coagulated with extract of cardoons rather than rennet, and two exceptionally deep-tasting, white-mold-rind sheep's cheeses, Emlett and Little Ryding (named after fields on the farm).

Less surprisingly than it may seem at first sight, Leon Downey turned to cheese after a successful career as a musician. His grandparents were farmers, and as a boy he spent every weekend helping with the cows and watching his grandmother make Cheshire. Choosing a career meant a tug-of-war between music and farming: music won, but only for a time.

After fifteen years as co-principal viola player with the Hallé Orchestra, he reverted to his second love and bought Llangloffan, teaching himself to make cheese, as he often says, by means of genes and a cheese-making kit. However, although he has given up music, he still performs. From April to October, he invites the public into his dairy to watch him at work. Partly because cheese making seems to have the same appeal as cookery demonstrations, but also because of his personality, people come, often by the hundreds. Perhaps following his example, other dairies have now opened their doors, which promotes not only interest in cheese but trust. When you actually see the makers exercising their skill and judgment and observe the impeccable hygiene that is maintained at every stage, you cannot doubt the outcome's wholesomeness.

Charlie Westhead is not exactly a

211

downshifter, since he rebelled from the start. "I was a product of the Thatcher generation. Everything was very materialistic, and I didn't want to have any part of that. I was into punk rock and didn't know what I wanted to do. I kept racking my brains for something that was sound, good, honest, and would never do anybody any harm." Instead of going to university and following his father into a profession, he wandered around London picking up work where he could and eventually found himself on the cheese counter at a delicatessen in Balham, which he enjoyed. From there, he went to a cheese shop in Belgravia, where he met Juliet Harbutt, and at her suggestion he asked for a job at Neal's Yard Dairy, the famous cheese shop in Covent Garden that specializes in British farmhouse cheeses. At first, he was told that no jobs were available, but he was so enthused by the staff and the atmosphere that he returned every Saturday until Randolph Hodgson, who runs the shop, gave in and let him stay. He graduated from selling cheeses to collecting them from the farms, which brought him into contact with the makers and set him thinking about cheese making himself. The Dairy had begun as a real dairy, selling yogurt and fresh cheeses that were made on the premises: after Randolph branched out into selling a wider range of cheese, space became an increasing problem and Charlie, seeing his opportunity, offered to take the production of the original yogurt and cheese elsewhere. He thus moved, first to a tiny farm on the crest of the North Downs, which had a view at least as spectacular as he has now, and subsequently to Herefordshire.

Goat, ewe, and buffalo

The remarkable revival in British farmhouse cheese that has taken place over the last fifteen years owes much to Randolph Hodgson at Neal's Yard Dairy, and also to James Aldridge, who for a time ran a similar shop in Beckenham. When they began trying to sell artisanal regional cheese, they found that hardly any was made, and had to seek it out in order to stock their shops. The immediate cause of the shortage was the policy followed during and after World War Two, which meant that until the mid-1950s, farmhouse cheese making was effectively prohibited: during this time, nearly all the traditional cheese makers disappeared. In actual fact, the decline began in the last century with railway transport and refrigeration, which encouraged farmers to sell liquid milk rather than bothering to turn it into cheese. Cheese factories, colonial imports, and the formation of the Milk Marketing Board in 1933 also contributed. It did not help that, in contrast to the French, the British had never regarded cheese (except perhaps Stilton) as a fashionable, gastronomic item; until people took holidays abroad and tasted Continental cheeses in all their variety, cheese was generally regarded as merely a cheaper substitute for meat.

One particularly helpful factor is that knowledge of Continental cheeses has helped to break down the prejudice that had long prevailed in Britain against goat's and sheep's products. This has opened an uncontested field for the new makers—as also, in the last couple years, has buffalo cheese. All three have the further advantage of being exempt from the milk quota that, by inhibiting expansion, has been a further factor in encouraging cheese making on small and middle-sized farms. However, we still need more real (that is, unpasteurized, handmade) cheese and, as this can only be made in small quantities, more cheese makers. With the new millennium, there is a more holistic, less consumerist feel in the air—and we still have plenty of hills with splendid views. What we need now, as I have said elsewhere, are accessible, comprehensive courses designed for the small cheese maker. Alan and Karen made no money for a year and had to sort out their problems with the help of James Aldridge, who now acts as an unofficial consultant. We also need greater recognition of our new *real* cheese abroad. We are a natural dairying country, with arguably the best grazing in Europe: our cheeses are now of commensurate quality and can stand comparison with any in the world.

Cheeses

Alan and Karen Reynolds

Penybont. A semi-hard goat's cheese with a slight lemon-like tang and hints of flowers in the summer. 1.8–2 kilogram truckles.

Mary Holbrook

All Mary's cheeses are warm-tasting and subtle but distinctive, with flavors of earth, mushrooms, and nuts.

Sleight. A fresh goat's log, plain or coated with pepper, rosemary, or garlic and herbs. 115 grams.

Tymsboro. An unpressed goat's cheese with a penicillin rind coated with ash. 225-gram pyramids.

Tilleys. A semi-hard or hard goat's cheese according to age, made with extract of cardoons rather than rennet. 1.2-kilogram rounds.

Emlett. An unpressed sheep's cheese with a penicillin rind. 175-gram rounds.

Little Ryding. Similar to *Emlett* but more powerful. 200-gram rounds.

Tyning. A hard sheep's cheese that gains strength with maturity: at a year it makes an ideal substitute for pecorino. 2.3–3.2-kilogram baskets.

Feta. A fresh sheep's cheese preserved in brine. 900-gram blocks.

Leon Downey

Llangloffan. A hard cow's cheese with a soft, buttery taste; mild or stronger according to age. Plain or flavored with chives and garlic. 1.4 kilograms, 4.5 kilograms, or 13.5 kilograms.

Llangloffan Red Cheese. A semi-hard cow's cheese, remarkable in particular for its airy, melting texture. Also plain or flavored with chives and garlic. 4.5 kilograms or 13.5 kilograms.

Charlie Westhead

Neal's Yard Creamery Goat's Curds. Fresh curds: in particular, excellent for cooking. Sold by weight.

Perroche. A fresh goat's cheese: very mild and sweet, with an exceptionally light texture. Plain or flavored with rosemary, tarragon, or dill. 150-gram rounds.

Ragstone. A goat's log with a penicillin rind and flavors of herbs and honey. 200 grams.

Wealden Round. A singularly delicate fresh cow's cheese flavored with tarragon, chives, parsley and garlic, or spring onions. 200-gram rounds.

Finn. An unpressed cow's cheese with added cream and a penicillin rind: mild but with a distinctive, cheesy tang. 200-gram rounds.

Chapter TWELVE

Wines and Vines

TWELVE:1

CONFORMITY

Hugh Johnson

It has recently become part of the accepted wisdom of the wine world to speak with foreboding about universal homogenization.

The ABC movement (Anything But Chardonnay/Cabernet) is agitated by two very different causes. One is personal boredom. Surely wine can be more varied and interesting than this? The other is an environmentalist's concern for loss of genetic variety and the threat to endangered species.

The wine industry has not been slow to react to the first concern. The range of varieties being planted and promoted today in nearly all the New World regions is becoming impressive. Not just Shiraz and Merlot, Sauvignon Blanc and Semillon, Riesling and Pinot Noir, but many more obscure varieties are getting a trial. Their prospects will be decided first by the farmers (if they are hard to grow their chances are slim) and then by us, the market. My feeling is that really good varieties are not likely to be overlooked, at least in the long run.

There is a strong urge among older regions, in Italy for example, to revive even forgotten specialties to help boost regional identity. In Switzerland, I understand, the Vallais is a hotbed of archaeological viticulture, with Humagnes and Arvines popping up everywhere.

There is a tendency to confuse the widely marketed popular wines with the more discriminating specialist market. There have always been at least two levels of market. It is good to know that wine is now a regular part of the diet of Britain, Australia, even of parts of the United States—countries with little or no popular wine tradition. But one should not expect the mass market to be discriminating. It is doing very well, it seems to me, to have retained the names of a few grape varieties where it used to buy just Mateus, Piat, Liebfraumilch, or some other brand.

The educated market with real curiosity about wine is quite another thing. It is young (older "connoisseurs" were rarely very curious) but growing, and willing to pay. Such books as Remington Norman's *Rhône Renaissance* have an eager audience. There is a thriving class of wine professionals in restaurants and retail stores whose stock-in-trade is the latest knowledge. I see this as a fertile ground for imaginative trials of old grapes in new places, or indeed old places.

Meanwhile, we should remember that in some of the most successful and popular wines in the world the grape variety(ies) is a given. No discussion. Nothing is better value (especially in recent splendid vintages) than Villages and Crus Beaujolais, or that unique but under-appreciated wine, Muscadet. What we are talking about here is not the variety (okay, Muscadet is a variety) but essentially the *terroir*, the local soil. Why have these wines never been imitated with the remotest success? Because they are specific grape-and-ground statements that work where they work.

The work for pioneers is discovering other such natural unforced winners. Have the Australians done it with Sauvignon Blanc, the Argentines with Malbec? They certainly have, and the future will hold lots more of these marriages made in heaven.

THE SECRET OF DIVERSITY

Jancis Robinson

Life would be oh so dull if all we wine drinkers had to choose from were Chardonnay, Sauvignon Blanc, Merlot, and Cabernet Sauvignon. And yet, to judge from the sample bottles that come through my door most frequently, it sometimes seems as though this is the logical conclusion of today's wine market—at least the markets as envisioned by the supermarkets and the agents of mass distribution.

Whites

The following grapes present those of us interested in diversity with some rays of hope. Around the world, **Viognier** has touched a nerve. Until recently found only on a few acres of vineyard in the northern Rhône valley in southeastern France, this headily scented grape has been planted at a remarkable rate all through southern France and in pockets of California, and is worn as a badge of wine-producing chic from Chile to South Africa to Australia. The wines, smelling of dried apricots or May blossom, should be full-bodied yet nervy, a trick few of them achieve (although Calera usually manages it despite sky-high alcohol levels, and the successful Italian producers keep the refreshment factor gratifyingly high). Too

many Viogniers, especially from young vines, just taste like liquid air-freshener.

The northern Rhône has yielded two more fashionable white wine grapes, the ingredients in white Hermitage: racily perfumed **Roussanne** and the heavier, marzipan-like **Marsanne**, sometimes blended with each other or with blander varieties. Some seriously deep-flavored Roussanne is produced in southern France, following the archetype at Château de Beaucastel in Châteauneuf-du-Pape. The Australian state to Victoria is also making much of its ancient Marsanne vines.

The great sweep of vines around the French Mediterranean coast, the Languedoc–Roussillon, harbors all sorts of occasionally ancient and fascinating vine varieties. The ambitious new generation of fine-wine producers are making much of Marsanne and lively Roussane, but there are others. **Grenache Blanc** tends to flab but is usefully full-bodied for matching with highly spiced foods. The tangy, delicate **Vermentino** is also grown in Sardinai and is probably the same as the **Rolle** of Provence (an issue that makes us grape nuts' hearts beat faster). **Picpoul** is the lemon-scented specialty of the village of Pinet, while minerally **Terret** is so ancient it has mutated to give us Blanc, Gris, and Noir (white, pink, and black berried) forms. Such wines, even from top domains, are rarely expensive. Perhaps the most fashionable white grape among grape enthusiasts now is **Petit Manseng**, the tangy ingredient in Jurancon in southwestern France, which is being planted by cutting-edge producers in the Languedoc and California.

The big bottlers are also trying to interest us in **Chasan**, but that is a relatively recent, decidedly expedient crossing of Chardonnay with Listan (a.k.a. Palomino), the sherry grape whose chief virtue is not its intrinsic flavor but the commercial allure of the first three letters of its name.

Italy, especially southern Italy, has a host of great but underappreciated grapes of both colors, but it will take time and tenacious importers to fully expose them to the outside world. For years the Italians, who have saved Piedmont's pear-scented **Arneis** from extinction, have done all they can to persuade us that Pinot Grigio is a boring grape, perhaps to satisfy consumers' need for something not too challenging, or the wine trade's desire for yields to match their profits. Happily, however, we are starting to see more and more Italian Pinot Grigio that displays the daring density of its French cousin in Alsace, **Pinot Gris**. This is a grape that could really catch on, the white wine for red wine food, smelling of bacon fat and tropical fruit and calling for game or almost rank cheese on the plate. Oregon vintners, especially old-timer Eyrie and brash newcomer King Estate, are latching on to Pinot Gris with a vengeance and the results are generally more successful than the state's effort with Chardonnay.

For moment, we Italophiles can content ourselves with a small revival in the fortunes of the classical, extremely well-traveled grape **Malvasia Bianca**. It was traded around the Mediterranean in the Middle Ages and has since somehow found it way to Madeira, Spain and California, where Bonny Doon sells it under the Ca' del Solo label. However dry it is, the wine tends to taste slightly sweet, but nobly, classically so with a certain ancient sheen.

219

Another grape with a long history that is strutting its stuff most dramatically in the New World is **Verdelho**. The vine was grown on Madeira and gives its name to one of the drier, longer-lived styles, but nowadays is responsible for some seriously vibrant, tangy, full-bodied dry white table wine from Australia, particularly some of the hotter vineyards of western Australia.

Reds

Australia leads the field in the hot red of the moment, the Rhône Valley's **Syrah** or, as the Australians call it, **Shiraz**. They have thousands of acres of this ancient vine (unlike California's Rhône Rangers, who yearn for more) and can turn out all manner of styles, from chocolate-rich Barossa soups to peppery, nervy numbers from the higher vineyards of Victoria. It also makes a fine blend with Cabernet Sauvignon, as Provencal winemakers have demonstrated for decades. The fashion for all things viticultural associated with the Rhône is also apparent in some serious bottlings of the spicy, meaty grape that dominates the southern end of this French valley, **Grenache.** In Cali-fornia it may be associated with vapid sweet pink stuff, but northern Span-iards are just coming to grips with how good their Gernacha (Gre-nache) can be if produced from low-yielding old vines.

Another extremely fashionable grape whose origins are probably Spanish but which is also grown in southeast France is **Mourvèdre**, known as **Monastrell** in Spain and **Mataro** in California and Australia. Many growers are rapidly renaming their Mataro in an attempt to give it French cachet, but in fact it is a decidedly unsuave grape, producing in-tensely gamy, animal, full-blooded wine that is usually best blended with something a little more structured, such as a Syrah or Merlot. And what, I hear you ask, will be the next Merlot? I put my money on its Bordeaux blending partner **Cabernet Franc**. All over wine world, from Washington State to New Zealand via Chile and Bordeaux, with all sorts of interesting stops en route, I hear growers and winemakers eulogizing the aromatic crispness of this cousin of Cabernet Sauvignon—a candidate, like Merlot, for delivering the thrill of Cabernet Sauvignon without the astringent pain, but one with a bit more finesse.

The grapes I think wine producers *should* be chasing is another question, of course.

Spain has some great white grapes, notably **Albariño** and **Godello** from the northwest corner, and many a grower elsewhere is already experimenting with Spain's noble red **Tempranillo**, the **Tinto Fino** of Ribera del Duero. The lean white **Assyritiko** of Greece is clearly a grape to watch. South Africa's rich red **Pinotage** can perform beautifully there. And Austria's own **Grüner Veltliner** can behave remarkably like dill-scented white burgundy.

But these are likely to remain local specialties for the moment. The two most underrated grapes in my view are also quite widely planted throughout the world, which may not be a coincidence. **Sémillon** makes sweet wines as sumptuous as Château d'Yquem as well as full-bodied, lemony dry whites for long ageing in Bordeaux, the rest of south west France and Australia. Washington's Semillons are wonderfully gusty dry whites—far more characterful than the state's generally insipid Chardonnay—and the grape could also do well in Chile, South Africa, and New Zealand.

And then, finally, there is aromatic, nervy **Riesling**. The great grape of Germany is capable of making tingling essences of place that can outlast any Chardonnay, and follow very much the same ageing pattern as a fine red Bordeaux. Riesling is the true insider grape. When two or three wine professionals are gathered together, it is a fair bet they will agree on the ethereal but under-appreciated quality of Riesling at its best (mostly from Germany's Mosel Valley, Austria's Wachau, and Alsace). Unfortunately, however, far too many Rieslings on sale today taste like particularly dull, stinky sugarwater, so making new converts is difficult. Never mind. All the more for us grape insiders.

THE ORIGINS OF CHAMPAGNE

François Bonal

In 1718, Canon Godinot of Reims, a philanthropist and owner of vineyards, wrote a book entitled *Manière de cultiver la vigne et de faire le Vin de Champagne:* "For the past twenty years," he declared, "the taste of French people has confirmed the success of sparkling wines from Champagne." We can therefore assume that champagne was invented around 1690. This is also supported by the appearance in 1700 of the first literary text to mention the wine. In a poem entitled *"Epitre à la duchesse de Bouillon,"* Guillaume de Chanlieu invites a lady to come to his home and drown "tomorrow's troubles in the sparkling froth."

The appearance of froth in wines from the region of Champagne was the result of new wine-making techniques. In the late 17th century, in all wine regions people began to realize that wine would keep and travel better in bottles than in wooden vats. Heavier bottles were thus produced, inducing the economist Savary de Brulons to write that some glassmakers had specialized in the production of "thick bottles, whose use and demand have rapidly increased since everybody knows that wines keep better in them." Producers also started to bottle at the onset of winter, when the wines had yet to complete their fermentation. It was a process of trial and error that generated residues of yeast and sugar. With the warmth of spring, fermentation started up again, producing carbon dioxide that accumulated in the bottle. In 1801, the famous chemist Chaptal wrote that "sparkling wines derive their properties from being shut in glass before fermentation has been completed."

The frothiness of the wine could vary considerably from one vineyard to another. The cold climate of northern areas—it was colder than it is today—enhanced the effervescence of the wine for two main reasons. Firstly, the grapes were never perfectly ripe at the moment of harvest, so they were rich in malic acid, which fostered malolactic fermentation. Secondly, fermentation was slowed down by the cold and was therefore far from being over at the moment of bottling.

Champagne was not invented by a single person. Indeed, the English journalist who wrote, with typical British humor, that champagne invented itself was pretty close to the mark. As I have shown in my book about Dom Pérignon (*Dom Pérignon: Vérité et légende*, Langres: 1 Editions Dominique Guéniot, the wine revolution responsible for the birth of champagne appears to belong to a framework of collective changes whose origins are still unknown.

Froth was initially considered an entirely negative phenomenon, and much effort was put into preventing it from forming, as many texts of the time reveal. However, a few producers understood the potential of the new drink. The joyous impertinence of champagne was likely to attract the young lords intent on pursuing pleasures in life during the last, gloomy years of the reign of Louis XIV. The production of this new sparkling wine thus became deliberate, and champagne eventually became popular at the dissolute court of the Duke of Vendôme. In 1715, Philippe d'Orléans and his lovers assured the lasting success of champagne at the convivial dinners held at the Palais Royal. As Richelieu himself wrote in his *Mémoires,* " . . . orgies did not start until everybody was in the state of beatitude brought on by Champagne . . ."

The fashion for champagne soon conquered England, Germany, Russia, and Italy, where in 1727, Paolo Rolli included the celebration in his *Di canzonette e di cantate:*

> In buona compagnia,
> Un fiasco di sciampagna
> Che i labbri e il cor vi bagna
> Col vivo suo liquor.

> Smozzata pria la fiamma
> D'ogni penoso assetto
> vi pon la gioja in petto;
> E l'allegria nel Cor.

> Gorgoglia in bianca spuma
> E fino alla pupilla

> Vivace vin zampilla
> Dal colmo del bicchier,

> Va poi dal seno in mente
> E grato a chi ti beve
> Le sue più care idee
> Risveglia nel pensier.

(Book I, Song XVIII)

By the early 18th century, champagne had become the perfect wine for high society parties. However, its organoleptic qualities fell far behind its great renown. It was produced by means of a process of continuous fermentation, and unlike today, no sugar was added at the outset. Indeed, to achieve greater sparkle the juice of unripe grapes was used. As late as 1799, Cadet-de-Vaux wrote in his book *L'art de faire le vin* that " . . . sparkling Champagne wine is produced with grapes harvested when they are not fully ripe . . ." So those early champagnes must have been incredibly acidic. In fact, it was only later that sugar was used as a sweetener prior to adding the liqueur d'expédition. And it wasn't until the beginning of the 20th century that wine makers began to remove the deposits formed by the agglomeration of vegetal organic matter. Champagne was originally so cloudy that a modern wine expert, Emile Manceau, did not hesitate to define it as "revolting dishwater." And yet, incredibly enough, that horrible wine was terribly expensive, since so much in its production depended on chance. Nobody knew how to control it, though it was found that it kept its

223

sparkle best when bottled during a full moon in March, possibly even in April. In 1816, a good century after the appearance of champagne, André Jullien made the following comment in his *Topographie de tous le vignobles connus*: " . . . the events that bring about the sparkling character of this wine are so astonishing that they cannot be explained . . ."

In those days it was taken for granted that wines produced either too much froth or too little. Some producers turned to all sorts of additives to give flat wines the right sparkle. In the treatise mentioned above, Godinot himself refers to some alarming practices: "It is also true," he relates, "that there were wine merchants who, in the light of the ever increasing success of these sparkling wines, added alum, wine spirits, pigeon excrement and other drugs to make them extraordinarily frothy." When wine was too effervescent, the bottles exploded. This was the scourge of the *casse* (breakage). Out of a thousand bottles placed in the cellar, as many as 800 might burst at the start of the second fermentation.

Because of the irregular production of bubbles, there were various kinds of champagne on the market that differed in relation to the intensity and quantity of the froth. The *mousseux* was the most common product, with a pressure of about two atmospheres; then there were the *demi-mousseux*, whose light froth vanished rapidly; and the *grand-mousseux*, also know as *saute-bouchon* (cork-poppers), which were highly appreciated by party-goers.

In the 19th century, champagne was still fairly expensive. In 1850, its price was 6 francs per bottle, while a Saint-Estèphe or a Pommard were sold for 2 francs. Nowadays, if we consider the price of a non-vintage brut champagne, the ratio has been reversed.

Thanks to an annual production of over 250 million bottles and reasonable prices, everybody now has the chance to taste this king of wines. Since proven techniques have replaced the earlier trial-and-error methods, the quality of champagne is now flawless and constant. The 1996 vintage of these wines was undoubtedly one of the best of the 20th century.

TWELVE:4

PEST, PRESENT AND FUTURE

Giovanni Ruffa

The world of wine has had its personal Deluge. The disaster struck unexpectedly in the second half of the 19th century, right at the peak of an immensely florid period for European viticulture. The 18th century had been one of growing fortune, with French wines dominating the world (despite the expropriation and the selling off of many of the most important properties after the Revolution) and, in Germany, the revival of whites from the Rhine and the Moselle after the damage caused by the Thirty Years War. The Age of Enlightenment also brought major improvements in both theoretical knowledge and practical techniques of wine making. In the second half of the 18th century, studies by Lavoisier, a research chemist who managed to quantify the transformation of sugar into alcohol, contributed to describing the mechanisms of fermentation, and during the same period, increasing numbers of cellars availed themselves of wine presses with iron screws and pressing cages, the forerunners of modern hydraulic presses.

The 19th century began in an atmosphere of optimism for producers and merchants. Enthralled by the fortunes to be made, they turned a blind eye to worrisome matters such as wine adulteration and the indiscriminate growth of vineyards. To meet production levels that were by now reaching abnormal proportions, American varieties were often being introduced, more resistant and with a higher yield. These were the carriers of the diseases that put an end to the carefree salad days, that caused the "disappointment" mentioned by Hugh Johnson in his *Story of Wine* (Mitchell Beazley, 1989).

A first warning came with oidium, a fungus that attacks the vine, jeopardizing the quality and quantity of the harvest. This disease was eradicated after around ten years when it was discovered that sulfur is an excellent antidote. At this point, however, another, far more serious danger arose in the form of a lethal parasite, an aphid that feeds on the vine's leaves and roots and which, once settled in, does not leave a vineyard until it has destroyed it completely.

Vine-pest, originally from the American continent, disembarked in France at the mouth of the Rhône during the years when steamships had reduced the time for crossing the Atlantic to around ten days, permitting this parasite to survive a voyage that it had probably taken many times before without ever arriving alive in Europe.* From the port of arrival, the previously unknown *puceron* spread throughout Europe, North Africa, the Middle East, and even to India. Not even Australia, New Zealand, or South Africa were spared. The devastating effects were noted for the first time in Arles in 1863. Identified and named in 1868 by Jules-Emile Planchon, an agronomist from Montpellier, the *Phylloxera vastatrix* was already active in 1871 in Switzerland and Portugal. In 1875, it appeared in Austria/Hungary, and from here infested central-eastern Europe, from Greece to Russia. In 1876, it was in Bordeaux, two years later in Meursault, Burgundy, and Spain. In 1879, it came to Italy, in 1880 to Germany, and by the end of the century was present in Algeria and Champagne.

Some forty years passed during which vine dressers tried everything to no avail; the systematic "work" of the vine-pest continued up to World War One and beyond. In Greece, for example, it was still active in the 1940s in Attica and in the 1960s in the Peloponnese. Gilbert Garrier, whose book *Le phylloxéra: une guerre de trente ans* (Albin Michel, 1989) is essential reading, recalls how the invasion of the vine-pest was seen by some as Nature's revenge for Man's repeated aggression, and by many farm workers in religious rural France as God's punishment. Real experts took to the field together with improvisers and charlatans, drawn by the reward that producers' organizations and the government were offering. Many of the suggested remedies were more fanciful than effective. At first, the only valid method seemed to be that of spraying vineyards with chemical

---

*This is the most widely accepted interpretation, even though not all historians agree. Tim Unwin, in his book *Wine and the Vine: An Historical Geography of Viticulture and the Wine Trade* (London: Routledge, 1991), suggests that here was a twofold reason: a new supply source of American vines to be imported to Europe between 1850 and 1860 and the consequent arrival of a special strain of vine-pest to which the vines of Europe would have been particularly sensitive.

concoctions, but these were complicated and expensive operations. A decisive role was played by Professor Planchon, whose efforts largely contributed to the final victory. He was the one who discovered the American origins of the vine-pest, which helped him understand how American vines had developed a special resistance to the parasite with which they had lived for so long. Hence the technique of grafting European varieties onto American stock, thereby weakening the scourge. The savior vine was found. Many years of research and selection were needed to create the stocks suitable for European soil and climates, but in the end the battle was won.

The price paid was high, however. The geography of the European vineyard totally changed: in areas with a lower propensity for grape growing they ceased to exist altogether, while everywhere else the vineyards were totally replaced. As a result, it is probable that the taste of wine has also changed. The new grafts of American stock, the need for treatments (as well as sulfur against oidium, it soon became necessary to spray the rows of vines with "Bordeaux mixture" based on copper and calcium to combat peronospora, a grape mildew that, like vine-pest, came to Europe with American vines), and the use from the middle of the 19th century of new aids in wine making refrigeration, heating, and pasteurizing systems are all factors that contributed to opening a new chapter in the history of vine growing and enology.

On the threshold of the third millennium, a new danger seems to threaten the world's vineyards: homologation. A flood of cabernet and merlot, of pinot and chardonnay is persistently streaming out of Spain and Italy, the United States and Greece, Bulgaria and Hungary. This results in the loss of an immense heritage of indigenous varieties, the disappearance of territorial traditions, and thus also the standardization of the taste of wine and the trend toward "international" products that are likely to colonize the markets. The savior, this time, does not come from afar, but from the heart of the historical producing areas, where the rediscovery and relaunching of regional grape stock will uphold diversity and the multiplicity of models and flavors.

TWELVE:5

THE REVIVAL ROUTE

Michel Smith

In France, a new fashion is about to take the world of enology by storm. New labels extolling neglected or forgotten grapevines are sprouting up everywhere. The following is a brief *Tour de France* encompassing some of the unrecorded vines of ancient times.

Are you fed up with your Cabernet? Tired of the Chardonnay? Then why not celebrate the sweet Arbane Champénoise and sing the praises of the good old Carignan from Languedoc! In every French region, all the most renowned wine growers have been smitten by the urge to rediscover our underestimated viticultural wealth, saving neglected and often endangered grapevines from oblivion. The movement actually began in a rather tentative fashion back in the 1980s.

I can still recall a number of learned colleagues sniggering at a Burgundian wine grower complaining about the systematic elimination of indigenous vineyards such as those producing the Pinot Beurot (the younger brother of the Alsatian Pinot Gris, also known as Auvernat, or as Malvoisie along the banks of the Loire) or the Pinot Lieubault (a red grapevine virtually erased from the grapevine description and classification maps). We will be lucky if we still have any of these grapevines left a few years hence, so there is nothing to laugh about. Yet nowadays, a great many wine-growers have decided to revert to earlier species, to exploit their forgotten grapevines as an effective subject of communication. And an equal number of experts and consumers have succumbed to their charms.

Autochthons and emigrants

I started my search in Champagne, in Aube to be precise, a province not held in high esteem by established merchants such as Krug, Bollinger, and the like. A rather ungrateful attitude, since the grapes grown in Aube largely contribute to the mixes of the great brands, whatever may be said in exclusive circles about premium grapes coming from Marne! Some time ago, François Moutard, the manager of a small Champagne-producing company, decided to focus on a few Arbane grapevines that had been planted in 1952. The Arbane is a vinestock that used to be regarded as twice as precious as the common and highly prized Pinot Noir and Chardonnay. This year, for the first time, Moutard has decided to make a separate wine from this peculiarity that, he believes, is going to yield 1,500 bottles per year. The result is a golden wine with an intense and complex nose, lively on the palate, marked by hints of dried fruit and great persistence.

A few steps from Champagne is Burgundy. Around Chablis, in the village of Irancy, the César, a black, hard-skinned grape producing a white juice, continues to yield colored, full-bodied wines rich in tannins on the farms of traditional wine growers like Patrice Fort. The Yonne is the only province where growers can produce a red or rosé Burgundy from this type of vine, which is said to have reached these hills with the Roman legions. Moving eastward, the rather touristy vineyard route of Alsace leads to Heiligenstein, an immaculate little village that takes pride in being the cradle of the Klevener, not to be mistaken—God forbid—for the Klevner, the Alsatian word for the Pinot Blanc, also called Auxerrois. Given that nothing is simple in Alsace, the true name of Heiligenstein's Klevener is Traminer, the local name of the Savagnin rosé from which the Gewürztraminer is made. This grapevine is so warmly supported by the wine growers of the village that in the surrounding area the two-hectare vineyards of the 1970s have gradually expanded to around eighty. "Apparently, it was transplanted here by some Austrian settlers a long time ago," explains Charles Boch, who cares for nothing but his Klevener. Michel Mastrojanni, a French expert who knows Alsace fairly well, reminds us that the word Traminer derives from Tramin, the name of a Tyrolean village in Italy. Whatever its roots, when vinification is performed correctly, the Klevener is an excellent white wine with a strong candied fruit aroma mixed with hints of *pain d'épice*.

A splendid Gamay

Between Alsace and Blois Castle there is only a small gap . . . on the road map, of course. A few kilometers south of the banks of the river Loire, not far from the woods and ponds of Sologne, the Cour-Cheverny denomination protects less than one hundred hectares of the bold Romorantin, the vinestock of a white

229

grapevine that is said to have been introduced by the French King Francis I, who brought it from Burgundy to the small town of . . . Romorantin. Whatever its history, this grapevine presently yields rare, precious, and highly delicate wines, such as those produced in the old vineyards of Michel Gendrier.

Not far from there, Henry Marionnet, an expert in fruity wines, has become a master of production using carbonic maceration of the Gamay, which is also found in the Beaujolais. He's also committed to protecting old vineyards through the marketing of three original *cuvées* at reasonable prices. His *"Cépages Oubliés"* (Forgotten Grapevines) have revalued the red juice Gamay (the one used for the Beaujolais gives a white juice) with its deep flavor and soft tannins. "It is the traditional grapevine of the Cher valley whose fruits we used to drink when we were teenagers," Henry says. "We would tap it from the *demi-nuid* of our parents. When the DOC officials turned down its request for recognition, it ran the risk of disappearing forever. When I realized that my neighbor was about to uproot the last plots, I persuaded him to rent them out to me."

Another *cuvée* named "Vinifera" (the equivalent of "wine-producing") is the fruit of a non-grafted Gamay from a French vineyard that Henry vinifies through intracellular fermentation, as he does with his classic Gamay. Oddly enough, this wine looks much darker, besides being marked by great persistence and a spiced black cherry aroma. It is a light wine that makes you merry if you are wise enough to drink it cool, with a few friends, on a summer evening, eating grilled meat on skewers, and avoiding intellectual exertion. Besotted with his Gamay, Henry has also vinified an extraordinarily fruity *"Première Vendage"* (First Grape Harvest) with no added sugar and sulfur. As he himself likes to say, this eleven-degree wine must be drunk without reserve! And, believe me, he is absolutely right.

A few steps from the Charmoise area, where Henry Marionnet lives, Charles Buisse, a shopkeeper, is busy bringing back distinction to the taste of the Fié, a grapevine that is grown on less than fifty hectares in all France. Fié is the local name of a Sauvignon Gris, the younger cousin of the Sauvignon Blanc, a renowned grapevine of Sancerre and Pouilly-Fumé. Paul presents his delicious white wine in a beautifully eccentric bottle. The delicacy, body, and fruit of the contents are remarkably well balanced.

While we are on the subject of Pouilly-Fumé, we should also add that since 1937, the village renowned for this white wine has also hosted a much less pretentious controlled denomination featuring the name of the village itself: Pouilly-sur-Loire. This is a light white wine, often pleasantly flowery, only produced from the Chasselas grapevine. Nowadays what remains of the species is apparently only sufficient to produce a few thousand bottles a year, which are mostly managed by Guy Saget, a wine merchant who makes an "old vineyard" *cuvée*.

Let us continue our trip to the Jura and Savoy, where certain grapevines such as the Poulsard and the Trousseau are presumably endangered since they grow nowhere but in their places of origin.

As we head down the Rhône valley, we will come across a micro-denomination at the gates of Aix-en-Provence. Its name is Palette and it derives from a 23-hectare vineyard in which René Rougier has lovingly preserved a few Manosquin vinestocks beside his other grapevines.

At the tip of the Côte d'Azur, the Niçois de Bellet (a wine produced in a 45-hectare area) can still boast a few specimens of the Folle Noire, which owes its name to its fluctuating yields, and the Braquet, named after a local family. We strongly recommend tasting the wine of this vinestock at Ghilslain de Charnacé's cellars in Bellet Castle. The sparkling version is produced in nearby Piedmont (Brachetto), where it is usually savored together with the first strawberries of the season.

The lavish Carignan

If we make a U-turn along the Mediterranean coast toward Montpellier, we will come across the first vineyards of Languedoc and Roussillon, two French regions whose Cabernet and Chardonnay have attracted the attention of Mondavi and Gallo. This is the home of Olivier Jullien, a sort of mischievous elf and a poet entirely devoted to his vineyard. He was the first to name one of his *cuvées* "Les Vignes Oubliées" in the 1980s, and since then he has been emulated by innumerable vine growers. A great joker, unable to take himself seriously, insensitive to the siren calls of the media, he dresses his bottles with "Etats d'âme" (Moods), as he has called one of his *cuvées*. Jullien obtains his "Vignes Oubliées" white wine from several ancient species, including the Terret-Boulet and the Carignan blanc. The result is a wine with a full-bodied finish that almost resembles honey after some years in the cellar.

Originally grown in the Cariñena region of Spain, the Carignan was introduced into southern France in the 12th century. It is not exactly a rare grapevine, since it is widespread in France and until very recently ranked fifth worldwide for its crop. Largely exploited from the beginning of the century till the 1960s to obtain industrial wines from flatland vineyards, where it used to be planted for maximum yield (200 hectoliters per hectare), the Carignan is presently abhorred and indeed uprooted by most grape-producing farms, which tend to favor popular grapevines such as the Syrah. These wine growers have evidently forgotten that the Carignan can yield excellent wines when the vines are relatively old (between thirty and one hundred years) and when the grapes are harvested fully ripe from vineyards grown on the poor hills of the French Midi.

Sylvain Fadat is a welcome exception to the general rule. He produces a deep Carignan as a *vin de pays* that can be pleasant in spite of its strong but harmonious tannins. Such tannins are the emblem of his 1994 red wine, maliciously sold at a few francs more than his extremely elegant, DOC-labelled Côteaux-du-Languedoc-Montpeyroux. The Carignan is also flourishing again in Minervois thanks to the Domergue family, whose "Carignanissime" *cuvée* bears fine witness to the grapevine. They have also rehabilitated another ancient grapevine, the Cinsault, with an excellent *cuvée*.

It is a widely held conviction that the South is unable to produce a good white wine. Nonsense! Simply taste the bright, sweet Malvoisie that Suzy Malet and her son Jerome produce just opposite the prison of Perpignan. This Catalan grapevine known as Tourbat, which is harvested rather late in the season and presented under the nice label of "L'Abandon," produces a tender, mild, light wine.

Toward the Spanish border, in the Banyuls denomination region, Christine Campadieu and Vincent Cantié are reviving the Grenache Gris, which was once regarded as destined exclusively for the production of specially fermented or alcoholic wines. A thick, spicy, full-bodied, powerful *vin de pays* (14 degrees) that goes well with many Mediterranean dishes.

Toward the end of uniformity

This *Tour de France* could stop at many other locations. Still in the south, we should not forget the Pyrenees and the famous Southwest region, where many denominations include such odd grapevines as the Fer Servadou for Marcillac, the Petit Manseng for Juranon, the Négrette for the Côteaux-du-Frontonnais area, and so forth. Robert Plageolles is almost a local landmark, renowned for his extraordinary knowledge of these ancient grapevines and the causticity of his humor. He is also a first-class wine grower for the Gaillac denomination. After rehabilitating the Len de Lell (i.e., *Loin de l'oeil*, "out of sight") a rigorously local grapevine, Robert has now fallen in love with another white, indigenous vinestock, the Odenc, which he has planted over 2.5 hectares of land to save it from

oblivion. The product is divided into three *cuvées* that produce a golden white wine whose fragrance may range from overripe to candied applies. Three grape harvests are made for a threefold sorting. The first offers a rather dry white wine with a ripe, intense, fruity flavor; the second, the "Grain d'Ondenc," is even more explosive, while the third, called "Vin d'Autan" (the Autan is the hot, dry wind that dries grapes) tends to be fortified with a honey touch. Each *cuvée* produces no more than three thousand 5-cubic-centimeter bottles, much sought after by collectors.

Coming to the end of our quick *Tour de France*, we can say that this wealth of unusual grapevines on our labels—and many others should be mentioned—may indicate a turning point in vine growing as if, at the dawn of the third millennium, wine growers felt bored and somehow sick of banality and uniformity. The curiosity shown by wine lovers toward the forgotten French grapevines is perhaps also a sign of incipient contempt for the soulless international wines that are flooding the planet. Wait a minute! Isn't that Bacchus pointing a reproaching finger at the Chardonnay, Cabernet, and other Sauvignon wines? . . . You don't believe me? Well, dreaming is not forbidden. . . .

TWELVE : 6

ZINFANDEL

Bob Thompson

A wintry night of lowering skies and rising winds. A fisherman's restaurant on a small bay north of San Francisco. A steaming bowl of the stew called crab "cioppino." Thick sourdough bread. A bottle of honest Zinfandel.

Nowhere else. Nowhere else on earth can all of these pieces come together the way they do here, especially when Zinfandel is one of the party.

For more than a century, Zinfandel has been California's own wine, its origins shrouded in the mists of time long past, its tangy, berry-like flavor bolder and more immediate than any other.

A Colonel Agoston Haraszthy claimed to have brought the grape variety to California from Hungary in the 1860s, but researchers have found records proving that a nursery in New York was selling cuttings of it twenty years earlier. In the 1970s, ampelographers linked Zinfandel to Italy's Primitivo da Gaia, but Zinfandel turned out to have been in America before Primitivo turned up in Italy.

Now, scientists using DNA tests are about to reveal Zinfandel's parentage. Almost certainly, the ancestral variety will come from the eastern side of the Adriatic. It may be Croatia's Plavic Mali. A few hasty people have come out and said Zinfandel *is* Plavic. Do not be surprised if Zinfandel has one last genetic trick up its sleeve.

In any case, do not fret for lost mystery. Plenty of comforting ambiguity will continue to surround Zinfandel. The most entertaining confusion begins with when to harvest, and continues with what sort of wine to make once the grapes have been picked.

Range of styles

A tired and tiresome cliché has it that Zinfandel is a perfect rosé, America's Beaujolais, a claret to rival Cabernet, or the basis of a good port-type. The cliché has gotten tired because, pretty much, it is true.

Picked early enough to provide brisk acidity and just-ripe berry flavors, then elaborated with little or no time in oak, Zinfandel will produce intensely flavorful dry rosé, or light and light-hearted red with some kinship to Beaujolais (more to Côtes-du-Rhône-villages).

Picked not much riper, and given a subtle touch of oak, Zinfandel will make a more claret-like red. Add time in bottle, and it can rival Cabernet Sauvignon. Give both a great deal of time in bottle, and expert tasters cannot tell them apart.

Grown as ripe as it can be, Zinfandel produces wine that makes Amarone di Valpolicella modest both in degree of alcohol and fierceness of tannins. (If you see 14.4 percent alcohol on the label, ask for tea instead. If you see a higher figure, quietly excuse yourself from the table and go to the cinema.) Zinfandel of such ripeness is the kind that succeeds in port-type dessert wines. Long term, claret is the style to aim at.

How it grows

It takes wine makers a long time to learn to see whether the grapes in front of them are candidates for rosé, or port. Zelma Long learned the lesson in her first year at Simi. She measured the sugar in some Zinfandel and decided the potential alcohol was a perfect 13.3 or 13.4 percent. Next morning, the must had almost 3 percent of alcohol and more sugar than she had measured to begin with.

Sneaky Zinfandel will do that because it ripens so unevenly. A single cluster will have green berries on the shoulder, raisins at the tip, and every ripeness in between. A single row will have more raisins than its neighbor. The block containing that row will have more green berries than the next one. Old vines exaggerate the tendency.

Zen helps.

Where it grows

Nobody has proven that the New York nursery sold Zinfandel vines to growers in California. Maybe Haraszthy did bring the variety to California, New York or no. In any case, Haraszthy was a Sonoman, and Sonoma is where Zinfandel reaches the peak of its performance. Always has.

Within Sonoma, Dry Creek Valley grows the purest expression of Zinfandel's wild berry flavors, but only on slopes where there is not much moisture in the soil. The adjoining Alexander Valley produces riper, softer wines. Not far away, Sonoma Valley Zinfandels are leaner, racier.

If Sonoma is best, second-best does not lag far behind in neighboring Napa and Mendocino counties. Napa's east hills and the flat at Oakville shine brightest. Mendocino's inland valleys around Ukiah are a fine source, the coastal hills above Anderson Valley a superb one. The Sierra Foothills are yet another congenial home, especially vineyards at higher elevations in El Dorado County.

Chapter THIRTEEN

In the Raw

COLDWAVE

Otto Horse

Mad cows do not seem to have curbed the consumption of *carpaccio*, and sea pollution does not appear to have quenched the passion for live seafood. And yet reticence hovers around these foods. Vegetarian medicine and enthusiasts of raw food have done a lot to disseminate the consumption of vegetables, both uncooked or squeezed in a glass. A hundred vitamins and no fats: this is the secret of such cold but palatable diets. Beyond this framework, however, raw meat and fish continue to elicit suspicion, suggesting primitive tastes and uncivilized customs. We have tried to understand why, thereby expanding the horizons of a gastronomy that has no flame or fixed abode. Our journey of discovery has taken us far afield.

Raw food is a source of prejudices.

Even vegetables have to conform to a code of taste that prefers flowers to leaves and leaves to roots, while ruling out tubers. The history of raw meat is more problematic. The first to gain access to international restaurants was the *steak tartare,* beef (or horse) fillet minced with a fresh yolk. It became popular in France in the early 1900s, acting as a pioneer. Before then raw food conjured up unattractive negative images and was excluded from grand hotels. After all, not many kinds of meat can be eaten without cooking them: nobody accepts the idea of eating pork loin or sliced chicken breast, even after intense and modifying marinades.

Raw food nevertheless exercises considerable attraction for the modern culinary age with its bent for minimal cooking and its taste for lean, thin cuts that can be transformed by acidic agents. Mince with lemon or tartare is no longer an isolated phenomenon. Over the last forty years, restaurants have gone several steps further in whetting the curiosity of youthful customers, and in so doing have created a number of interesting and successful dishes like beef *carpaccio* and tuna tartare. Our search for raw foods has taken us far and wide. We trust that the fruits of our gastronomic *wanderlust* provides readers with an enticing coldwave of flavors.

THIRTEEN : 2

THE GREEKS CALL IT καρπατσιο

Dimitris Antonopoulos

Far be it from me to suggest that the Greeks, as a nation, are relatively free of prejudice when it comes to food. Yet in Athens, which is a large city where people are likely to be more open-minded than elsewhere in Greece, you'd be surprised at what goes on. The casual observer can witness some wonderfully contradictory scenes. For instance, that of a delicate young lady practically fainting at the sight of a single drop of blood dripping from her steak, then tucking into a tasty veal *carpaccio*!

So what's the explanation? Nothing that a little gentle psychoanalysis can't help place in perspective.

In theory—and practice, too—the

237

human is an omnivorous animal. Of course, there are other creatures on earth who share this quality. Pigs, for instance, eat all kinds of food. However, by and large we don't appreciate comparisons with these nice creatures. Up go our defenses and out come our claims to belonging to a superior species. Of course we're not like other animals. The very suggestion! Such creatures doggedly follow their survival instinct, whereas we think and therefore we are legitimately entitled to rank first in the hierarchy. Granted, we must eat to survive, but this need of ours is part of the aesthetics of gastronomic pleasure, probably spiced with worries about our health and plenty of preconceived ideas.

In his book *The Sacred Cow and the Abominable Dog,* reissued as *Good to Eat: Riddles of Food and Culture* (Prospect Heights, Il.: Waveland, 1998), anthropologist Marvin Harris makes effective use of a famous maxim by Claude Lévi-Strauss, pointing out that "we think some food is good" and some "is bad." This is the gist of it. There are no absolute values in nutrition. In order to survive, humans are able to violate even the most deeply rooted taboos. If necessary, they can even practice cannibalism (you may remember what happened to the people who survived the plane crash in the Andes a few years ago). So exactly what it is that induces a satisfied pursuer of gastronomic pleasure to take the giant step and turn utter disgust for steak tartare into mad love for *carpaccio?* Don't waste too much time thinking about it. *Fashion* is what calls the tune.

But let's go back to the Greek example. One day at the end of the 1980s, the famous *carpaccio* served at Harry's Bar in Venice began to make its appearance in the fashionable clubs of Athens. People went wild about it. As if by magic, the "raw meat" taboo no longer applied. What people were enjoying was a new gastronomic fashion, and there couldn't be anything wrong with that. Today *carpaccio* is hallowed and nobody cares about its profoundly raw nature. Since it is never out of fashion, *carpaccio* has also obligingly prepared the way for other delicious raw meat dishes. *Sashimi,* or thinly sliced raw fish, is unthinkable outside

Japanese restaurants. Yet describe it as swordfish *carpaccio,* as certain enterprising restaurateurs in Athens have done, and you'll find that raw or marinated fish dishes go down a treat all over the place. The problem with fashions is that they are quickly forgotten. But since *carpaccio* and *sashimi* are particularly delicious, I hope they will not lose their charm. Perhaps, like Martini Dry, they can become *all-time classics,* proof of the fact that the culinary art is very delicate technique, even when it doesn't involve cooking.

Next time you wonder: "How can that savage eat his fillet so underdone?"—just think that his dish has been a little tortured over a flame. By contrast, *carpaccio* continues to defy your mind and nutritional ethics with its pure rawness.

THIRTEEN : 3

MY FATHER AS A TARTAR

Giampiero Rigosi

We've never got on, me and my old man. Right from the beginning, he took me the wrong way. He expected his son to be strong, with a healthy complexion and lively manner, whereas he ended up with a pale, sickly child lacking in appetite. Everything that he wasn't. Who knows, perhaps my mother, for once in her life, had had the courage to do something of her own accord and had been unfaithful with one of humanity's lesser beings, a tramp or a drunk, or a stunted postman even. If I try and think back to the past, I can see my old man's fat face atop a huge body, scrutinizing me in silence and frowning with disappointment. He's never liked me, and for my part I've always harbored a deep-rooted hatred for him. On the other hand, there are very few people in my life that I haven't ended up hating. One thing is certain, my old man has done his utmost to correct me, strengthen me, and toughen me up. In short, to make me how he wanted.

Our fights over food began early on. My lack of appetite has always enraged him more than anything else. That I was lazy, sickly, or lied was at least bearable. But all the fuss I made over eating was too much for him.

"But why," he would bellow, moaning to my mother about me. "Eating is a pleasure, and more than that, a necessity! At his age, I'd have done anything for a mouthful of cheese, whereas he refuses to eat everything you put in front of him. Look at him pushing the food round his plate with that fork, he makes me mad." Not that it took much to make my old man mad.

Only now, after all these years, can I see the funny side of this expression. Now that he's sitting there looking depressed and disoriented—and still he won't accept what's in store for him. Clearly he balks at the idea that this time it's him being forced to eat what I have prepared for him. And I bet you anything he'll even find fault in the recipe I've chosen for him.

I wonder how I've managed to put up with it all. In twenty years, not a day has gone by without my old man filling my head with nonsense. Don't leave the fat, don't play with the bread, don't leave food on your plate. But

why? Because in Africa there are children dying of hunger, and food shouldn't be wasted. Fair enough, but what could I do to save those children from their fate? Would they really have wanted to eat the fat off my meat? Well, feel free!

My old man's blood would boil. He'd thump the table hard, bellowing at my mother about how heartless I was, an appalling monster with no feelings. Then he would force me to swallow the rest of my soup that had gone cold, the spongy fat off the meat, and even the little bits of dry, dirty bread that I had wrapped around my fingers. It wasn't just about the children in Africa, but about him and my mother, if I really wanted to know—when they were young they had experienced hunger. Finding something to eat wasn't that easy in those days, and you never dreamt of leaving anything on your plate. I had these stories coming out of my ears, and I'd have eaten the cutlery as well rather than listen to the same old record yet again. But when the old man got going there was just no stopping him. And on he went, telling me for the umpteenth time about all the hardships they'd had in their lives. Fascism, the war, the Germans, and all the misery there was at the time. But I couldn't have cared less about their war. And while the old man went on blathering, I forced myself to swallow those mouthfuls, chewing as little as possible so as not taste the food and get rid of it quickly in the hope that sooner or later his batteries would run out. I could feel those dead lumps plopping like stones into my stomach, and thought that the Germans couldn't have been worse than my old man. Him, his war, his damn hunger of the past. Later on, as soon as I was alone, I would lock myself in the bathroom and throw it all up in the toilet.

Compared with the recipe he used to use, the one I have decided to follow is slightly more fancy. Just a few ingredients, well measured. The secret of this dish lies in the freshness of the meat. Isn't this just what he used to say to me time and time again?

My old man is nothing more than a tyrant, an endless stream of clichés with an insatiable appetite.

He would look down on me from his hundred and twenty kilos and repeat his favorite comment: "This child looks as if he's just been let out of a sanatorium. I can hardly believe he's really my son."

He would enjoy humiliating me with his barrack-block jokes. I can still hear him reciting his endless list of damn proverbs. *Good food keeps you going. The appetite grows with what it feeds on. A glass of wine a day keeps the doctor away. Red wine makes for good humor. A hungry man is an angry man.* And of course his favorite, the most horrific and nauseating of them all: *Raw meat, cooked fish.*

"Believe you me," he would pontificate, "leave that raw fish to the Japanese. As far as I'm concerned, you can't get better than a beautiful rare steak, *carpaccio* dressed in oil, pepper, and Parmesan, or freshly minced steak tartare."

I still wonder how I managed to stand and listen to him without throwing up in his face. But the worst of it is that he wasn't happy just praising the virtues of food, the pleasures of the table, the taste of his favorite recipes. He would do anything to get me to taste them. And the more I tried to refuse, the more he dug his heels in. I absolutely had to try at least one mouthful.

What were his favorite dishes? The most revolting things you could ever imagine. Blood-sausage, boiled tripe, ox testicles in piquant green sauce, pig's trotters fricassee, braised tongue, sliced heart Genoese style, pan-fried kidneys, liver Venetian style, fried brains, chicken giblets in sweet and sour sauce, calf's head in Barolo wine. And then meat, meat, meat. Especially raw.

"It's absurd to be frightened of blood," he loved repeating. "Blood is the best way of becoming a man."

My head would spin out of sheer nausea.

"What's wrong with this meat? It's excellent. When will you see that you are just biased? On the other hand, you just have to think that some populations eat mice, ants, worms, grasshoppers, and snakes. What you eat or don't eat is just a question of custom and habit. Personally, if I was about to die of hunger, I wouldn't think twice about eating human flesh, I can assure you. In fact there have been cases—it's not that shocking. Just listen to me—if you want to be a man, you must show them you've got guts. Man is a carnivore, a hunter. Cooking is great, but it's in the taste of raw meat that you are aware of your true nature. You really must taste this steak tartare, my word!"

To be honest, he isn't a great example of virile strength, sitting there whimpering and moaning, tied to the chair. A while ago when I started the job, he even wet himself. I felt more disgust than pity, and I went on cutting. I've learned the lesson; I can put up with the sight of blood, but he doesn't seem all that impressed. And to think that I'm making him one of his favorite dishes: steak tartare. Beautiful, fresh meat, just how he likes it. Now that I've finished garnishing the plate, he's even stopped moaning. Every so often he looks up, and stares at me with those tearful, desperate eyes of his. He avoids looking down at all costs. I can quite understand. He can't be too enthralled by the sight of the stump instead of his leg. Moreover, he can't be too happy at the thought that the minced meat for this tartare that I've made him has come straight from his thigh. He has an expression of total failure. Perhaps because he is forced to admit, for the first time in his life, that he too at the end of the day harbors some absurd prejudices towards certain foods.

Steak tartare with an egg
(For one person)

Grind 150 grams of steak, add salt and pepper and a few drops of Tabasco. Sprinkle on a spoon of olive oil and a generous squeeze of lemon juice. Mix together, place on a plate, and cover with a spoonful of finely chopped parsley. Make a small hollow in the middle and place the yolk of a raw egg in it. To serve, place small heaps of gherkins, capers, and chopped onion around the meat, with a series of sauces of your choice to accompany it.

THIRTEEN : 4

RAW RECIPES: MARINATED
SARDINES

Have you ever opened up a sardine straight off a fisherman's boat by slipping your thumb into its belly? The experience is more interesting than you might imagine. Moreover, it is the only way you can possibly taste the unexpectedly delicious raw flesh of what is otherwise considered a very common kind of fish. Along the Catalan coast, sardines—was well as anchovies, a real local specialty—are still caught on summer nights by lamplight: thousands of tiny silvery bellies shine through the water under the light. All you have to do is to haul in the net, the *sardinal,* and catch the darting fish.

Rumor has it that sardines are best at grape-harvest time, but for the moment we shall not tackle this debatable question. Some say that Mediterranean sardines are smaller than Atlantic ones . . . but this too is an assertion that needs to be proved.

Those who watch me when I'm gutting sardines tell me that I look as though I get a sensual kick out of breaking their little necks. Perhaps there is a certain malicious pleasure in the way I like to tuck into them from June on . . .

First of all, you have to slip your finger into their bellies in order to remove their entrails. Violence is strictly forbidden: you must be very delicate and kind with these poor, tiny creatures. Then, taking one of their backbones firmly between your thumb and forefinger, let you fingers slowly slide from head to tail. Practice a bit; you will learn very quickly. If the sardines are very fresh, you will realize that opening them up is not complicated at all. You will thus smell the strong sea aromas and obtain compact and whole sardine fillets. Put them on a board and chop their tails off with a knife. Now you just have to get rid of the scales. Sardine scales are so large and thin that it is better to remove them when you eat raw fish, though they are not a problem when you grill sardines or cook them in any other way. The ideal solution would be to remove their skin, but it's so thin that the operation would prove too risky, even with a razor blade. At times, when I am starving, before chopping the sardines' heads off and separating the fillets, I remove the scales as best I can (I find dishcloths and paper towels particularly useful) and I rinse the fillets in a bucket of sea water as I was taught by a friend of mine, Jean-Marie Patrouix, a cook who is almost obsessed with respect for fish and its freshness. Rinsing the fillets in sea water is very important. Tap water deprives sardines of their typically strong, iodized flavor. Do not forget that these tiny creatures are delicate and fragile. I like sardines

243

like that, uncooked, with just a few crystals of sea salt. I wait a couple of minutes—the time salt needs to produce small white burns on their brown flesh. The only exception to the rule in this raw meal is a slice of rough bread I toast and flavor with a sprinkle of virgin olive oil. Then I put my fillets on bread and sometimes I also add fresh lemon-scented thyme leaves, tarragon leaves, a sprinkle of paprika-scented oil, and a few garlic slices minus their green shoots.

Jean-Marie—who traveled for years on large cruise ships and has finally decided to settle at La Littorine, just at the entrance of Banyuls-sur-Mer, not far from the symbolic Spanish frontier—loves marinated sardines with diced tomatoes. "A real summer dish that you can also have on the beach," he says. Sardines, coarse salt, freshly ground pepper, a few garlic cloves crushed under the blade of a thick kitchen knife, the juice of a freshly picked lemon, olive oil, diced tomatoes, and—the final touch—two tufts of wild fennel stolen from the hillsides on which the Banyuls vineyards are perched. Two or three hours later, the dish can be served on a terra-cotta plate together with a few slices of bread. Uncork a bottle of rosé with a great personality, but fruity, like a Gérard Gauby rosé. Now the moment has come: a taste of paradise. I pray to God that the shoals of my beloved sardines will no longer be decimated by large and ugly industrial fishing boats!

Marinated Sardines
(For one person)

INGREDIENTS:

12 very fresh sardines

60 grams coarse sea salt

Freshly ground pepper

1 washed and diced tomato without the seeds

The juice of half a lemon

4 crushed garlic cloves

3 spoonfuls olive oil

2 tufts of slightly crushed wild fennel

Cebiche

INGREDIENTS (for 6 people):

500 grams angler or hake, cleaned of skin and bones and cut into cubes OR
500 grams filleted anchovies which, after cooking in lime, are rolled up and held together with a toothpick

200 milliliters lime juice. Alternatively, use lemon juice, but add a couple of pieces of rind to give it a more intense bouquet.

2 long, hot chili peppers, crushed in a mortar or blended in an electric food processor (minimum setting) with a drop of oil. If it is not the fresh chili season, use a quarter of blended red pepper together with a teaspoon of dried chili.

1 onion, finely chopped

Lettuce leaves, to garnish around the fish like a crown

Whole boiled sweet corn

Boiled sweet potatoes, chilled and cut into slices

Small boiled cassavas, chilled and cut into slices (both the sweet potatoes and cassavas can be found in shops selling early produce and exotic foodstuffs)

In its golden age, Peru overlooked an icy ocean teeming with life. Then, for a long, long time, these waters were totally exploited and plundered of all their riches. During the 1970s and 1980s, there were fish meal factories that fouled the air along those white, sandy coasts. Today, at long last, they have been shut down and the fish may even return in their immense shoals to the crystal-clear ocean as the birds flock back to the *guaneras* islands. Only in this way will the region regain its earlier charm.

Fish has always been one of the staples for the population along the coast, and history books relate how the Incas devel-

[continued next page]

oped a system of fast couriers who not only carried daily news and information concerning the accounts in all regions, but also fresh fish.

Cebiche is the national dish of Peru, an institution, like the *pisco sour*, an aperitif made with lime juice, *pisco* (a spirit distilled from local white wine), egg whites beaten to a froth, and syrup of cane sugar. And mention should also be made of the *anticuchos*, kebabs of heart and meat marinated in water, vinegar, and spices for a few hours and then roasted on small grills (the best *anticuchos* can be eaten on Sundays from the stalls around the Lima stadium).

Cebiche is either made with a large, white fish with fine meat—black umbra, similar to hake or angler—or a small fish, the *pejerrey*, a sort of giant anchovy with sweet white meat, which is rolled like the Swedish *roll-mops*.

Clean the large fish by removing the skin and bones before cutting it into large cubes. Open and bone the small fish (anchovies can be used as well). Lay the fish in one single layer in a dish with sides at least 1.5 centimeters high. Cover it with finely chopped onion, fresh chili crushed in a mortar or ground in the food processor with a touch of oil, and pour the lime juice on top. Let the fish "cook" in this juice for at least two hours, then drain most of the juice. Dress it with oil and salt and decorate with lettuce leaves. It is served with sweet potatoes, boiled sweet corn, and boiled cassavas. The sweetish side dishes douse the fire lit by the *ají* (chili).

—Elena Giovanelli

Sea Urchins

The Pacific Ocean is not pacific at all. It is an immense, fierce, and ice-cold sea. An enormous mass of water that crashes violently against the rocks of the southern coasts of Chile. This is the route taken by those early navigators who managed to sail around the terrifying Cape Horn, opposite Antarctica, in their search for the true passage to the East, the most feared and dangerous of all.

At such extreme latitudes, where the world comes to an end, lives one of the strangest and most elusive marine delicacies: the sea urchin. These invertebrates can be found in other seas too, but sea urchins from Chile, from the Pacific Ocean, taste like the ocean itself. The sea urchin *(Loxechinus albus)* has a spherical bony shell made of calcium carbonate. It moves about the seabed by means of its spines, which it also uses to defend itself. Its eggs are edible. Each urchin has five tongue-like sex glands, 5 to 10 centimeters long, which can be removed from the body after breaking the lower part of the shell.

They are best eaten as they are, raw and fresh, even alive, to enjoy their full flavor. They taste of iodine, salt, and fury, and to appreciate their full beauty one has to learn to let them linger in the mouth for a moment before swallowing them. Thus consumed they conjure up the entire Pacific Ocean.

Sea Urchins in Piquant Green Sauce
Place the urchin tongues on a plate, uncooked. Prepare a green sauce with onion and chopped parsley, adding olive oil and lemon. This dish should be served with a robust white wine, aged for a long time in the barrel, so as to counterbalance the urchins' penetrating taste of iodine.

Urchin Prawns
Within the sea urchin lives a small, parasitic prawn with a light, fairly tender shell. The fishermen generally eat the prawns and sell the urchin eggs. The prawn is eaten raw: put it to your mouth, squeeze it, suck the juice, and spit out the rest.

—Miro Popic

Gazpacho Andaluz

INGREDIENTS:

4 cloves garlic

Dried bread, not crusts

1 fresh tomato, peeled

Extra virgin olive oil

1 cucumber, 1 tomato, 1 green pepper, 1 onion

Salt and Jerez vinegar

METHOD:

Crush the ingredients in a mortar until you have a compact lump.
Mix in the oil, stirring continually. Add the salt and vinegar and then
dilute with cold water
Serve with pieces of pepper, cucumber, and tomato

Gazpacho is the fruit of popular wisdom: a cheap, easy, and quick-to-make chilled soup that counteracts the sizzling summer heat as well as offering complete nutrition. *Gazpacho* has now transcended its humble origins to assert itself as one of the most widely appreciated creations of modern gastronomy.

Making a virtue of necessity and turning want into healthy eating, with *gazpacho* the Spanish country folk of Andalusia, Extremadura, and Mancha achieved a nourishing meal-in-itself that is both light and non-fattening. The secret of its vitality lies in the utter simplicity of the basic recipe: a mixture of extra virgin olive oil, garlic, and vegetables, all diluted in cold water, with the addition of salt, vinegar, bread, and various ingredients that change from one place to another. Everything is raw and fresh. No wonder the famous nutritionist, Dr. Maranon, described it as "an extremely wise empirical combination of all the basic principles of healthy eating."

—Carlos Delgado

Chapter FOURTEEN

Animals and Meat

MEAT ON THE MOVE

Manfred Kriener

On the highway, near Frankfurt: the policemen patrolling the Walldorf exit notice a Spanish truck with a strange liquid leaking from its trailer. They stop the truck. When the policemen get closer, they see something red dripping onto the road: blood. An inspection explains the "leak": the transporters have loaded almost twice the permitted number of pigs for slaughter. In the crush, the animals at the sides have been pressed up against the metal grating, breaking a few bars, which have penetrated their flesh like knives.

Hegyeshalom feeding station: the animal feeding point on the border between Slovakia and Hungary is packed. The truck drivers stop here with their cattle, on the road to Trieste and Rasa, Croatia, where they will load them onto ships heading for Africa. Only 8 of the 119 trucks inspected entered the animal feeding station by the prescribed time. Swindling is the rule. Some trucks stay in line for another three to four hours before the animals can eat and drink. The most impatient drivers poke a water hose in through the ventilating holes. Others just get their documents stamped and carry on without feeding the animals at all.

Beirut harbor: a ship from Germany is docking, with a cargo of eight hundred head of cattle. While unloading, some animals collapse with exhaustion on the ramp; the injured or dead remain immobile. Unbeknown to the authorities, a troupe from "Frontal," a TV network ZDF program, is there filming everything. The camera follows a bull with a broken hind leg up to the slaughterhouse. These pictures are shown back home and are watched by the Brandenburg farmer who raised the animal, the cattle dealer, and then the exporter: a black bull that keeps falling, standing up, and falling again.

All shocked, no one to blame

Three scenes in the everyday life of international animal transportation, three cases of ordinary cruelty. Only rarely do journalists and cameramen

devote their attention to cows, pigs, sheep, goats, and chickens on their way to the slaughterhouse. A brief burst of indignation follows, followed by business as usual and platefuls of succulent steaks. "Animal slaughtering" says Karen von Holleben, veterinarian in Schwarzenbek, "is one of the last big taboos. Once it was a feast, now it is a black spot." Today, those who eat meat know almost nothing about animal transport and slaughtering practices. Apart from brief encounters with doleful eyes gazing from the air vents of large trucks, the occasional magazine article is about as close as we ever get to this particular aspect of reality.

In 1995, 277 million live animals were transported within the European Union (EU); 105 million were taken to countries outside the EU. After the collapse of livestock breeding in Eastern Europe, exports from the EU have increased dramatically. According to Brussels statistics, exports of cows and calves have increased by 400 percent since 1990—especially toward countries in North Africa and the Middle East.

Germany has traditionally supplied Turkey, Lebanon, and Syria with cattle and calves, and is ranked with Ireland as the largest EU exporter. The EU grants huge subsidies for every animal for slaughter that is exported to a non-EU country. Last year, the EU gave a contribution of 660 Deutsche marks for a young bull weighing 300 kilograms. "Public money for bone breakers": this is what animal rights' activists call these subsidies.

The truth is more complicated. EU contributions not only apply to live animals, but also to those that have been freshly slaughtered. Yet the export of frozen meat, which would solve so many problems and alleviate so much suffering, is not always looked upon favorably for the following reasons.

• In North Africa and the Middle East there are no transportation, refrigeration, and conservation facilities. Lebanon, for example, is ready to buy frozen meat, but wants the necessary infrastructures to be partly financed by the EU.

• Many countries try to exploit their own slaughterhouses. Why pay for slaughtering and cutting up within the EU, when all this can be done at home with lower costs and local labor? This is why countries like Turkey levy higher taxes on imports of frozen meat than on live animals.

• Consumers in these importing countries like fresh meat from freshly slaughtered animals better than frozen goods.

• Sometimes, to refuse imports of frozen meat, they say that European slaughter practices do not comply with Koranic precepts. The statement is wholly untenable, since slaughtering by the ritual cutting of the throat after stunning the animal is now carried out in Europe, too, and even certified by Muslim experts.

For all these reasons, long-distance transportation of animals is not likely to diminish in the near future. But even within Germany, millions of animals are transported live—and not only to the nearest slaughterhouse. So long as there are minimal price variations between the north and the south of the country, so long as the slaughterhouses in eastern Germany are able to undercut their western competitors price-wise, so long as meat production and consumption differ from region to region, animals will continue to be loaded onto trucks and carried up and down the country. And "inhuman" conditions would seem to be part and parcel of this trade.

pH and PSE

Stress begins with loading. Pigs, calves, and bulls raised in dark stables are suddenly expected to climb a steep ramp in full daylight to enter a narrow truck. All around there are people waving, yelling, pushing, and pulling, and if an ox refuses to budge, it gets a shock up its backside. Once the animals have finally been more or less violently transferred to the deck, stress prevails within. Sheep refuse to drink during stops, bulls follow their sexual instincts and try to mount each other, calves cannot find their usual troughs, while cows after hours of travel have painfully clogged udders. Add to this fights between animals, vibrations, drafts, noise, heat, overcrowding, drivers under pressure, bends, braking, traffic jams, never-ending lines of traffic on crowded highways, and it is no wonder that the animals are prey to fear and bewilderment.

The vets at the BSI (a Schwarzenbek-based institute devoted to the study of less stressful ways of handling cattle and animals for slaughter) have dealt with pigs as they would athletes, applying electrodes to measure their body temperature, heartbeat, and breathing during the journey, and the pH level and conductivity of their meat after slaughtering. Not only have

these studies shown that every transfer is a huge source of stress for animals, but also that there is a surprising relationship between the state of the animal and the quality of its meat. In other words: the better the animal feels, the better its meat tastes, since its condition at slaughtering has a fundamental effect on quality. Long-distance transportation not only makes the animal suffer, but also leads to lower-quality meat for consumers.

Pigs are animals that easily suffer from blood circulation problems, particularly at high temperatures: they cannot sweat, and after a long and hot journey they really need a shower. Body temperature and pH level clearly show the effects of transport fatigue. When animals are packed into narrow places, their temperatures rise rapidly to 40–41° C, as opposed to the 38° C of a relaxed animal. When animals travel on a fully loaded truck for over two hours to the slaughterhouse, one hour after slaughtering the pH-level of their meat is distinctly lower. Just like a marathon runner, their muscles are full of lactic acid. This gives rise to the infamous PSE (pale, soft, and exudative) meat of the sort that shrinks and turns tough in the pan. High body temperature and excess acid damage the membranes of the muscle cells, thus considerably reducing the "water-retention power" of the meat.

With such instruments, the BSI vets managed to identify one particularly ruthless truck driver. Their statistics revealed that all pigs transported by driver number 37 had a strangely low pH level with a high percentage of low-quality, PSE meat, regardless of where they were bred. By the same token, it is also possible to detect the most cautious and disciplined drivers: the meat of the animals they carry is better, their PSE rate lower. However, slaughterhouses rarely measure pH levels. It is the quantity and not quality of lean meat that counts. Yet compliance with EU norms in this sector now requires cattle-truck drivers to undergo training at the BSI institute.

Stressed meat

Scientific studies also show that an increase in outside temperature and humidity levels have a negative effect on the quality of meat; the same is true when excessive numbers of animals are packed into trucks or when electric power is used during loading. Loading and unloading remain the most difficult moments. The pig's pulse can reach hummingbird rates and its fragile circulatory system can lead to "transportation death" right there on the loading ramp. Pigs are bred to obtain the highest possible amount of lean meat, and are subject to far greater strain than other animals with less muscle and more fat during transportation. Mother nature made pigs fat and never intended them to be fashion models.

Cattle suffer from different stress factors. As veterinarian Karen von Holleben tirelessly explains to truck drivers, cattle are particularly exposed to centrifugal forces during a journey full of bends, because of their high center of gravity, their great body weight, and their thin and feeble legs. Keeping upright is a constant struggle. If one animal falls, the whole lot go down like dominos, since every cow pushes down the one next to it. Only with an adequate load density—not too many animals, and not too few—can animals stand crosswise to the road and counteract the truck's movements by means of little steps. The narrowness of each space ensures that they only lie down when they are exhausted—that is, after a minimum of eight hours.

Cattle drink a lot. Each animal needs 30 to 60 liters of water a day, meaning about fifteen drinking sessions. Thirst makes the animal weaker and diminishes the quality of its meat. The troughs, if they exist at all, are likely to be full of dung, in which case the cattle will not drink from them. Overhead guards would

253

forestall the problems incurred by cattle jumping up and down, and electrolytic drinks would counteract the negative effects of high muscle stress. Yet few if any farmers are likely to go to such lengths. After all, once the animals have been sold for slaughter they can be dispatched on their final journey with no further thought.

Cattle show journey stress by losing weight. During a 24-hour transfer, they can lose up to 10 percent of their body weight. Scientists have shown that even ten days after a 300-kilometer journey, cows yield 20 percent less milk. After a 1,500-kilometer transfer, they need four weeks' rest before they can eat the usual quantity of fodder.

The last signs of journey stress are detected by the vets who inspect the meat of slaughtered animals. The three letters DFD—dark, firm, dry—mean poor quality. If animals from different herds are loaded onto the same truck, the rate of DFD meat skyrockets. Likewise, journeys full of bends, nervous drivers, and frequent jumps also use up the sugar reserves of the animals and increase their adrenaline production. The direct consequence is meat that is dark, firm, and difficult to preserve. The pH level rises from an ideal value of 5.5 to 5.8–6.2.

When our steak is too chewy, it is often pointless arguing with the cook: the blame is on those drivers and breeders who are prepared to shift their animals up and down Europe to obtain what are often minimal price advantages. Those who do not buy meat in supermarkets but patronize the local butcher who knows where his meat comes from, those who avoid beef that is excessively dark and red and pork that is too light and shiny, those who do not faint at the sight of a little piece of fat positively contribute to the well-being of their stomachs and to the quality of the animals' lives. One thing is certain: food lovers and animal rights' activists have much more in common than they might imagine. Shoulder to shoulder they could make a very influential and effective lobby.

FOURTEEN:2

FEATHERS AND PLUMES: OSTRICH FARMING

Emilio Senesi

Ostriches originated in distant lands. Their habitat used to extend from Africa to Syria and Arabia, but in recent times their territory has shrunk to the driest and sandiest areas of Africa. Ostrich farming developed this century in South Africa, in particular in the region of Outshoorn where there are still at least 200,000 of these earthbound birds. Things began to change in 1986, however, when the United Nations sanctions against South Africa, its apartheid domestic politics, and its imperial attitude towards Namibia spurred the creation of the first ostrich farms in the United States, to supply the required skins for Texan cowboy boots.

Ostriches are now farmed in several countries beyond South Africa: Namibia, Zimbabwe, Botswana, Israel, the United States, Australia, and Brazil. They can also easily be bred in European climates. In Italy there are about 700 farms with a total of 15,000 birds; moreover, farms have been set up in France, Spain, and Great Britain as well.

Ostriches have not been domesticated. They are wild animals in captivity, and their natural characteristics are only slightly mitigated. They usually run away very quickly to avoid confrontation, but if they are driven to the wall and are injured, they can attack. And when they attack, they give kicks with the two very strong toes of one foot, which can cause lethal injuries. Men and horses have been killed during such assaults. Sometimes ostriches emit a shrill hiss to scare intruders and prepare for attack. In our age of adventurous tourism, this information should be included in any survival handbook for ignorant daredevils.

70 kilometers per hour

A closer look at the subject reveals that ostriches are not quite such remote creatures as we might think. Their origin dates back to the Eocene epoch (40 to 50 million years ago), and they were first domesticated by the ancient Egyptians and Romans, who used them to pull their triumphal chariots. The various symbolic meanings attributed to ostrich feathers over the centuries prove that the bird was highly rated. Pharaohs and court dignitaries had ostrich feather fly-whisks as tokens of their role as men of law. Crusaders returning from the Middle East, where there were still thousands of ostriches, used the plumes to decorate their helmets as symbol of power

255

Ostrich meat was the focus of a merry encounter organized by the Michiana convivium in the United States, at Buchanan, close to the border between Michigan and Indiana. This report is by Paul Landeck, convivium co-executive with Larry O'Neil.

We felt the event was a great success in every way. There were twenty-nine members and one guest in attendance and we all learned a lot about ostrich and what it takes to get it from the egg to the dinner plate.

For instance, did you know that an ostrich can run 45 miles per hour and easily make 20-foot strides? At present, ostrich can be butchered as early as nine months old, though most are at least ten months. They are dumber than a gourd, as their brain is only about the size of a pea. They are extremely powerful and can rip open a car door with one swift kick if they want to. Their meat is considered a dark meat and is much like beef in my estimation. The way it was prepared for us, there was no "fowl" taste whatsoever, and we found it very tasty in all of the three variations we were served. Our dinner was held at Pebblewood Country Club, which happens to be operated by the same individual who raised the birds. He (Nick Stama) is quite a character and certainly had his trials and tribulations setting up the business of raising these birds. His first bird committed suicide on the day he turned it loose in its pen: a motorcycle drove by the pen and so scared it that it ran into the fence and killed itself.

That bird was served in my restaurant on that very night, as they had to butcher it right away. Here is the menu for the evening.

MENU

A "nest" of sautéed angelhair pasta served with meatballs of minced ostrich in a light Béarnaise sauce

Salad of baby mixed greens and wild mushrooms with a raspberry dressing

Vegetable soup made with shredded ostrich meat
(from the neck)

Ostrich tenderloin stuffed with crab and topped with
a lemon cream sauce

Skewer of ostrich and fresh vegetables garnished
with fresh asparagus and yellow rice

Warm bread

Chocolate heart stuffed with frozen raspberry yogurt served
over a light cream sauce garnished with raspberries

• • • • • • • • • • • • • •

Overall, the entire meal was very good. However, I think the ostrich
vegetable soup was the course people enjoyed most. Everyone was
encouraged to have the beverage of their choice, which is usually
how we do things. Being the wine maker that I am, my choice was a
glass of Tabor Hill Merlot from our wineries. It complemented the
bird quite well.

—Paul Landeck
Tabor Hill Winery and Restaurant,
Michiana Convivium

and virility. Since those days ostrich feathers have appeared in many coats of arms, most notably in that of the Prince of Wales since the time of Edward III. Over the years, ostrich feathers progressively became the prerogative of kings and queens, and later of the beautiful women who took their cue from royalty. Ostrich plume trimmings reached their zenith during the *belle époque*, when several farmers in South Africa's Cape colony made their fortunes. Initially a symbol of force and virility, these feathers finally became the ultimate symbol of femininity.

The ostrich is the largest living bird in the world, but it cannot fly since its feathers, wings, and tail are not functional. From a zoological point of view, it is the only living member of the Struthionidae family, belonging to the order Struthioniformes. Apparently there are no closely related species, even though a few zoologists consider emus and rheas to be their relatives. An adult ostrich is on average 2.5 to 3 meters high and 2 meters long. It usually weighs from 70 to 130 kilos, but some can reach as much as 180 kilos. Wild ostriches weigh 100 to 115 kilos on average, but farm-raised ostriches are usually slaughtered when a little less than that.

In the past there were a few species of birds even larger than the ostrich, like the giant elephant bird of Madagascar, which could weigh as much as 500 kilos. However, such creatures have long been extinct. Although the ostrich is a flightless bird it is a very rapid runner, reaching peaks of 70 kilometers per hour and maintaining constant speeds of 50 kilometers per hour for about fifteen minutes or more, with giant bumping strides of 4 to 5 meters each. The two toes of the foot are united by a web that enables the ostrich to run smoothly on unstable surfaces such as sand. High speed and perfect eyesight have always been—and still are—the ostrich's main defense against enemies and predators. Indeed, they account for its survival.

1 e g g , 1 2 p e o p l e

Though not without pitfalls, ostrich farming is a relatively straightforward affair. Since their natural habitat consists of deserts and savannas, ostriches are naturally resistant to major temperature drops at night and during the cold season. They do not like heavy rain and high humidity, but can endure snow and temperatures below 0° C. They feed more or less like chickens and turkeys, meaning that they are basically granivorous—herbivorous birds whose diet should be supplemented with fodder, medicinal herbs, and birdseed when they are chicks.

Definitive feathers grow when they reach sexual maturity, at about 16 to 18 months of age. Male ostriches are black, with snow-white feathers on the wings and the tail. They are easy to tell

from female ostriches, which are grayish brown all over. Ostriches have been bred for several years in order to obtain two very valuable products: plumes and skin. By contrast, until recently, ostrich meat was only eaten locally and its nutritional value was largely underestimated.

Nowadays we use everything in ostriches. Their skin is soft, but strong and easy to tan. Ostrich skin has always been considered a precious hide for luxury leather items such as shoes and bags. Furthermore, it is decorated with a natural pattern deriving from its quill marks. Plumes are still used in the fashion trade, but nowadays it is the commercial value of the meat that has made ostrich farming really profitable. Eggs are much prized, less for nutritional purposes than for breeding. (An ostrich egg is 14 to 18 centimeters long, 12 to 15 centimeters across, and can weigh from 0.7 to 1.9 kilos, 1.1 to 1.6 kilos on average; one ostrich egg corresponds to twenty-four hen's eggs and would suffice in an omelet for at least twelve people!) The very fine, short, soft neck plumes are used to produce sophisticated brushes for electronics and precision instruments since they are antistatic. In addition, bones are used to produce supplements for zootechnical fodder. By the way, did you know that ostrich corneas are similar in size and shape to a human's? For the moment, they are a marginal subproduct, but they could one day be successfully used in transplants. The species of ostrich bred for money and

FARMING · If ostrich meat is such a new, resourceful product, why is it so hard to find? There are many reasons for this, but it is worthwhile explaining at least a couple of them. The first is that the South Africans used to hold a monopoly of both eggs and breeders. In Zimbabwe, farmers either had to capture wild ostrich breeders in the savanna or incubate fertile eggs taken directly from ostrich nests. The new farms thus had to start from scratch.

The second reason is that many legislative obstacles had to be overcome. In Italy, the first ostrich farms opened a few years ago, but it was only in 1996 that laws prohibiting their slaughter were repealed. However, those in the trade are still awaiting the approval of norms defining the characteristics of slaughterhouses for ostriches, such that the creatures can be slaughtered in ordinary abattoirs as well. In the meantime, live ostriches are transported to foreign slaughterhouses and then their meat is reimported into Italy. This game of snakes and ladders neither promotes a serious commercial policy nor encourages the spreading of ostrich meat.

admitted for international trade is the *Struthio camelus australis*, the only species that is not endangered. All the other species and subspecies—*S. camelus, S. masaicus, S. molybdophanes*—are protected and, as a consequence, not marketable. The species *S. syriacus* has already become extinct, as the last specimen was killed in 1960 along the border between Syria and Jordan. The species *S. camelus australis* includes several types of ostriches that are mistakenly called breeds—Blue Neck, African Black or Black Neck, Red Neck—but most farm-raised specimens are mixed subjects whose characters tend to converge.

A 10-kilo tenderloin

Fresh ostrich meat is rare in South Africa, where it is generally served as *biltong* (jerked meat). Paradoxically it is becoming more popular in Europe than in its country of origin; in fact, it is no longer a rarity in supermarkets and restaurants. A slaughtered 12- to 15-month-old ostrich of 90 to 110 kilos live weight provides about 35 kilos of meat, 10 kilos of which are prime choice cuts such as tenderloin. Ostrich meat is also served on planes. British Airways has included ostrich meat in the meals of first-class passengers on overseas routes. Belgium and Switzerland compete for the position of greatest per capita consumption in the world. Probably this phenomenon is closely related to the phobias caused by Mad Cow disease, cholesterol, and unsaturated fats. The interest in ostrich meat is not just a matter of gastronomic curiosity, but a possible sign of new nutritional patterns.

The geographical and cultural diversity of ostrich meat diminishes as its sensorial and nutritional features are analyzed. To put it briefly, ostrich is half way between beef and poultry. It has the same dark red color as beef, often with a cherry red nuance. It is as tender as poultry, since the muscular fibers are quite short. It has a particular taste, less pronounced than beef, but more characterized and intense than ordinary poultry. It is easy to digest because it is so tender that it requires only brief cooking; moreover, no sauce or gravy are required to embellish its taste. It is low in fats (less than 1 percent) and cholesterol, but high in unsaturated fatty acids. Proteins account for more than 21 percent, and the level of essential amino acids is the same as in other types of meat. It is rich in minerals, especially iron and phosphorus, and low in sodium. One hundred grams of ostrich meat give 105 kilocalories. Hardly surprisingly, many Swiss clinics and nursing homes have been serving it for many years now.

The fact that ostrich meat is not taken into account by recipe books should excite the imagination of gourmets, but for the moment nobody has gone beyond a good ostrich fillet or stew. Ostrich meat could also be an ingredient for hamburgers and meat rolls, stuffed vegetables, ravioli, and cold cuts. As to cooking methods, apart from the traditional grill, we could also try dry heat (baked, baked in paper) and moist heat (steamed) preparations or the microwave.

FOURTEEN : 3

SINS OF THE FLESH

Tom Bruce-Gardyne

Time and again, the European Ministers of state are presented with the most compelling argument yet for dropping the export ban on British beef. With every trip to Britain comes the sensual delight of meat at its most tender—each succulent mouthful a poignant reminder of what they are missing back home. Whatever the cut, whether it's a rib or a rump steak, the beef is invariably prime Aberdeen Angus from the damp Scottish hills. As the ministers return to Brussels and continue with their blockade, one can only marvel at such an orgy of self-denial.

On a more serious note there is a depressing sense of inevitability over the way the beef crisis developed. Once the British government had made its statement last year about the possible link between bovine spongiform encephalopathy (BSE) in cattle and Creutzfeld-Jakob disease (CJD) in humans, the media circus took over, showing all the usual restraint and sensitivity for a complex and still unresolved issue. But here is not the place to rake over the past and point fingers. Suffice to say that the crisis is not just about Britain and it is not just about beef. The real issue concerns our willingness to pay the price of a cheap food policy and the sacrifice of quality and possible risk to health that lie behind it. If the industrialized chicken is at the end of the scale, then surely the humanely reared, grass-fed Aberdeen Angus is at the other.

The *doddies* or *hummles* as they were known, have been roaming the grasslands of northeast Scotland for as long as anyone can recall. However, it is only over the last two centuries that these rugged, black beasts have evolved from their local roots into the most famous breed of beef cattle in the world. The first real pioneer was Hugh Watson of Keillor in the county of Angus, who began in 1808 to build up an all but closed herd on the likes of Tarnity Jock and Old Grannie. Before being struck by lightning at age thirty-five, Old Grannie produced no less than twenty-five calves, including the famous Strathmore, sold to the Emperor Napoleon III in 1856. These vital early bloodlines were developed and strengthened by William McCombie of Tillyfour in Aberdeen-shire and by Sir George MacPherson-Grant, who died just as the breed was getting established on the other side of the Atlantic. Every winter, ranchers from the American Midwest and the Argentine pampas would come to the sales in Perth, Scotland, and bid for pedigree stock with which to improve their herds back home. By the 1950s, farmers from the United States were

261

paying so much money that one could sell a prime Angus bull and buy a farm on the proceeds. In 1963, prices peaked at £63,000 for what proved to be a rather pricey piece of beef, since the young bull was later found infertile. The prevailing fashion overseas was for smaller bulls, and breeders made the mistake of pursuing size to the exclusion of other attributes, as well as ignoring the domestic market. British farmers turned increasingly toward continental breeds such as Charolais, Limousin, and Simmental, which could provide the bigger carcasses that were in demand. Today, thanks largely to crossbreeding with bigger Canadian Aberdeen Angus, the breed appears very much back on form.

Rain, grass, and carotene

The ancestral home of Aberdeen Angus is in the eastern foothills of the Grampian mountains that lie between Perth and Inverness. For a good eight months of the year they live a life in the open, grazing on the lush grass and clover that cover these hillsides. Whether gently bathed with rain or belted by hail and sleet, under their tough coats as black as Guinness these cattle seem impervious to the vagaries of Scottish weather. They are compact and stocky with no horns and somewhat stumpy legs, and with their well-rounded rump and broad backs they are quite clearly bred for beef. There is no evidence of a previous vocation as with those continental breeds that evolved from the plough. According to the Scots, Aberdeen Angus don't melt in the winter, meaning they retain their body weight thanks to the healthy layer of fat they wear beneath their coats. Calving is in spring, and the young are kept on their mother's milk for six months—a far cry from the dairy herds where calves are weaned at a few days old and effectively raised as orphans. In the winter months, the cattle are usually brought indoors and fed on silage, which is dried, fermented grass, perhaps enriched with molasses, barley, oats, or potatoes.

It seems a better life than most breeds of beef cattle that live inside, chained to a feed lot and fed on a concentrated diet of cereal for the fastest possible growth. Grass certainly gives the beef more flavor, but the carotene in the grass helps turn the fat a buttery yellow, which nanny supermarket has decided we don't want. Apparently what we do want is cherry-red beef, with the least amount of Persil-white fat possible, and this can only come from cereal-fed cattle. To what extent we choose our food on appearance is a moot point, but our big buyers certainly seem to—try looking for a bent carrot in a British supermarket. However, there are signs of progress with companies like Marks & Spencer actively selling Aberdeen Angus beef from grass-fed Scottish herds, and interestingly their sales are up compared with two years ago—well before the Mad Cow debacle began.

Pure as the Queen Mother

All the efforts of rearing the heifers (the females) and the steers (the males) to produce good beef could be undone by what follows. Humane slaughter with the minimum of stress undeniably benefits the quality of the beef. On the Glenbervie estate in Aberdeenshire, the animals are taken to the slaughterhouse in the evening to allow them to calm down before being killed early the next morning. Initially the meat is tender—to quote the scientists Harris and Shorthouse, "The Carib Indians, from whom we derive the word cannibal, would eat their victims very fresh, before the tightening effects of rigormortis." Thereafter it is best to wait and not chill the meat too soon. To achieve the tenderest and most succulent beef, you need to hang the carcass for a good three weeks at

BEEFSTEAK · A well-hung sirloin of pure Angus beef cooking in its own juices and fat sounds faintly immoral in these days of lean cuisine. So much of our meat sold as "fresh and fat-free" approaches supermarket chicken for sheer lack of flavor. Luckily, the prime cuts of Aberdeen Angus beef have their own tissue of subcutaneous fat. Known as marbling, this is what keeps the meat sweet and juicy in the oven. Steaks should be a good 2 centimeters thick and after seasoning need to be brushed lightly with melted butter or oil before being grilled or fried in a heavy cast-iron pan for four to five minutes each side. Best of all, grill them on the red-hot embers of an open fire. Then sit down with the finest bottle you can lay your hands on, slice through that wonderful burgundy flesh, pop some in your mouth, and let it slowly, slowly melt.

The Aberdeen Angus Cattle Society
Secretary: Bob Anderson
6 Kings Place, Perth PH2 8AD Scotland
Tel. ++44/1738/622477
Fax ++44/1738/636436

around 3°C to give the natural enzymes time to break down the protein in the muscle tissue. If it is hung on the bone, rather than in a vacuum pack, as is more common, this can further help concentrate the flavor into the meat.

Over the last thirty years, consumption of beef in Britain has been falling at roughly the same rate as wine consumption in Italy and France. Of course these factors are unrelated except that they share similar causes: a population shift from manual to sedentary work, vague concerns over health, and the fact that these victuals have long been cheap, plentiful, and taken for granted. Until the export ban began, prime Angus beef from producers like Donald Russell in Aberdeenshire have been better appreciated abroad. Like other companies, they are keeping up their contacts with top chefs from around the world for the happy day when the ban gets lifted.

As Aberdeen Angus bulls trot round the ring at Perth or parade about the Royal Highland Show in Edinburgh, there's no doubting their pedigree, with bloodlines as pure as their patron, Queen Elizabeth the Queen Mother. However, checking the pedigree of the fillet of Angus beef on your plate is another matter. The agreed minimum is that it should come from cattle sired by a purebred bull registered with the Aberdeen Angus Cattle Society. To tighten these constraints would limit supply. There is certainly a strong demand for Aberdeen Angus, at least in name. It is said that in Italy before the export ban, only a sixth of what was claimed to be Aberdeen Angus was actually genuine, but who knows how much this was due to deceit or ignorance. Perhaps Aberdeen Angus had become a generic term for *Bistecca inglese*. In Britain, one of the positive outcomes of BSE has been the move to ensure traceability, whereby meat can be tracked from field to shelf, and this will help protect prime beef from a specified breed. It may also encourage the better farmers to come closer to the consumer and move away from the anonymity of producing just a commodity.

SOS FOR DOMESTIC ANIMALS

Anna Mannucci

Once upon a time there was the Val D'Adige gray cow, the Friuli black pig, and the Calabrian, Sicilian, Sardinian, Neapolitan, and Apulian horses. They have all recently become extinct. In the same way, Paduan hens, Bergamo sheep, Calvana cows, Lamon sheep, Casertana pigs, white Garfagnina sheep, Giara horses, Amiata donkeys, and many others have become endangered species. These breeds of domestic animals, as the names suggest, had time-honored environmental and traditional ties with particular Italian regions. About thirty years ago, people began to realize that they were almost all dangerously close to becoming extinct. Some species, such as the Agerolese cow, Turchessa sheep, and Valfortorina goat were officially recognized as "relics."

Whenever the word extinction is mentioned, several wild animals spring to mind almost of a conditioned reflex: the first is often the panda, followed by tigers, elephants, and so on. Those who have a basic knowledge of the natural world will also add a few wild plants to the list, such as cacti, mahogany, and some species of orchid; linguists will think of dialects and cultural traditions. Yet farm animals are rarely mentioned. However, back in the 1970s, the the United Nations Agriculture and Food Organization (FAO) set alarm bells ringing. In 1976 in Italy, the National Research Center (CNR) launched the "Defense of the Genetic Resources of Animal Populations" project directed by Professors Rognoni, Ferrara, Velfré, and Finzi. This came to an end in 1982, and the next year the *Atlante etnografico delle popolazioni bovine allevate in Italia* (Ethnographic Atlas of Bovine Breeds Raised in Italy) and the *Atlante etnografico delle popolazioni ovine e caprine allevate in Italia* (Ethnographic Atlas of Breeds of Sheep and Goats Raised in Italy) were published. The first stage involved a census, and only later did the rare creatures become the object of scientific study and conservation programs.

The National Center for the Conservation of Animal Germoplasm in Extinction (CeSGAVE) was set up at the Casaldianni estate in Circello (Benevento) by the then minister for Agriculture and Forestry, the Italian Association of Breeders, and the Commune of Circello. In 1992, the Center became a part of a Consortium for the experimentation and application of innovative biotechniques (ConSDABI), commonly known as the Circello Estate), whose official aims are the "conservation, multiplication, knowledge, genetic improvement, and zootechnic use of indigenous breeds threatened by extinction." In 1994, an

265

Artificial Insemination and Embryo Production Center was also set up on the estate. Furthermore, since 1992, the European Community has financed the rearing of breeds threatened by extinction under EC Rule No. 2078.

Indigenous breeds and master breeds

These and other projects were set up to counteract the situation that arose after World War Two when the Frisian and Alpine Brown cows arrived in Italy. Their advent was almost an invasion: in 1940, a year considered to be crucial by experts, there were 188,000 Frisians, whereas by 1983 there were 3,486,000. These are "cosmopolitan" breeds, able to live anywhere and are suited to industrial-type breeding, with no links to the surrounding landscape. The productivity of these cows was certainly excellent, and thanks to them, Italy experienced a boom in the consumption of meat and other animal-based products. Hens and pigs were also intensively farmed, whereas sheep and goats were excluded, although many breeds were also lost or almost lost, since where farm animals are concerned, those that do not produce (in a certain sense, those that are not eaten) become extinct.

Farms became animal-protein factories and the animals were selected according to whether they could survive and produce in unnatural conditions, which often cause them great suffering. A system evolved that favored only a few breeds, those that were highly productive (even if with high social and environmental costs), capable of surviving in factory-farm conditions, in large numbers, eating industrial fodder, with constant medical care. This was detrimental to many less productive stronger breeds used to living outdoors in small groups and eating local fodder, however more economical these breeds were overall. Of course at the time, horses and cows were more useful for their manure and for pulling plows and carts than for milk and meat. The tractor, and mechanization in general, have made cart horses, mules, and oxen redundant.

After a few decades, the error of merely pursuing the productivity myth was acknowledged, because the choices that were made proved detrimental both in natural and socioeconomic terms. The "reduction or absence of genetic differences," according to an article by Donato Matassino of the Federico II University of Naples and a director of CeSGAVE, in *L'allevatore* of 7 July 1996, "leads to a fall, or the disappearance in extreme cases, in the homeostatic or self-governing abilities of the biological system, with the risk of losing information that cannot be retrieved." Matassino continues, "Indigenous animals form an integral part of the countryside, and as such, should be considered part of the public heritage, indeed the cultural heritage."

The recovery of indigenous breeds does not necessarily imply some museum-like project or a zoo of traditional cows. In their paper presented at a conference on "The Conservation of Biodiversity in Umbria" (28–30 May, 1996), G. Gandini, A. Caroli, and L. Catellani pointed out that "the exploitation of a breed passes through various states, including the recognition of productivity, genetic and managerial improvement, the creation of infrastructure, the commercial promotion of production, the development of markets." Typical indigenous breeds

evolved in specific circumstances. Both environmentally and culturally, safeguarding them entails not only the defense of their zootechnic biodiversity and genetic heritage, but also the preservation of their ecological niche, which includes farmers, local traditions, and tastes, as well as agricultural and cultural systems.

Tarentaise and Abondance

A remarkable example of saving, which is often cited by those in the field, is the Reggiana cow, typical of the plains of northern Italy. It was saved by Parmesan cheese. In the above-mentioned C.N.R. Atlas, the breed was considered in 1983 to be a "semi-relic," with only 1,125 examples left (there were 84,000 in 1940 and 130,000 in the 1950s). However, since 1990, with the help of the Consortium for the Promotion of the Ancient Reggiana Breed, this cow has been saved since it produces excellent milk used to make Parmesan cheese. Thus we are not advocating a bucolic return to bygone times, but suggesting that the economic benefits of diversity and quality should be evaluated accurately, possibly at the expense of intensive farming. One of the first exemplary experiences of the link between breed and product, quoted by G. Gandini, A.

267

Caroli, and L. Catellani, was the French experiment with Beaufort cheese, which acquired a denomination of protected origin as early as 1968, but which was threatened by the expansion of Frisian cows in the 1970s. In 1986, the producers stipulated that Beaufort could only be made from the milk of Tarentaise and Abondance cows; furthermore, since 1993, the milk can come only from farms with production below 50 quintals per milking.

In some cases, the impulse for conservation is more scientific; for example, the region of Tuscany finances the safeguarding of Pontremolese and Garfagnina cows (from the localities of the same name), two breeds that were considered "desperate cases" by Emanuele Villa of the Italian Breeders Association. In 1940, there were 15,000 Pontremolese cows, but by 1983 (when some were already kept in special centers), there were only 13, and in 1995 the number had risen only to 23. These cows produce little milk and "poor" veal, but the fact that they are suited to their surrounding is an intrinsic value. Their genetic characteristics are still little known, and they should therefore be "put in the safe," or rather in the fridge, which is the procedure followed by the ConSDABI using the most up-to-date technology. Besides rearing ancient breeds, the Center conserves *in frigido* gametes and/or zygotes, and carries out in-vitro fertilization, embryo transfers from one mother to another, cytogenetic tests, and molecular biological analysis.

Darwin and breeders

On account of its geographical reality, the presence of the Apennines, numerous valleys, and a variety of historical factors, Italy is one of the richest countries in Europe in terms of "taxonomic species and ethnic groups," to quote from a ConSDABI paper that also deals with plants. At the other end of the spectrum, in a country such as Holland, made up exclusively of plains, the local breed is synonymous with the cosmopolitan or national breed. However, according to Antonio Saltini, author of the four-volume *Storia delle scienze agrarie*, Italy has paid little attention to this wealth: "Italy is an emblematic case, because it is one of the countries that has most abandoned and sacrificed their traditional zootechnical heritage." Saltini locates the date of several fundamental choices back in 1870, when it was decided not to select or improve local breeds. A census of local breeds was taken shortly after Unification, when they began to be replaced by English and Dutch animals. At that time, there was still a great variety of farm animals in Italy (various colored dairy cows, white oxen, white pigs with black stripes on the abdomen), although they were almost always kept in dreadful conditions.

Saltini describes the very different situation in England, where a short time earlier Darwin had studied the way breeders worked and their criteria for selection. He could do this in

England and not in Italy because selective breeding of work animals and animals for meat had begun in the 18th century. The English meat market was rich and demanding, great competitions and auctions were held, butchers proudly displayed their animals to the public before they were slaughtered, and all English counties had their own traditional breeds.

By 1993, however, many of the diverse breeds that were of zootechnical interest in Europe in the first half of the century were in danger of extinction. Yet the problem is more general. In 1995, the UN's Food and Agriculture Organization published its *World Watch List for Domestic Animal Diversity*, featuring the domestic animal breeds in danger of extinction throughout the world, from the Koto-koli pony of Benin, to the Botswana Tswana pig, the Brazilian Cardao donkey, the Cambodian Monn khmer chicken, the Chilean Chaku llama, and thousands of others. By the 1980s, people had begun to realize that the intensive model of farming exported to Third World countries is destructive both to nature and society, and that it is preferable, worldwide, to recover local breeds using up-to-date technology.

Chapter **FIFTEEN**

Leftovers

A LEFTOVER CULTURE

Alberto Capatti

There are many ways of thinking about the scraps of food and the leftovers from a meal. The most obvious is familiar to the down-and-out, who live on the streets and rummage in trash cans for the only free comfort society has to offer. Yet other perspectives spring readily to mind if we think about how we procure and consume food. In our economy of abundance, the concepts of food saving, recovery, and reuse no longer get much consideration; they seem to belong to some distant past. These days, leftovers have to be eliminated. There is the real danger of overproduction, whereby food has to be destroyed before it is ever distributed. The challenge of eliminating food cleanly, filling up trashcans to save

money, has become more complex and burdensome than the problem of producing and conserving food. This paradox prompts us to address questions not to economists but to consumers and to adopt the chicken or cow's perspective in taking a long, hard look at the infernal machine that churns out legs and wings, carcasses and ribs, which are then frozen, minced, and converted into animal feed or trash.

The cooking of leftovers takes us back to a subliminal past, which surfaces in our thoughts and our tastes. The very history of gastronomy is a "leftover" history, in that it is concerned with supplies, ingredients, portions, and ephemeral objects of taste, mixed together and subsequently destroyed. What is superfluous is inedible because it is more than our appetites can manage, and like the scraps that become the ingredients for new dishes the following day, can provide "food for thought" concerning the values that have formed our eating habits and our culture. It's easy to throw away a dented tin or a thawed-out fish, but it's hard to do the same with the leftovers of a dish that has cost us patience and hard work! The sacrifice is so intolerable it's as if we were getting rid of our own tastes and pleasures. In many European cultures, the art of recycling leftovers has always been the cook's salvation and her vindication—a sort of extreme confirmation of her role. Yet the exact opposite is true in China.

After all, isn't avoiding leftovers by eating more than one's fill a good way of appreciating the banquet?

Today, leftovers are viewed with suspicion for health reasons, which are used as an excuse to dump provisions, packages past their sell-by date, and poorly refrigerated foodstuffs. Here we have a second paradox, since the strategy of strict control leads not to rational, balanced consumption, but to the programmed liquidation of foodstuffs. In the past, society was a body that held onto food for as long as it could, and that called all social strata around its table. When there wasn't a crumb left, its celebration could be deemed complete. This was society's way of being healthy.

Today the body politic puts evacuation on a level with nutrition, practicing disposal with the same profit-inspired tenacity. Devoid of religious, civil, economic, and political values, waste has penetrated its way to the heart of the nutritional act, ultimately reducing the problem to indifference and insignificance. Since it would be hard to imagine returning to an autarkic or self-sufficient lifestyle, and since the mega market generates it shown negation, let's consider the brief steps it would take to recover what used to be good to eat—and perhaps still is. In other words, let's re-examine leftovers: they could be undigested gastronomic possibilities.

RICE AND FISH BONES

Françoise Sabban

L'Art d'accommoder les restes is the French equivalent of the Italian writer Lindo Guerrini's *L'arte di utilizzare gli avanzi della mensa* (the art of using leftovers). Both allude to a skill that was indispensable to every good housewife in the past, in France as in Italy. In China, on the contrary, such an "art" is unthinkable, and no one would dream of writing books of the kind. Not that Chinese writers and poets can't pen culinary treatises: in fact, most if not all culinary treatises are the work of great literary minds, one of the best known of whom was the prolific 18th-century poet Yuan Mei, dubbed the "Brillat-Savarin" of China. His magnificent cookbook, *The Menus of the Garden of Suiyuan,* is a collection of the finest recipes of his time, gleaned over the years by his cook, whose job it was to take note of the preparation of dishes that gratified his master's palate whenever he happened to be eating out.

No, the reason why it is impossible even to contemplate books about leftovers in China is the low esteem in which they are held there. Though leftovers may be commendable symbols of surplus, of wealth so great as to allow for waste, they are also the waste of eating, and hence contemptible, unfit for any further noble use. In China, kitchen scraps enjoy no consideration whatsoever and are thus necessarily devoid of gastronomic value.

True, practical reason has justifications that inflexible theory often tends to ignore, which is why certain indelicate restaurateurs bent exclusively on gain are capable of dressing a half-eaten fish in sauce to deceive subsequent diners into believing that they are being given the genuine article. But it would be wrong to confuse unscrupulous innkeepers with professionals for whom scrimping and saving is an alien practice. Like the star chefs of our own Western firmament, such cooks aim exclusively at satisfying a clientele unperturbed by financial concerns. They are thus prepared to strip away the tender outer leaves of Chinese cabbages to get to the straw-yellow heart. The outcome is cuisine for the elite, and the question of leftovers simply does not arise. What remains on the dish, if anything, is an insignificant detail; incorporated in the price, it is no more than a whim of the diner, and no one pays the slightest attention to it.

Excused from the sin of gluttony

As in Western Europe, in China the great chef focuses on *haute cuisine* with no concern for leftovers. Even the initial selection of the finest ingredients implies discarding elements that would normally be regarded as perfectly edible. In China, the only person interested in what remains in the dish at the end of a meal is the hungry beggar prowling round the table ready to snatch scraps before the waiters dispose of them. When eating in contemporary China you can still occasionally feel the eyes of some wretched creature bearing down on your hypernourished Western person. As soon as you get up and go, he will swoop down to get whatever remains on your plate.

Within the sumptuous context of great banquets, the host spares no expense, to the extent that it is virtually impossible to eat all of each dish: as the Chinese say, surplus connotes well-being, ostentation, and generosity. Of course outside this sphere, leftovers are fastidiously recovered and eaten without qualms at the next meal. In normal households, they are kept and served later without even reheating them. At the restaurant, today as yesterday, they are carefully wrapped up, either at the client's request or at the restaurateur's suggestion, and taken home. This system works well for the solo diner, because it is often hard to order single portions in restaurants. In this way he can order a full meal—always far too abundant anyway, since the Chinese menu is based on the concept of sharing—without having to feel embarrassed about leaving half the food on the plate under the half-amused, half-accusatory stares of the restaurant staff. True, you may not know what to do with all those boxes full of food, especially if your only home is a small hotel room. But at least for the moment your honor is salvaged. Once out of the restaurant, however, weighted down by the precious boxes, you have to find a way of discreetly disposing of them. And your heart fills with shame at the thought, with so many people dying of hunger around you. This happened to me one late spring evening on the streets of Kowloon. I had my hands full with a huge box of Cantonese pasta, which the staff of a restaurant—where my eyes had been bigger than my stomach—had foisted on me by way of a punishment. I didn't know how to get rid of the burden without feeling guilty. Then fortune suddenly smiled upon me in the shape of a semi-naked giant of a man, whom I recognized as one of the many poor tramps who used to roam Hong Kong. His hair was like matted wool and he wore faded rags. His woebegone gaze was from another world, and he had the timeless appearance of someone who had stepped out of an album of faded photographs of gray, pre-war China. Locked in his poverty, he enthralled me. The big man must have been relatively young because his long, twisted hair was still jet-black. Bare-chested, he crouched in the middle of the pavement, idly scratching his backside. Before I had time to realize what I was doing, I put the box of still warm pasta at his feet. Then I rushed away, blushing but happy, with his expression of gratitude following on behind me. It was in this way that I *a)* ingloriously expiated my sins of gluttony, and *b)* shamefacedly returned the poor soul to his sad condition as a hopeless outsider by offering him the leftovers of my dinner.

Daily meals and banquets

But let's think further about the impossible art of using leftovers in China. There is no actual contradiction between the fastidiousness with which the recoverable is recovered and a gastronomic contempt for leftovers. The apparent paradox can be justified on at least two grounds. The first is the fact that everyday meals, however fine, and banquets staged for special occasions imply two clearly distinct, if not opposite, situations. The daily meal is invested with vivifying powers, and its main aim is to nourish. It has to be based on the consumption of a given number of cereals: boiled rice, steamed bread, pasta. The dishes that accompany this staple diet are enjoyable accessories designed to satisfy taste, pleasure, and gourmandise (although nowadays some people can

virtually afford to do without the indispensable—i.e., starchy cereals—and nourish themselves, in the full sense of the word, with the accessory—i.e., meat-based dishes). The banquet for special occasions follows exactly the reverse order to the daily model. The cereal element is served for solely symbolic purposes at the end of the meal, when diners, satiated by the finest courses served without accompaniments, have no appetite left to eat even the tiniest morsel. In this context of gastronomic grandiosity, the recovery of any leftover food would be inconceivable, forbidden by the morals of lavish ostentation. Again, in everyday meals, whose function is sustenance, the opposite is true. Even if only as a question of economy, it would be inconceivable to waste food without compromising true morals—Morals with a capital "M."

And this leads me to a second problem with leftovers, which derives from the Chinese concept of "culinary preparation." Making a dish is a one-way operation in which each sequence is conducted in a climate of extreme tension and has to be performed at exactly the right moment. It is essential to respect a whole series of imperatives dictated by the nature of the ingredients, by how they are cut, by the heat of the flame, the condiments, and the cooking methods. The result is a finished, non-modifiable, ready-to-eat dish. In theory the cook, the master of an art, uses fire to elaborate dishes whose heat, flavor, texture, and smell combine to create perfect harmony. Eating the dish means destroying this harmony once and for all. No amount of culinary intervention on the left-overs of a fine meal can recover it. Even when everything that can be recycled has been recovered and con-served, leftovers are always leftovers, and have to be consumed as they are. An item of food that has become a left-over cannot be magically restored to nobility, not even as a raw material for culinary rehabilitation. We therefore have two reasons why the "art of using leftovers" does not exist in China.

Nevertheless, there is an exception to the accepted rule, whereby the cook should know how to create a meal in proportion to the appetite of the din-ers, thus limiting leftovers to a bare minimum. Cooked rice can be fried in a pan and thus recooked, and leftover steamed bread can be heated up the day after to accompany the main course of another meal. Indeed most cookery books avoid mentioning the provenance of the cooked rice required for frying, which is quite likely to be rice previously cooked and left over from the day before. A beautiful book (called *Zhongguo mishi*, or *The Chinese Rice Book*) on rice and rice-based recipes, published in Taiwan, is the only case I have ever come across of a deliberate effort to deal with the problem of the leftovers that haunt the Chinese housewife. Hardly surprising-ly, it was declaredly educational in its aims. So fried rice recipes using pre-cooked rice are the only example I know of recycling leftovers.

Indispensable dishes

Rice is the staple food par excel-lence, and indispensable source of nourishment that ensures our survival. To waste it is unthinkable. While elab-orate dishes belong to the sphere of pleasure, rice resides in the sphere of necessity. This is why it may be recov-ered and recooked. The daily methods of cooking rice allow for a second culi-nary operation that would be incon-ceivable for other foods. As the basic element of a meal, rice is boiled with-out salt in the right amount of water. Cooking rice this way makes it edible but is not considered a "culinary oper-ation." The preparation provides us with a nourishing foodstuff whose neutral flavor sets off the tasty dishes it accompanies. When it is subsequently fried, it at last takes part in a true culi-nary procedure. It is then dressed and mixed with other ingredients, with other flavors and aromas, to become a "complete" dish.

Reading the culinary treatises pub-lished in China today, I have the impression that Chinese family cook-ing produces no leftovers. But this does not mean that the authors pay no attention to household economy. On the contrary. A 1995 book entitled *Chufang xiao qiaomen 1300 li* ("1,300 Tricks in the Kitchen") leaves no doubt about the need for sound man-agement and avoiding waste. The fol-lowing is a translation of an amazing recipe for cooking fish bones:

It would be a real pity to throw away fish bones, which contain important nutritional elements such as calcium and phosphorus. Cooked as follows, they are particularly appetizing, delicious, and both crunchy and soft. Chop up the bones and fry them in plenty of oil. When they are golden, drain and dry them. Marinate them immediately in vinegar until they are cold. Fry them a second time for three or four minutes, drain them, and serve immediately.

Far be it from us to mock the Chinese who, in this instance, mask a remarkable sense of economy with dietary considerations. Wasn't the great chef Massaliot, author of the *Cuisinier royal et bourgeois* (1691), moved by the same spirit in asserting that: "Anchovy bones may be fried. Dipped in a batter made of white wine, flour, salt and pepper, you can use them as a garnish for another dish or serve them as a *hors-d'oeuvre*, dressed with orange and parsley . . ."?

The choice between the *siècle d'or* French approach and the more recent Chinese one is entirely up to you!

FIFTEEN : 3

GOD IN THE CRUMBS

Dominique Prédali

For centuries, monasteries and convents were bastions of gastronomy. To this day, two- or three-star itineraries follow virtually the same "routes of taste" that have connected up monasteries, convents, abbeys, and great religious centers since the Middle Ages.

The reputation of these famous centers of gastronomic luxury has never faded. Monks were the researchers, breeders, herbalists, and apothecaries of the Middle Ages. They had the finest produce, the best-equipped kitchens, and the personnel best trained in culinary matters. Though they asserted themselves as masters of festive cookery, it was during periods of fasting that their great treasury of cunning and imagination emerged to fullest effect. Monks compensated for the limited choice of ingredients available with remarkable culinary skill. Since food is a gift of God, it is forbidden to waste it. All the various orders thus became masters of exploiting leftover flour, apples, milk, honey, and so on. Some developed or perfected methods of preserving cheese, biscuits, spice bread (in Austria they invented *Oblaten-Lebkuchen*, spice bread on a wafer base to make it keep better), hydromel (a low-alcohol, watery mead), cider, and wine. At first, spices were added to mask the acidity of the wine, then techniques were discovered to conserve and improve the taste.

In the austere Middle Ages, nothing could be wasted and leftovers had to be "recycled." This was particularly so with bread, imbued as it was with symbolic values. According to a German legend, the devil collected any crumbs that fell from the table, turned them into burning coals, and threw them at sinners roasting in hell. Anyone accidentally allowing crumbs to fall from the table would be punished. The Benedictine rule, which was echoed in the Statutes of Peter the Venerable, the 12th-century abbot of Cluny, clearly states that at the end of the meal one of the monks should use his hands, a knife, or a brush to carefully gather up the crumbs and put them in a special basket. These same crumbs were used to make a soup at the end of the week to be eaten hot on Saturday evenings. The same ingredients could be used to make a humble pudding for the poor. A similar tradition has survived in Spain, where on Christmas Eve they eat in *las migas del Niño*, the Crumbs of Baby Jesus.

To this day, in monasteries and the lay world alike, stale bread is not wasted and instead is used to make the sweet fried pancake that the French call *pain perdu* and the Spanish *torrijas de Santa Teresa*. The recipe, which originated in the convents of Castille, is repeated all over Europe with the same ingredients: slices of bread soaked in milk, dipped in beaten egg yolk and fried, and sprinkled with sugar and cinnamon. In Sweden it is served with black currant jam. Another, slightly more elaborate variation on the theme is *sopa dourada*, a soup that always features on feast-day menus in Portuguese monasteries. Its sole ingredients are great quantities of egg yolks, syrup, and almonds. In France the same dish is called *soupe dorée;* in Savoy it becomes *soupe crute* and in the Creuse region *soupe rousse*.

Stale bread is also one of the ingredients of *mendiant*, a very compact sweet pudding originally named *quatre mendiants* in honor of the mendicant orders: the Augustines, the Carmelites, the Dominicans, and the Franciscans. In this recipe, the four orders are represented by raisins, hazelnuts, figs, and almonds, the colors of which evoke those of the habits of these orders.

Celestial nourishment

Eggs are an inexhaustible source of inspiration in monastic cookery. According to popular legend, the ban on eating eggs during Lent, in force since the 4th century, derives from the fact that Christ was pelted with eggs after the flagellation. The ban translated into a surplus of this ingredient in the days following the "lean period." The egg-yolk-based confectionery of Portuguese and Spanish convents in the Middle Ages undoubtedly constitutes the most original and creative way of using surpluses or leftovers in recipes that would make a saint swoon.

Why the yolks? Because the whites were used to lubricate the rigging of ships and to clarify sherry and sometimes red wine as well. It would have been out of the question to waste all the yolks, so the common practice was to donate them to convents. The nuns had Saracen maids whose flair and skill with egg yolks and sugar could be harnessed to bake an infinite variety of delicate sweetmeats. It was the Saracen maids who initiated the nuns to the secrets of Arab confectionery, a direct legacy of the refined cuisine of the aristocracy. For the greater glory of confectionery, these women invented a thousand and one variations on the theme of egg yolks and sugar, adding almonds, coconut, walnuts, cheese, candied pumpkin, milk, flower essences, vanilla, cinnamon, and liqueurs, all with sublime delicacy. Some of these creations have disappeared today, but in both Portugal and Spain, the traditional fare of religious festivals survives as a delicious reminder of the Arab presence in the Iberian peninsula.

In Portugal, the names attributed to these specialties sometimes assume religious connotations. This is the case, for example, of the so-called "celestial nourishment" and its several variants. Some are made with almonds, others with cheese. There are also many recipes for what in Spain is known as "celestial lard." These confections are made of egg yolk, syrup, and caramel, but none includes even the slightest amount of lard! The names of these cakes oscillate between the erotic, the amusing, and the evocative: "nuns' belly," the cinnamon-scented "angel's breasts," "angel fleece"(dainty, pale, round cakes filled with an egg custard, cream, and sugar), "damsel's nectar," "sighs," "widow's dessert." The more austere Spanish convents invested their egg-yolk cakes with more prosaic names: "almond marzipan" or simply "yolks of Saint Teresa" or "yolks of Saint Paul," depending on which religious order baked them. These "yolks" are a sort of deliciously nauseating candy floss traditionally eaten in Castille at Easter or on other religious feast days.

So not all these good, old-fashioned customs have been lost. The Spanish Clarissan nuns offer the following tips in a cookbook they once published: "nothing must be thrown away. Stale bread can be used to make delicious *torrijas*, and with fish leftovers it is possible to make marvelous croquettes." One year when the fruit harvest was a disaster but there were plenty of cucumbers, Father Hugues of the priory of Saint-Benoît de Chérence decided to make cucumber jam. The leftovers served to prepare delicious soups, always popular in monasteries and convents because, as St. Teresa of Avila said of the cooking pot, "God exists even in a *pot-au-feu.*"

ITALIAN MEATBALLS

Marco Guarnaschelli Gotti

The image of *polpette*, or meatballs, is as contradictory in Italian cuisine as it is in the culinary repertoire of many other countries. Meatballs are made of leftovers, which means that they are looked down upon as impromptu fare, outside the canons of fine food. Yet particular versions of

them can also meet with accolades from gourmets. As the 17th-century aristocrat Vincenzo Tanara enthusiastically declared: "Cooks called the *polpetta* the queen of foods." The basic distinction to be made in the realm of meatballs concerns the nature of their main ingredient. Raw meat or cooked meat? Though I list other distinctions below, this is the one of the most important because it concerns the social significance of *polpette*. The Venetian comic playwright Carlo Goldoni, who was as astute a social critic as any of his time, made the point in *La cameriera brillante*: "meatballs of cooked meat" or "meatballs of raw meat," this was the question. Those made with precooked meat are first cousins to ravioli, to old-fashioned soup with dumplings, *Knödel* in German, *canederli* in the Veneto. The genre, which can achieve true wonders, came into being with the medieval custom of serving meat on large slices of bread. The bread, which served solely as a support, soaked up the meat juices and together with other leftovers was returned to the kitchen to feed the servants. The latter would strive to create variations on the theme, thus inventing a whole new branch of modern cuisine. It is no accident that bread soaked in sauce or stock or water (or, in more refined ver-

sions, milk) forms the basis for cooked *polpette*.

Raw *polpette* are a different matter altogether! They provided a way of making acceptable (chewable) use of inferior cuts of fresh meat from aged animals (the word "fresh" here is a euphemism, and the most wild and wonderful sauces and spices had to be used to "disguise" the quality of the meat). Armed with these basic concepts, let us now take a look at the variegated world of Italian meatballs. Their humble origins have become a distant memory and they are now considered a distinguished chapter in the story of Italian gastronomy.

From south to north

We set out from the south, from Sicily, which boasts a multitude of *polpette* made with raw mince. Flavored with egg, piquant cheese (*pecorino* with pepper) and breadcrumbs, they are often boiled in chicken or other meat stocks. However, they may also be simply fried (in lard, known as *saìmi*), dressed with tomato sauce, wrapped in lemon leaves and grilled (exquisite!), or fried with the addition of a generous tablespoonful of sugar and vinegar to create a stunning sweet and sour effect. Also worth mentioning are *polpette di melanzane*, eggplants balls, whose alternative ingredients are cooked in the same way as meatballs.

Meatballs of all shapes and sizes play a leading role in Neapolitan cuisine. Made of fresh mince, with soaked breadcrumbs, garlic, egg, parmesan, and—a characteristic touch—pine nuts and raisins, they are fried without breadcrumbs and then served in tomato and onion sauce. This is the concoction, designed to dress pasta, so popular among Italo-Americans of Neapolitan origin. *Polpetta d'uovo*, on the other hand, is made with egg, herbs, and Parmesan—no meat. It is interesting to note that southern meat *polpette* are made of fresh minced veal. The fact that precooked meat fails to get consideration may mean that there used to be no leftover meat to rehash in southern kitchens. The habit was to buy meager quantities of poor cut soft meat and use the *polpetta* approach to make it cookable. But, albeit in modest quantities and for only those who could afford it, it's fresh meat we're talking about.

Generally speaking, the apotheosis of meatballs from leftover meat begins in Rome. Roman *polpette* are made of chopped leftover beef (enriched with bread first soaked in stock and then squeezed dry), egg, and Parmesan. Garlic and lemon peel are used as flavoring, and the whole mixture is shaped into largish balls, then dipped in egg and breadcrumbs and fried (formerly in lard, now in oil). This is a supreme version of the *polpetta*. A variation involves frying them coated in flour rather than breadcrumbs and serving in a sauce. No so very different is the "regular" Tuscan *polpetta* described by Artusi. He enriches it with ham, raisins, pine nuts, and lots of spices. Artusi also talks about interesting *polpettine* made with tripe (very Tuscan!), but he devotes not a word to another monument to the genre, the *stracottata*. As the name declares, this is a *polpetta* made from *stracotto*, braised beef. It was once made with leftovers, but now the meat is specially cooked for the purpose. The texture of the aromatic, flavorsome *stracottata* is inimitable, and a delicate tomato sauce to accompany it adds zest as well as depth. Outstanding!

Another great repository of this national dish is Lombardy in general, Milan in particular. But beware of the linguistic trap: in Milanese dialect, *polpetta* means meat roll not meatball. The European *polpett de verz* is stuffed cabbage and the *polpett de la serva*, the serving maid's meat roll, also sounds very tempting. But they aren't meatballs. No, in Milan, *polpette* are *mondeghili*, a Spanish word of Arab origin,

281

from *albondiga* and *albondeguilla*, which mean meatball. How come? Possibly the Spanish grandees were actually a bit down on their luck and found themselves eating lots of meatballs, so much so that they imposed their own name for them. So what does a *mondeghilo* actually consist of? The base is more or less the same as usual, though the mixture may also contain liver sausage, potatoes instead of bread (in which case, soaked in milk), chopped parsley, and garlic. That all sounds Spanish enough, but doesn't really explain the whole story.

Besides the two versions of the *polpetta* Goldoni mentions, the Veneto region offers other interesting variations. These owe much to the influence of Jewish cuisine, which was noteworthy in both Venice and Padua: in particular, interesting spinach balls with pine nuts and raisins, and *pinzette*, lean mince patties that are comparable to hamburgers. Whether *polpette di baccalà* are real *polpette* or not is a moot point; they exist, so we mention them.

Polpette don't exactly abound in Piedmont, unless we include *polpettine in carpione*, balls of raw minced veal fried and then marinated in a mixture of vegetables, herbs, and vinegar with the same procedure used for tench. They are eaten cold, and are, similar, curiously enough, to the sweet and sour preparations of Sicily. But let's not go out of our way to find mutual influences. The only thing that is really similar is the original function, which was to enhance poor-quality meat in the days before refrigerators. What remains of this tradition today is the gastronomic content, which is fascinating throughout the country.

FIFTEEN:5

PEBBLE BROTH

Pier Luigi Manachini

Believe it or not, a soup made of stones! I found out about it in a funny little book I picked up on an antique bookstall. Printed in a limited edition in Livorno in 1939, it is the work of one Giovanni Petagna, a great admirer of he Liv-ornese gastronomic tradition.* In it the author entertainingly draws on his firsthand experience to describe the ingredients, cooking methods, and destiny of *brodo di sassi*, or pebble broth

The principal ingredients were (past tense is *de rigueur*) the "spongy" pebbles found on the seafloor at Livorno, part of a sedimentary rock conglomerate known as the "Livornese bench." Once fished out, they were immediately placed in a bucket and covered with water so that the pebbles did not come into contact with the air, which would have imbued the stock with an unpleasant taste. Petagna recalls that, as a child in Livorno, he would get home and give the bucket to his aunt, Zia Teresa, who used to sift the pebbles and some of the seawater into a pan and add fresh water and a few vegetables. The contents of the pan were then boiled, and the resulting broth was both tasty and hygienically safe because the heat killed off any harmful microbes in the seawater. After cooking, the stock was filtered with a cloth to remove the inevitable grains of sand and served very hot as a soup with short pasta, sometimes with a sprinkling of olive oil.

So much for the recipe. But it is also worth mentioning the dish's equally curious fate. The author recalls that Zia Teresa forced the pebble broth on her husband to bring him around after his Pantagruelesque drinking sessions (he couldn't hold his drink). Clearly the uncle had what Artusi would have described as a "weak or paper stomach."**

Seawater

Reading Petagna's account, I was struck not only by the strangeness of the recipe, but also by the fact that seawater was used to make the pebble stock. "[It] was a way of saving salt," a

---

*Giovanni Petagna, *Brodo di sassi: Curiosità gastronomiche della storia livornese*. Petagna's daughter Laura, also an expert in gastronomic traditions, intends to have the volume reprinted.

**Pellegrino Artusi, *La scienza in cucina e l'arte di mangiar bene*. Florence: Salvatore Landi, 1910.

precious commodity at the time. Since seawater can't be drunk, how did it fit into food preparation? Is Zia Teresa's recipe the only one we know about?

These are pretty obvious questions for someone like myself, born and bred in a corner of the Po valley that lies south of Novara, a land of ricefields and canals, springs and *marcite* (meadows irrigated during winter to protect them from cold, so as to provide fresh fodder for dairy cattle in early spring). Thanks to my origins, I developed a close relationship with freshwater. With the exception of freak events such as drownings and illnesses, the relationship has always been a positive one, closely bound up with the vital need to appease the pangs of hunger through practices that combine farming and cuisine: ricefield-rice-risotto (Novarese *paniscia*) or *marcita*-forage cattle-milk cheese.

Yet I developed a very different relationship with the water of another "plain": the sea. It was a relationship based on what I read. The sea was adventure, the conquest of new land, an enemy to be tamed and vanquished, a place where terrible monsters lived, a potential spectacle, a joy for eye and mind. Only rarely did the sea—salt water—have a fun dimension, and I never thought of it as edible. After all, what sort of a culinary fate could a liquid containing an average of 35 grams of salt per liter hope to have? Yet it is possible to imagine culinary uses for seawater: apart from tasty dishes such as Zia Teresa's pebble broth, the preparation of brines or foodstuffs on board ships, for example. In an era when crossing the oceans meant weeks at sea without a port of call, it was necessary to manage freshwater supplies carefully. I did a little research on the subject and came up with one or two items of interest. In *De re conquinaria*, the cooking manual written by the famous, ancient Roman gastronome Apicius, I discovered precise instructions concerning the use of seawater in the kitchen. The ancient Romans used it to cook wild boar meat: *Aqua marina cum ramulis lauri aprum elixas quosque madescat. Corium ei tolles. Cum sale, sinapi, aceto inferes.* ("Boil the wild boar in seawater with bay leaves. Remove the skin. Serve with salt, mustard, and vinegar.")

From Apicius's boiled wild boar to Petagna's pebble broth: two stages in seawater's long, strange voyage in pans.

Suggested Reading

Christian, Marie. *La soupe aux trois cailloux en France: de la campagne à la ville*, Geneva: Metropolis, 1997.

Dimitris Antonopoulos ("The Greeks Call It καρπατσιο," "Souvlaki"), *Greece*, wine and food writer, general secretary of Slow Food Greece.

Arnaud Apoteker ("Transgenesis"), *France*, head of Greenpeace France.

Françoise Aubaile-Sallenave ("Frying"), *France*, researcher.

Enrique Bellver ("En Sevilla"), *Spain*, food and wine journalist; executive, Slow Food Seville.

Stefanie Böge ("Insidious Distance"), *Germany*, engineer at the Department of Traffic of the Wuppertal Institut für Klima, Umwelt, Energie.

Françoise Bonal ("The Origins of Champagne"), *France*, wine historian.

Barbara Bowman ("In the American Ark: Wild Rice"), *United States*, board member of Slow Food U.S.A.

Tom Bruce-Gardyne ("A Broken Heart," "Sins of the Flesh"), *Great Britain*, wine and food critic.

Alberto Capatti ("A Leftover Culture"), *Italy*, food history academic.

Lesley Chamberlain ("Fish and Chips," "Latter-Day Religion: Vegetarianism"), *Great Britain*, author of books on philosophy, travel, and cooking.

Elizabeth Clift ("Pickles"), *Great Britain*, cook and innkeeper.

Mary Davis ("Puritanical Proscriptions"), *United States*, professor of psychology, Arizona State University.

Carlos Delgado ("Without a Tablecloth: Tapas"), *Spain*, vice-president of the Slow Food Movement, editor-in-chief of *Vino y gastronomi*, wine and food writer for *El País*.

Jorge De'Angeli ("Tacos"), *Mexico*, restaurateur, contributor to Slow Food Editore.

Sarah Freeman ("Farm with a View"), *Great Britain*, journalist.

Vincenzo Gerbi ("'Toma': To Be or Not to Be"), *Italy*, professor, Turin University.

Ivana Gribaudo ("The Vine and the Engineer"), *Italy*, researcher at Centro miglioramento genetico e biologia dell vite at Grugliasco, Turin.

Marco Guarnaschelli Gotti ("Italian Meatballs"), *Italy*, journalist and expert in gastronomy.

Sylvie Guichard-Anguis ("Squid and Sweet Potatoes") *France*, expert in Japanese culture and society, freelancer for the Centre National de la Recherche Scientifique.

Otto Horse ("Coldwave"), writer.

Annie Hubert ("The Convict's Diet," "Khao Soy and Other Noodles," and "Sunday Morning in Limogne"), *France*, director of the Centre National de la Recherche Scientifique, Bordeaux.

Michael Jackson ("The Post-Industrial Pint," "For Stout Lovers"), *Great Britain*, journalist, consummate beer and whiskey expert.

Aïda Kanafani-Zahar ("The Lebanese Calendar"), *Lebanon*, historian and anthropologist.

Radha Kapoor-Sharma ("Tandoori," "Chutneys") *India, France*, lecturer in comparative and French literature at the University of Delhi.

Manfred Kriener ("5,000 Varieties," "Spoilt Chickens," "The Second Revolution," "Meat on the Move"), *Germany*, journalist, expert in consumer and environmental issues, contributor to *Der Spiegel.*

Nelly Krowolski ("In the Streets, at Home"), *France*, expert in Asian culture, researcher at the Centre National de la Recherche Scientifique.

Deborah Madison (foreword, "Native Chiles in Santa Fe"), *United States*, author of *The Greens Cookbook, The Savory Way*, and other books.

Maurizio Maggiani ("Farinata"), *Italy*, writer.

Pier Luigi Manachini ("Pebble Broth"), *Italy*, microbiologist; lecturer, University of Milan.

Anna Mannucci ("SOS for Domestic Animals"), *Italy*, journalist.

Massimo Montanari ("Unnatural Cooking"), *Italy*, professor of medieval history.

Carol Nemeroff ("Puritanical Proscriptions"), *United States*, professor of psychology, Arizona State University.

Charlie Papazian ("New Brews,"), *United States*, beer producer and executive of Slow Food Colorado.

Carlo Petrini (preface, "Building the Ark"), *Italy*, founder and president of the Slow Food Movement.

Uda Pollmer ("On Fats"), *Germany*, food chemist, lecturer, science journalist, and scientific director of the European Institute for Food and Food Science.

Dominique Prédali ("God in Crumbs"), *France*, historian.

Sarah Heekin Redfield ("Tumalo Tomme in Oregon"), *United States*, vice-chair, Federation of State Humanities Councils.

Giampiero Rigosi ("My Father as a Tartar"), *Italy*, writer.

George Ritzer ("Slow Food versus McDonald's"), *United States*, professor of sociology at the University of Maryland.

Marco Riva ("Magic Bullets and Philosophers' Stones," "Nutraceutical Food"), *Italy*, professor of food technology at Milan University.

Jancis Robinson ("The Secret of Diversity"), *Great Britain*, journalist and editor of *The Oxford Companion to Wine*.

Bernard Rosenberger ("The Smoke Market"), professor of medeival history, Paris III University.

Giovanni Ruffa ("Pest, Present and Future"), *Italy*, executive, Slow Food Italy; regular contributor to Slow Food Editore.

Françoise Sabban ("Rice and Fish Bones"), *France*, historian and sinologist.

Barbara Santich ("Vietnamese Snake Tavern"), *Australia*, food historian, writer, and researcher.

Piero Sardo ("Typical?"), *Italy*, wine and food critic; executive, Slow Food Italy.

Cinzia Scaffidi ("The Market at Ulan Bator"), *Italy*, journalist.

Hermann Scheer ("Region Is Reason"), *Germany*, president of the Agriculture Commission of the Assembly of the Council of Europe.

Emilio Senesi ("Feathers and Plumes: Ostrich Farming"), *Italy*, university researcher.

Vandana Shiva ("Genetic Freedom," "A Miracle?"), *India*, physicist, biologist, philosopher; head of the Research Foundation for Science Technology and Ecology, New Delhi; recipient of the Alternative Nobel Prize, 1993.

Philip Sinsheimer ("Falafel"), *France*, research fellow at the Ecole des Hautes Etudes en Sciences Sociales in Paris.

Michel Smith ("The Wretched and the Noble," "The Revival Route"), *France*, wine and food writer.

Grazia Solazzi ("Alkmaar: The Cheese Market") *Italy*, journalist.

Bob Thompson ("Zinfandel"), *United States*, journalist and writer specializing in wine.

Ettore Tibaldi ("Bicycle or Airplane Chickens"), *Italy* zoologist; lecturer, University of Milan.

Giorgio Triani ("Balsamic Vinegar"), *Italy* sociologist.

Gianni Vercellotti ("The Value of Time," adapted from *Africa. Gli ultimi fuochi*. Turin: Gribaudo, Cavallermaggiore, 1997), *Italy*, Slow Food director.

Luigi Wanner ("Drinkable Bread"), writer, journalist, editor of the German edition of *Slow*.

CHELSEA GREEN

SUSTAINABLE LIVING has many facets. Chelsea Green's celebration of the sustainable arts has led us to publish trend-setting books about organic gardening, solar electricity and renewable energy, innovative building techniques, regenerative forestry, local and bioregional democracy, and whole and *slow* foods.

More than 300 titles bring you the information that helps you lead pleasurable lives on a planet where human activities are in harmony and balance with nature.

For more information about Chelsea Green, or to request a free catalog, call toll-free (800) 639-4099, or write us at P.O. Box 428, White River Junction, Vermont 05001. Visit our Web site at www.chelseagreen.com.

For more information about **Slow Food USA** and local convivia, please contact the national headquarters at info@slowfoodusa.org or call toll-free (877) SLOW FOOD (756-9366). You can write to **Slow Food** at P.O. Box 1737, New York, NY 10021 or visit their Web site at www.slowfood.com.

Select back issues of SLOW MAGAZINE *are available*

through Chelsea Green — please call

(800) 639-4099

for more information!